Biblical Holy Places

an illustrated guide

Rivka Gonen

PAULIST PRESS
New York/Mahwah, New Jersey

Books of related interest published by Paulist Press
Bed and Blessings: Italy
Witnessing the Holy Land

Editorial	*Georgette Corcos*
	Frances Gertler
Design and Layout	*Constantin Presman*
Paging	*Margalit Bassan*
Production	*Rachel Gilon*
Maps	*Haim Eytan*

Front cover photograph: A view of Hebron

Planned and produced by The Jerusalem Publishing House, Jerusalem, Israel.
Copyright © 2000 by G.G. The Jerusalem Publishing House Ltd., 39 Tchernichovski Street, P.O.B. 7147, Jerusalem 91071, Israel.

Composition: Posner and Sons Ltd. Jerusalem
Printed in Hong Kong

All rights reserved. No part of this book may be reproduced or transmitted in any form or by any means, electronic or mechanical, including photocopying, recording or by any information storage and retrieval system without permission in writing from the Publisher.

ISBN: 0-8091-3974-X

Published for North America by Paulist Press
997 Macarthur Boulevard
Mahwah, New Jersey 07430

www.paulistpress.com

CONTENTS

PREFACE

*Over the ages the interested layman and the faithful pilgrim alike
have drawn inspiration from famous sites remembered for their
association with important biblical events and personalities. At
such places one can perhaps feel closer to the divine and gain a
sense of the spirit of the place and atmosphere of the event that
occurred there. Of course many of these places no longer exist in
their ancient form, shrines and monuments often having been
erected to enhance the site's significance and themselves destroyed
and reconstructed with time. A visit to a holy place can sometimes
be a rather confusing experience, the traveller being confronted
with sections of old buildings merging into one another or built one
on top of the other, thereby obscuring the original nature of the
site. The traveller also faces the problem still unsolved by
historians and archaeologists, of the precise identification of some
of the sites. The exact location in which an important event took
place is not always clear, the ambiguity often giving rise to several
traditions. The site of Emmaus for example, is variously located
in three different places leaving the visitor wondering how these
conflicting traditions developed. This comprehensive guide
explains some of these traditions and gives the historical and
architectural background of the place.*

*The 210 entries in this volume will lead you through the places
which have become sanctified, and clarify for you the nature of
the event and the traditions that surround it, the shrines and their
history. Each entry gives the relevant biblical reference often
accompanied by a quotation, location, a comprehensive description
of the site – its principle structures as well as contemporary
surroundings, and enough archaeological data to give life to the
ancient places. To further set the place and event in its context,
a historical table with significant dates and events can be found
at the beginning of the book. The photographs give an extra
dimension to the written description by familiarising the reader
with the sites, highlighting interesting details and showing
archaeological finds. The maps will orientate the traveller and
provide information on how to reach the site and acquaint him
with its geographical surroundings.*

*The entries are arranged by countries conveniently listed in
alphabetical order. Within each country the sites are again
arranged in alphabetical order, with the most important sites –
Jerusalem, Bethlehem, Nazareth and Rome – taking up a major
part of the book. Cross-references, printed in small capitals, refer
to related entries. The detailed index helps locate every site, giving
both its modern and biblical spelling.*

*Naturally, most of the important biblical places are in the Holy
Land, but the guide also covers other countries which appear in
the Bible, including Italy, Malta, Greece, Turkey, Cyprus, Syria,
Jordan and the Sinai in Egypt. This wide coverage will give the
reader a glimpse of the geography and history of the countries of
the eastern and central Mediterranean, where prophets and
apostles lived and acted and handed down the rich heritage of the
Bible to Judaism, Christianity and Islam.*

HISTORICAL OUTLINE

PERIOD	MAJOR EVENTS AND DEVELOPMENTS
Paleolithic ?-12000 B.C.	Early societies of hunters-gatherers living in caves and open sites. Stone tools.
Mesolithic 12000-8000 B.C.	Transition to cereal gathering and permanent settlements.
Neolithic 8000-4500 B.C.	Agriculture based on domestication of plants and animals. Invention of pottery; long distance trade. Fortified towns in Jericho.
Chalcolithic 4500-3200 B.C.	Invention of metal work, intensive use of copper. Economy based on herds. Impressive art. Large towns in Anatolia.
Early Bronze 3200-2200 B.C.	Network of towns throughout the ancient Near East. Kingdoms in Egypt and Mesopotamia. Canaanites in Syria and Canaan.
Middle Bronze 2200-1550 B.C.	Period of the Patriarchs of Israel. Fortified towns throughout the region.
Late Bronze 1500-1200 B.C.	Canaan ruled by Egyptian empire. Apex of Canaanite culture. Israelites in Egypt. Exodus.
First Temple (Iron Age) 1200-586 B.C.	Settlement of Israelites in Canaan. Philistines in coastal plain. Establishment of Israelite monarchy. David, Solomon and the Prophets. Old Testament written. Destruction of the Temple and Kingdom by Babylonia.
Second Temple 538 B.C.-A.D. 70	Return from Babylonian exile. Ezra and Nehemiah. The Hasmonean dynasty. King Herod. Jesus and the birth of Christianity. Destruction of the Temple by the Romans.
Roman 70-324	Entire eastern Mediterranean under Roman empire.
Byzantine 324-640	Christianity becomes state religion. Constantinople capital of the Roman empire. Arab conquest of Syria-Palestine. Byzantine rule continues in Asia Minor, Cyprus and Greece.
Early Moslem 640-1099	Moslem empire centres around Damascus (Umayyad Dynasty), then around Baghdad (Abbasid Dynasty).
Crusader 1099-1291	European-Christian thrust in the Orient, establishment of Latin Kingdom of Jerusalem.
Mameluke 1291-1519	Conquest of Syria-Palestine by Moslems of Egypt. Period of decline.
Ottoman (Turkish) 1519-1917	Ottoman conquest and rule. The entire eastern Mediterranean again under one empire centred around Istanbul. Decline continues.
British Mandate 1917-1948	Conquest of Palestine by the British. Major developments amid growing political unrest.

CYPRUS

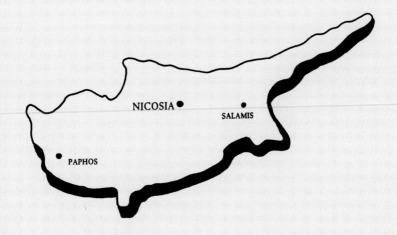

PAPHOS

On the western coast of the island of Cyprus are two ancient towns named Paphos. Old Paphos was established around 1300 B.C. by settlers from Mycenean Greece. It was the centre of the cult of the goddess Aphrodite and capital of the Kingdom of Paphos which, in the first half of the 1st millennium B.C., spread over much of western Cyprus. Towards the end of the 4th century B.C. the last king of the Kingdom of Paphos established New (Nea) Paphos.

At the beginning of the 2nd century B.C. it became the capital of the whole of Cyprus. Paphos (hereafter without the prefix New) reached its golden age under the Romans. It was visited by Paul and Barnabas who converted the Roman pro-consul, Sergius Paulus (Acts 13:6-13). After the Roman period, perhaps as the result of two severe earthquakes in 332 and 342, Paphos lost its importance. Nowadays its site is partially occupied by the village of Kato Paphos.

Not much of the large and prosperous city of New Paphos has been unearthed. The main Hellenistic period edifices seen today are several impressive underground chambers the purpose of which has not yet been determined, although two – the so-called Tombs of the Kings – are referred to as "catacombs". Also of the Hellenistic period are a 3rd-century B.C. theatre which has not yet been excavated and a rock-cut sanctuary to Apollo Hylates. More has survived of the Roman period. Most impressive are two large houses, that of Dionysos which was a private dwelling and that of Theseus, which may have been the residence of the Roman governor. These houses testify to the splendour of Paphos in the Roman period., Both have splendid mosaic floors with scenes from Greek mythology. Also noteworthy is the civic centre of the city with

(left) The Pillar of Flagellation of St Paul at New Paphos. (right) Remains of an ancient synagogue at Paphos.

an *agora* (market place), an *odeon* (small theatre for musical performances) and an *Asklepeion* (a temple to Aesculapius god of medicine).

The sites of Christian significance are St Paul's Pillar in the centre of the village of Kato Paphos to which, so a local tradition relates, Paul was bound and given 39 lashes as punishment for preaching the new faith. In the village are also the remnants of a very large early Byzantine (4th century) basilical church. The colourful mosaic floors which adorned the five-aisled basilica have been well-preserved. Near the coast lies an important Byzantine period castle built in the 7th century to guard the harbour against Arab raiders.

SALAMIS

An ancient city in eastern Cyprus, on the Famagusta Bay some 8km (5 miles) north of the town of Famagusta. Tradition holds that Salamis was founded by Teucer son of Telamon on his return from the Trojan War. In the Persian period (5th-6th centuries B.C.) Salamis was the principal city of the island of Cyprus. It flourished due to its good harbour and large scale trade.

In 58 B.C. it became a Roman province. In 22 B.C. the Romans transferred the capital of Cyprus to NEW PAPHOS but Salamis remained the commercial centre of the island. In Roman times there was a Jewish community in Salamis, and one of its members was Barnabas. In A.D. 46 he accompanied Paul on his first journey to Cyprus (Acts 13:1, 5). Barnabas suffered martyrdom in his native town and his reputed tomb is said to have been discovered in 477 next to the Monastery of St Barnabas. A small church is built over the tomb.

After the 1st centrury A.D. Salamis declined rapidly. It had been the centre of a great Jewish revolt against Rome in A.D. 116-117, when it was destroyed. Repeated earthquakes completed the destruction. In the 4th century Emperor Constantine rebuilt on the ruins of Salamis a smaller, but beautiful town which he named Constantia. It was destroyed by the Moslem Mu'awiya in 648 and was never rebuilt. Its ruins were used as a quarry for the construction of Famagusta.

The site of Salamis is almost completely covered with sand. Excavations have unearthed some of the treasures of its past, the best known of which is the "royal necropolis" of about 700 B.C., in which rulers were buried with horses and chariots, wooden furniture inlaid with ivory and splendid bronze cauldrons. Of the Roman period, the Great Stone Forum, measuring about 220 by 60m (700 by 200 ft) and one of the largest in the Roman world, has been unearthed. The forum was bordered by a peristyle of very tall Corinthian columns, later used for the construction of the Byzantine city. On the south side of the forum was a temple, and in its north side – a huge water reservoir fed by a great aqueduct which brought water from Kythrea 50km (35 miles) distant. The aqueduct dates to the Byzantine period. On the northern edge of the site is a smaller forum built of marble, perhaps dating to the 2nd century A.D.

EGYPT

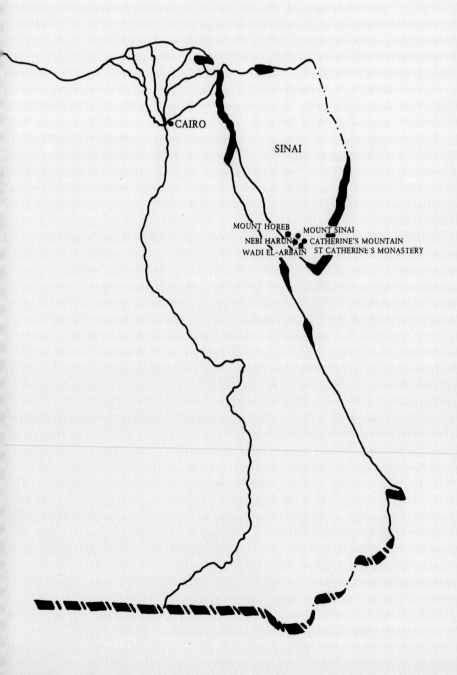

CAIRO

SINAI

MOUNT HOREB   MOUNT SINAI

NEBI HARUN   CATHERINE'S MOUNTAIN

WADI EL-ARBAIN   ST CATHERINE'S MONASTERY

SINAI

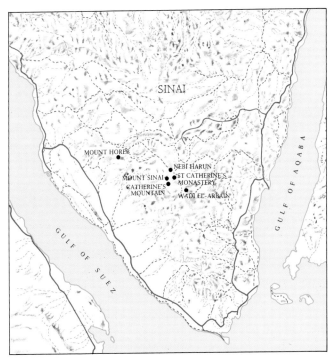

A large triangular peninsula between Egypt and the Holy Land. Sinai is bounded by the Mediterranean Sea on the north, the Suez Canal and the western arm of the Red Sea on the west and by the Gulf of Aqaba on the east. Most of Sinai is a low desert plateau which slopes gently from south to north, towards the Mediterranean coast. The southern part of the peninsula is a spectacular area of high mountains of ancient crystaline rock, mainly pink and grey granites. Because of their height, the mountains of southern Sinai receive more precipitaion than the rest of the peninsula and have several springs and oases which make the region somewhat more habitable. On the whole, because of the harsh desert climate, Sinai has always been sparsely populated, mainly by nomadic Bedouin.

Landscape in Sinai.

The Exodus of the Children of Israel from Egypt and their long wanderings in the desert on their way to the Promised Land undoubtedly took place in the Sinai peninsula. The exact route of the Exodus, however, and the places connected with it have not yet been identified with certainty. This is perhaps because nomads and travellers hardly leave traces in the landscape. Traditions that developed in the Byzantine period at the latest placed the most significant events of the Exodus in the mountains of southern Sinai and they point to MOUNT SINAI and MOUNT HOREB. Christians hermits were drawn to the region and built monasteries, the most important being ST CATHERINE'S MONASTERY.

CATHERINE'S MOUNTAIN – JEBEL KATERINA

Highest of the southern Sinai mountains, about 2,642m (8,700 ft) above sea level. The mountain is composed of various types of volcanic rock of different geological ages with geologically late instrusions of red granite. The landscape is wild and windy, with snowfalls every winter. The view from the summit, which can be reached by foot or on camel-back from the monastery at WADI EL-ARBAIN or by special vehicles from Wadi Rutig, is breathtaking and encompasses all of southern Sinai. Especially impressive are the sunrises. The monks at St Catherine's Monastery organise early-morning walks to witness them.

St Catherine was a Christian Egyptian woman who died a martyr for her beliefs. Tradition holds that many years after her death angels brought her body to the peak of the mountain. A monk from the Monastery of the Burning Bush at the foot of the mountain dreamt that on the summit was a treasure; it turned out to be St Catherine's body. Her skull and left hand are now said to be interred in a silver box in the monastery which was renamed St Catherine's in commemoration of the discovery of the body.

On top of Catherine's Mountain, over the pit in which the body is said to have been found, stands a small, white chapel, sometimes visited by monks and pilgrims. Many graffiti inscriptions around the chapel indicate that pilgrimage to the summit is an old custom. Every Sunday a resident of St Catherine's Monastery climbs the mountain and lights a candle in the chapel.

MOUNT HOREB – JEBEL SIRBAL

One of the highest and most spectacular mountains in southern Sinai, some 2,070m (6,800 ft) above sea level. Jebel Sirbal is a separate topographic unit, apart from the main mountainous core of southern Sinai, and is surrounded on all sides by sheer cliffs. The mountain, of hard, red granite rock with deep gullies, can be distinguished from a great distance because of its serrated profile which gives it an awesome appearance. Jebel Sirbal is especially impressive when viewed

One of the mountains in Sinai said to be Mount Horeb.

from Wadi Firan, which runs north of the mountain. It is no wonder that it has been venerated by local people and pilgrims and sometimes identified with Mount Horeb, the mountain of God (Exodus 3:1).

The region of Jebel Sirbal was inhabited only in the Byzantine period by determined Christian hermits, who practiced small-scale agriculture in the valleys. The inhospitable mountain is deserted and even the Bedouins do not venture there with their flocks.

MOUNT SINAI – JEBEL MUSA

A high mountain 2,285m (7,500 ft) above sea level, in the Jebel Safsafa range of southern Sinai believed to be the Mount Sinai where the Children of Israel received the Law (Exodus chapter 19). The entire mountain range is a red granite block, bounded by geological faults, giving it its spectacular features of sheer slopes and deep valleys. Northwest of the mountain range, in Wadi e-Deir, is ST CATHERINE'S MONASTERY, and southeast is WADI EL-ARBAIN. Between the mountain peaks are small valleys in which water and earth running off from the surrounding slopes accumulate. In many of these valleys are small chapels, often surrounded by orchards, which were built by hermits in the Byzantine and later periods. In one of these valleys – the Valley of the Cypresses – are three structures dedicated to the prophets Elijah and Elisha and to an Egyptian saint named Marina. The valley is about two-thirds of the way uphill from St Catherine's Monastery to the summit of Mount Sinai. The top of the Mount is reached on foot by 2,700 steps.

Steps leading up to Mount Sinai.

At the summit are two structures – one a chapel, first built in the Byzantine period; the other, an open mosque. In the corner of the mosque is a niche where, according to a Moslem tradition, Moses hid when God revealed himself to him. The view is magnificent and includes CATHERINE'S MOUNTAIN to the south and all the spectacular mountains of southern Sinai.

The first identification of this mountain with Mount Sinai dates to the 4th-5th centuries A.D., and is a Christian tradition. The local Bedouins accepted this identification and celebrate Id el-Adha, one of the most important Moslem festivals, on its summit.

NEBI HARUN

A low hill in the mountain of southern Sinai, surrounded by high mountains and overlooking ST CATHERINE'S MONASTERY. According to a Christian tradition, Moses' brother Aaron (Harun) cast the golden calf here, while Moses tarried on top of the mountain (Exodus 32:1-4). The Moslems accepted this identification and built on the hill a round structure dedicated to Nebi Harun. Inside is a tombstone covered with green and white cloth indicating its holiness – green, the colour of vegetation, and white, symbolizing purity, are colours venerated by Moslems. It is interesting that the Christian and Moslem tradition was not accepted by the local Bedouins who, although officially Moslem, have preserved many pre-Islamic customs and traditions. The Bedouin venerate the tomb and bury their dead at the foot of the hill in close proximity, but do not believe it is the tomb of Aaron. They themselves have no tradition as to who is actually buried there. In 1911 a Christian chapel was built on top of the hill, not far from the Moslem structure.

St Catherine's Monastery.

ST CATHERINE'S MONASTERY - SANTA KATERINA

A large monastery in southern Sinai, built by Emperor Justinian in the 6th century on the site of an older fortified church, which had been built, according to tradition, by Helena, mother of Emperor Constantine in the 4th century. The monastery was constructed to protect what was believed to be the Burning Bush in which God first revealed himself to Moses (Exodus 3:1-4:17). It is located at the bottom of Wadi e-Deir, on a site rather difficult to protect, since it is exposed to winter floods that sweep down the steep wadi. It was also often attacked by marauders, who took advantage of the slopes surrounding the monastery. As a protection against these dangers, Justinian had the monastery surrounded by a strong high wall, which is still one of its main features. Most of what is seen on the site today dates back to the 6th century. Over the generations, however, buildings were added to the compound, the last one being a hostel in the 1940s.

The monastery, first named after the Burning Bush, had its name changed to St Catherine when the body of the Egyptian martyr Catherine was found nearby.

Since its establishment the monastery has been the centre of monastic life of southern Sinai. At first it served as a place of refuge for the hermits who lived in solitude in the area, but as time passed the monks moved into the monastery. It served also the numerous pilgrims who came to see the holy

(overleaf left, top) Interior of the church of St Catherine's Monastery. (bottom) A corner of the library.
(overleaf right, top) Mosaic of the Transfiguration. (bottom) Altar in the Chapel of the Burning Bush.

mountains where God revealed himself to Moses and the Children of Israel during the Exodus and, later, to Elijah.

The 6th-century walls, much repaired in later generations, are a rare example of Byzantine fortifications. They surrounded an area of some 80 × 80m (250 × 250 ft) and are built of close fitting granite stones. There were four original gates in the walls – the three in the northwestern wall have all been blocked for hundreds of years. The one in the northeastern wall is about 9m (28 ft) above ground level, too high to be used in a normal fashion, and was reached by means of a basket and a pulley. This unusual way of entering the monastery was practiced until the middle of the 19th century when a new gate was opened in the northwestern wall.

The church dedicated to the Virgin Mary is the most important structure in the compound. It is a well-preserved Byzantine basilica with a nave and two aisles and an apse. It contains many exquisite works of art, the most striking of which is the very well preserved, 6th-century wall mosaic in the apse depicting the Transfiguration of Jesus in the presence of the prophets of Sinai – Moses to his right and Elijah to his left – and of his disciples Peter, John and James. This major work of art is surrounded by 30 medallions with representations of the Apostles and the prophets. There are also hundreds of icons, lamps, wood, stone and metal objects and beautiful wall decorations. Also worthy of special attention are the inner wooden doors, excellently preserved examples of ornate 6th-century Byzantine craftsmanship, and the outer doors which were made in Egypt in the 11th century.

Left of the main altar is the Chapel of the Burning Bush, with exquisite blue tiles covering its walls. In the courtyard

The 6th-century cedar wood door of St Catherine's Monastery.

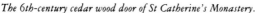

The Codex Syriacus at the library of the Monastery.

behind the chapel grows a trailing raspberry bush, believed to have grown from the original Burning Bush.

While the church was no doubt built by local masons who left their mark in the rather crude capitals of the pillars, each representing a month of the year and an icon of the saint of the month, its decorations were executed by first-rate artists and craftsmen commissioned from the great art centres of the day.

The other structures in the compound are the famous library with 3000 precious manuscripts and documents, about ten chapels and additional offices, monks' cells, and a refectory room with a 16th-century mural of the the Last Supper and doors decorated with carvings of names and weapons of knights of the Crusader period. There are also the lodgings of the Bedouins who work at the monastery, and a hostel for pilgrims. An imposing mosque was built inside the compound in 1106 behind the church. Its tower was, for hundreds of years, the highest structure, until a belfry was added to the church in 1871.

St Catherine's Monastery is most renowned for its unique collection of precious art objects accumulated over many centuries. As the monastery did not suffer any major destruction, and as it was secluded and not affected by the movement of iconoclasm that wrecked art objects in the major centres of the Byzantine Empire, St Catherine's collections are unique. Among them are some of the oldest known icons.

As important as the art objects is the library with its collection of old manuscripts, some with exquisite illuminations. For many centuries it was the home of the Codex Sinaiticus, a 4th-century Greek manuscript of the Septuagint, which was taken in 1844 by the German von Tischendorf, who brought it to St Petersburg. It was later sold to the British Museum, where it is now.

WADI EL-ARBAIN

One of the central wadis in the mountains of southern Sinai, formed by a strong geological fault. The roads to JEBEL KATERINA and MOUNT SINAI pass through it. The name El-Arbain – "The forty" in Arabic – recalls a local tradition concerning 40 monks who were killed here by the Saracens, and in whose memory the monastery Deir el-Arbain was built. The contemporary monastery, with its fortress-like appearance, is built on Byzantine foundations. It is surrounded by high walls with only one small, low entrance. The huge olive grove around the building, with some very ancient trees, is still productive, and at olive-picking time monks from ST CATHERINE'S MONASTERY come here. The rest of the time the monastery is kept by a Bedouin family.

Not far from the monastery, in the wadi, is a large rock known as the Rock of Moses. Christians and Moslems believe that this is the rock which Moses hit to draw out water (Exodus 17:6). Near the rock is a chapel, built in 1977, which serves the pilgrims on their way to Jebel Musa (Mount Sinai).

GREECE

PHILIPPI

THESSALONICA — SALONIKA

ATHENS

CORINTH

PATMOS

ATHENS

Capital of modern Greece, mother of democracy and an ancient city of great fame. Athens is world-famous for its historic sites and glorious cultural history. It was one of the main centres of religion in ancient Greece, its chief deity being the goddess Athena. But its claim to holiness for the modern pilgrim lies in the fact that it was one of the places visited by St Paul on his apostolic voyages where *disputed he in the synagogue with the Jews, and with the devout persons, and in the market daily with them that met with him. Then certain philosophers of the Epicureans, and of the Stoics encountered him. And some said... He seemeth to be a setter forth of strange gods; because he preached unto them Jesus, and the resurrection* (Acts 17: 17-18). Paul then went to the hill of AREOPAGUS where he preached again and won several converts, among them Dionysius – St Denis the Areopagite.

The Parthenon at Athens.

The history of Athens began in the 2nd millennium B.C., when a fortress was built on the acropolis. Since those early beginnings Athens has been a place of importance, its influence spreading far beyond its own city limits. Social and cultural innovations introduced there had a profound impact on world history. Athens was the home of the social reformer Solon (6th century B.C.); of Cleisthenes (507 B.C.), who laid the foundation of the Athenean democracy; of the statesman Pericles (5th century B.C.); of Socrates, Plato and Aristotle the philosophers; of Aeschylus and Sophocles the dramaturges; of the sculptor Phidias, and of many others who made the legacy of Athens one of the cornerstones of Western culture. The greatest period of Athenean glory spanned the 6th-4th centuries B.C. From the time it fell under the Macedonian yoke in 322 B.C. Athens knew successive periods of slavery and independence under the Hellenists and the Romans. Its cultural life, however, continued. From about the 3rd century A.D. there were considerable changes in the life of Athens. On the one hand, Athens – and the rest of the Roman Empire – suffered constant attacks by barbarian tribes, while on the other hand, Christianity, introduced by St Paul on his visit in A.D. 49, made great progress despite the active resistance of the neo-Platonist and other schools of philosphy that remained active until the 6th century. Only in 529 was the last school of philosophy closed, and the pagan temples converted into churches. Athens lost its supremacy when Constantinople became the capital of the Byzantine Empire. It knew another period of glory during the Crusader period, but assumed the status of a small and unimportant town after it fell to the Turks in 1454. Between 1821 and 1833 the town passed several times back and forth between the Turks and an allied army of European nations. In the course of these battles many of the ancient monuments were severely damaged. On April 12, 1833 the Turks evacuated Athens and the town became the capital of an independent Greece.

Athens is one of the world's most attractive places to visit, offering many famous sites which this short description does not attempt to cover. Only a detailed archaeological guidebook can do them full justice. The best known section of Athens is the Acropolis, a fortified enclosure centered around the Parthenon. This 5th-century B.C. temple was the main temple of the goddess Athena, and is a classic example of the Doric style. The Parthenon is approached through a monumental gateway of the Roman period, on the right side of which stands the small and delicate temple of Athena Nike. The Propylaea, the 5th-century B.C. entrance to the Acropolis, is a most impressive structure. Another well-known structure on the Acropolis is the Erechtheum with its Portico of the Caryatides, in which statues of six maidens (caryatides) replace conventional pillars in carrying the weight of the roof. At the bottom of the southern slope of the Acropolis is the Theatre of Dionysus where the yearly Great Dionysian Festival, which included dramatic contests, was celebrated. This was the birthplace of Greek drama. The theatre was first built in the 5th century B.C. and repaired and altered many times. West

of it is the Herodes Atticus Odeon, built in the 2nd century
A.D., where musical concerts were held.

Many other ancient monuments abound in Athens –
temples, market places, centres of culture and of political life,
streets and fountains. To these should be added the various
museums which house the treasures of the past. But to all
those who seek places of holiness, none of these impressive
remnants of the past is as close to heart as the hill of Areopagus
west of the Acropolis, where Christianity was first introduced
into Athens.

AREOPAGUS

A hill in Athens, west of the Acropolis. It was dedicated to
the Greek god of war, Ares (Roman Mars), who had a temple
at the foot of the northwestern slope of the hill. Another
temple connected with the hill was that of the Erinyes, or
Furies, goddesses of revenge, whose temple was a sanctuary
for murderers. This hill was the meeting place of the Senate
of Areopagus, the oldest council of the city of Athens, which
dealt with both political and judicial matters. Legend has it
that avenging gods and heroes, such as Ares himself and
Orestes, who murdered his mother Clytemnestra, were
brought to trial before this council. Later this senate was
deprived of its political powers but retained its judicial
standing and dealt with matters of corruption and treason. It
was also charged with preserving the constitution and the
customs of the land. This court most probably had its seat on
the summit of the hill. Somewhere *in the midst of Mars' hill*
(Acts 17:22), perhaps in the Royal Stoa of an agora that was
on the Areopagus, Paul delivered his message of the new
doctrine of Christianity (Acts 17:19- 34). Dionysius, believed
to have been a senator, was converted on the occasion, and is
known as St Denis the Areopagite. Every year on June 23 a
pilgrimage is held in memory of this event.

The remnants of the place where the Senate of Areopagus
met is marked today by two terraces, one higher than the
other, and linked by rock-cut steps. A square block above the
second terrace was either an altar to Athena Areia, or one of
the two stones where the contending parties sat. On the side
of the hill are traces of four rectangular structures which served
the Scythian guards who kept order in the place. Traces of the
sanctuary of the Erinyes are at the foot of the northern
escarpment of the hill. This temple was replaced by a church
dedicated to St Denis the Areopagite.

CORINTH

The modern Greek city of Corinth, on the Bay of Corinth on
the northern shore of the Peloponnesus peninsula, lies 6km (4
miles) northeast of ancient Corinth, one of the most important
cities of ancient Greece. It was a major trading centre,
occupying a bridge-like crossroad between Asia and the
Cycladic islands to the east and Italy to the west. In A.D. 52
Paul went to Corinth and stayed for one year and a half.

(left) Street leading from the centre of Corinth to the port of Lechaum.
(right) Remains of the agora.

At that time Corinth was already in the second cycle of its existence. The ancient city, founded perhaps already in the 19th century B.C., grew through the manufacture of purple dyes and textiles, painted vases, and bronze objects that were exported as far as Etruria in Italy. It even founded colonies in the 8th century B.C. among which was Syracuse in Sicily. Corinth was captured and completely destroyed by the Romans in 146 B.C. It was rebuilt about a hundred years later by Julius Caesar as a Roman colony and what can be seen on the site are mainly the remains of that city. This was the Corinth in which Paul stayed and which he found to be a city of very low moral values. There were a number of Jews, in whose synagogue Paul preached and was rejected (Acts 18:1-18), and from the time of Paul's visit, a newly formed Christian community, *the church of God which is at Corinth...* (II Corinthians 1:1). This Roman city reached the height of its development in the 2nd century A.D. and at that time was considered the most beautiful city in Greece. From the 3rd century A.D. Corinth suffered several devastations and in the 6th century the city was confined to the nearby hill of the Acrocorinth. Even this more defensible location did not save the city, which was captured nine times between the 12th and the 18th centuries. Major earthquakes in 1858 and 1928 further destroyed what was left of the ancient city, and what is seen on the site today is the result of excavations.

Excavations revealed substantial remnants, mainly of the Roman phase of Corinth. They include a central *agora* (market place), surrounded by rows of shops and public buildings. On the northern side of the *agora* is the lower Peirene spring, the upper one issuing on top of the Acrocorinth. Several structures connected with water have been built around the spring over the generations, the one now seen is a *nymphaeum*, a public pavilion, from the 2nd century A.D. Northwest of the *agora* stands a 2nd-century A.D. *odeon* (small theatre for musical concerts). Beyond it was a Greek theatre over which a Roman theatre for gladiatorial contests was erected in the 1st century. Further north is a temple of Aesculapius the god of healing.

To an earlier phase in the life of Corinth, belong the impressive South Stoa, a long building – one of the longest in Greece – which served, among other functions, as the seat of the senate. This stoa, built in the 6th century B.C., is one of the oldest surviving buildings in Corinth. It was restored many times, but its original plan was not changed. The largest of several temples found around the centre of the town, is the temple of Apollo, also dating to the 6th century B.C. This is a good example of a temple of the Doric Order.

On the Acrocorinth is an imposing fortress which was built, destroyed and rebuilt many times from the Byzantine period to the Turkish. The view from the Acrocorinth is magnificent.

PATMOS

A small, volcanic island in the Dodecanese, about 43km (27 miles) from the coast of Asia Minor. The island is formed of three short, rocky mountain ranges with two isthmuses which over the years have almost filled up to become salt flats between the mountains. The main bay, Skála, offers good shelter for ships and is the gateway to the island. Because of the poor quality of the soil, Patmos is almost bare of vegetation and grows only a few cereals, vegetables and some wine grapes. These rather hostile natural conditions have made the island an ideal place for seclusion, and in the Roman period it served as a place of exile for political prisoners. John the Apostle sought refuge there between A.D. 81 and 96, and tradition holds that he lived in a grotto between the bay of Skála and the town of Patmos, capital of the island. In this grotto John is said to have written the Apocalypse (Revelation 1:19).

In 1088 a monastery was founded at the place where an altar to the Greek goddess Artemis once stood. The monastery, dedicated to Ayios Ioannis Theologos, is still standing and has

View of Patmos.

St John's Grotto at Patmos.

maintained its medieval fortified character. The church of the monastery is beautiful. Some of the monks' cells are rented to tourists.

PHILIPPI

A town in Macedonia, in north-east Greece, some 185km (115 miles) north-east of THESSALONICA and close to the Bulgarian border. Philippi was built in 356 B.C. by Philip II of Macedonia (after whom it is named) on a precipitous hill, as a fortress to defend the border with Thrace. It became famous for the great battle that occurred there in 42 B.C. between the armies of Brutus and Cassius (who assassinated Julius Caesar) on one side and those of Octavian and Mark Antony (friends and supporters of Caesar) on the other. The victory of the latter was a turning point in the history of Rome and marked the end of the Republic, opening the way to the establishment of the monarchy. The second event was the visit of the Apostle Paul, for whom Philippi was the first landing point on European soil, and where he preached his first evangelical sermon in Europe (Acts 16:12). There he won over to Christianity a *certain woman named Lydia, a seller of purple, of the city of Thyatira* (Acts 16:14). Philippi was a prosperous city thriving on the trade which passed along the Via Aegnatia – the road built by the Romans to connect Asia Minor with Italy. Following the activities of Paul, it readily abandoned its pagan gods and adopted Christianity.

Extensive evidence of the worship of various gods is seen in the series of shrines cut into the rock at the foot of the rocky hill on which Philippi is situated, and elsewhere in the surrounding area. Innumerable reliefs carved into the rocks and carrying effigies of Greek, Thracian and eastern gods were found, and half-way up the acropolis are the remains of a shrine to the Egyptian gods, Isis, Serapis and Harpocrates. On the acropolis are the remains of the Macedonian ramparts and a theatre built in the 4th century B.C., but extensively altered in the 2nd century A.D. Considerable parts of the stage from this latter period have survived, despite the fact that in the 3rd century the theatre was altered again, this time to accomodate the combats of gladiators and wild beasts.

THESSALONICA – SALONIKA

The third largest town in Greece, capital of its northern province Macedonia, called now Salonika. It is situated at the head of the Gulf of Thermai on the Aegean Sea and rises from the shore in the shape of an amphitheatre. Thessalonica was founded in 316-315 B.C. and, according to tradition, was named after Alexander the Great's sister, Thessaloniki. It became the major port of northern Greece, and in 148 B.C. became one of the capitals of Roman Macedonia and prospered greatly following the construction of Via Aegnatia which connected Asia Minor with Italy. Paul visited the town during the winter of A.D. 49-50. As was his custom wherever he went, he preached on three different Sabbaths in the synagogue of the prosperous, well-established Jewish community that had its quarter near the port. He was subsequently expelled from the city (Acts 17:1-10). However, he founded a church there, to whose members he wrote (Epistles to the Thessalonians) to encourage them and give them direction in their new faith. Thessalonica thus became one of the earliest centres of Christianity and several churches were built there over the ages. All, however, were destroyed during the numerous sackings the city suffered at the hands of waves of invaders – Goths, Avars, Slavs, Saracens, Normans and Turks – as well as during periods of internal religious unrest in the late Middle Ages. At the end of the 15th century, when the population of Thessalonica was greatly reduced and extremely impoverished,

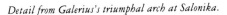

Detail from Galerius's triumphal arch at Salonika.

the town was given a boost by the arrival of 20,000 of the Jews expelled from Spain in 1492. The Jews contributed greatly to the demographic and economic revival of Thessalonica and lived in harmony with the local population until they were almost completely exterminated by the Germans in World War II. The prolonged Turkish occupation of Thessalonica between 1430 and 1912 gave the town a pronounced Moslem atmosphere with the surviving churches being turned into mosques. However, an enormous fire in August 1917 almost completely destroyed the centre of town which was subsequently rebuilt along modern lines.

The main sites of interest in Thessalonica are the remnants of the Byzantine churches of the 5th-15th centuries, most of them newly restored after the fire of 1917. Also of interest are the Galerius Arch, erected in A.D. 303 by the emperor Galerius and adorned with reliefs representing the victories of the Romans over the Persians, and the ramparts, the oldest sections of which date to the 4th century A.D. but with traces of older, Hellenistic ramparts visible here and there.

THE HOLY LAND

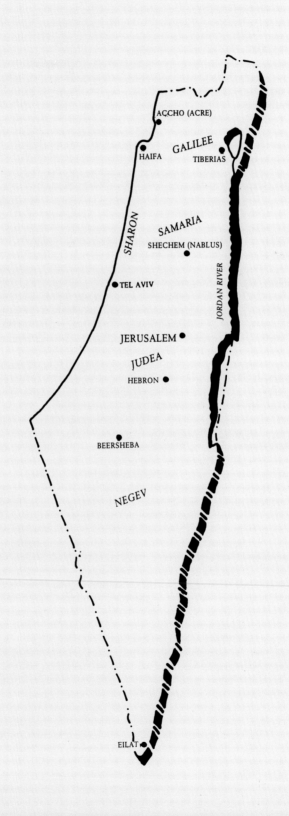

ACCHO (ACRE)

GALILEE

HAIFA
TIBERIAS

SHARON

SAMARIA
SHECHEM (NABLUS)

JORDAN RIVER

TEL AVIV

JERUSALEM
JUDEA
HEBRON

BEERSHEBA

NEGEV

EILAT

ABU GHOSH

Statue of the Virgin overlooking the village of Abu Ghosh.

Sometimes a tradition of holiness attaches itself to a place for no apparent reason other than convenience and accessibility. This is the case of the village of Abu Ghosh, erroneously identified by the Crusaders as EMMAUS, where the Risen Jesus made himself known to two of his disciples (Luke 24:13-35). The Crusaders did not know of – or perhaps did not accept – the identification of Emmaus with LATRUN, and, in their desire to locate Emmaus, measured the distance of 30 furlongs (11km; 7 miles) from Jerusalem given by Luke (24:13). This brought them to the village of Kiryat el-Anab, the former name of the village now known as Abu Ghosh – the name of one of the town's most powerful chiefs in the early 19th century.

It is interesting to note that Emmaus has been also identified with another site, the village of EL QUBEIBA.

The Tenth Roman Legion was stationed at the village after it had captured and destroyed JERUSALEM in the year A.D. 70 and built a water reservoir over the spring in Abu Ghosh. Later, in the 9th century, the reservoir was incorporated in a roadside inn. It thus became known to the Crusaders, who visualized this as the place where Jesus and his disciples rested and ate (Luke 24:28-30). The knights of the Order of the Hospitallers built a fortress-like church over the reservoir in the middle of the 12th century. This church has been preserved intact and is one of the finest examples of Crusader architecture. In the crypt under the church one can see the walls and steps leading to the original Roman reservoir, with a Latin inscription reading *Vexillatio Leg(ionis) X Fre(tensis)*.

The village of Abu Ghosh is situated, as mentioned, about 11km west of Jerusalem. Sometimes, as in the Roman, Crusader, and more recent periods, the main road connecting Jerusalem with the coast passed through it, increasing its importance. In the early 19th century, a period when law and order were not strictly enforced, the villagers harassed travellers on the road and extorted toll fees for the right of passage. Uncooperative victims were imprisoned in the Crusader church. Later, when other roads were preferred, Abu Ghosh lost all importance. Now the new Jerusalem-Tel Aviv highway passes south of the village.

(left) Stone bearing the imprint of the Roman Tenth Legion in the wall of the Crusader church. (right) Tomb in a niche near the church.

Earliest settlement of the site dates to the Neolithic period, when a small village existed there. In biblical times it was called Kirjath Jearim, "The Town of the Groves" – Kiryat el-Anab being an Arabic translation of the name. Initially one of the four cities of the Gibeonites (Joshua 9:17), it was taken over by the tribe of Judah and was located on the northwest boundary of the tribe's territory (Joshua 15:60). The Ark of the Covenant was housed here for a period of 20 years, from the time it was returned by the Philistines (I Samuel 6:12-17) until it was brought by King David to Jerusalem (II Samuel 6:12). On the assumed site of the biblical town, on the hill west of the village, stands the church of Notre Dame de l'Arche d'Alliance (Our Lady of the Ark of the Covenant) built in 1924, surmounted by a great statue of the Virgin and Child. During its construction remnants of a Byzantine church with a mosaic floor were found on the site; they can be seen in the new church. From this hill is a breathtaking view of the Judean mountains to the east and the coastal plain to the west.

ACCHO – ACRE

An ancient coastal town (given as Accho in the Bible) situated on the northern point of the Bay of Acre, opposite the town of Haifa and Mount Carmel. Accho was the only natural harbour on the coast of the Holy Land and one of the finest in the eastern Mediterranean. The fertile Plain of Acre opens into the Valley of Jezreel which is its agricultural hinterland and connection with the interior of the country. With such excellent natural conditions, Acre has known days of greatness, but also periods of desolation.

Accho was an important Canaanite town, mentioned as early as Eyptian sources of the 18th century B.C. It was also

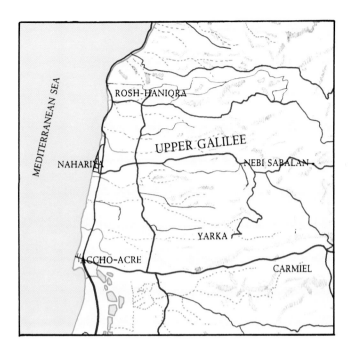

mentioned in letters and lists of places from 15th, 14th and 13th century B.C., all indicating its central position in the Land of Canaan. The Old Testament has little to say about Accho. It was included in the territory of the tribe of Asher but was not taken by the Israelites (Judges 1:31), at least not in the first stages of the conquest. Excavations in the mound of ancient Accho show that the site was inhabited in the 12th century B.C. by one of the tribes of the Sea People, who probably resisted Israelite assaults. During the First Temple period Accho was a Phoenician town, and thus outside the boundaries of Israel. It belonged to the territory of Sidon, and very little is actually known about its fate.

Only with the advent of Alexander the Great in 333 B.C. did Accho regain its importance. Alexander granted it the privilege of minting its own coins, and established a mint there. Ptolemy II Philadelphus (285-246 B.C.) of the Hellenestic dynasty of Egypt enlarged Accho and bestowed on it the special favour of bearing the dynastic name Ptolemais. This was a period of glory for the city which, for the first time, spread beyond the traditional confines of the ancient mound towards the sea coast. In the days of the Maccabean Revolt (135-132 B.C.) Accho-Ptolemais played an important role in the struggle for independence of the Jews, but, as in the first Temple period, it was not within the boundaries of the Jewish state. In the Roman period, Ptolemais became a colony and the Romans settled army veterans there. It was in this Roman town that St Paul spent a day on his return from his third missionary voyage (Acts 21:7). By then a Christian community was already established in Accho, and because of its largely gentile population, Christianity spread quickly in the city. In the year 190 the city already had a bishop.

Accho reached perhaps its most significant period in the time of the Crusaders, when its name was changed to St Jean

View of Acre from the sea.

d'Acre. It was first conquered by King Baldwin I in 1104, and became the main link between the Latin Kingdom and Europe. Recruits, pilgrims and supplies reached the busy docks of Acre aboard ships of Italian city-states. These city-states were so vital to the life of the city that they were granted the right to establish their own autonomous quarters in Acre, alongside the quarters of the military orders of the Templars and the Hospitallers. During the last hundred years of the Latin Kingdom, Acre was its centre, flourishing on the east-west trade. Its size in those days was about three times that of the walled city of today. The end of the Latin Kingdom came in 1291 when Acre fell to the Mamelukes.

For the next 450 years Acre lay in ruins until it became the centre of a small, independent fiefdom created by Daher

(left) An 18th-century khan (inn). (right) Entrance to St John's Crypt.

al-Omar and Ahmed Pasha in the second half of the 18th
century. The walls of present-day Acco were built in those
days, and withstood a 60-day siege by Napoleon in 1799.

The main sites of interest in Acre today are all within the
old city surrounded by the 18th-century walls. The wall is
complete with towers, gates ditch and counterscarp. The
domed mosque of Ahmed Pasha, known as al-Jazzar – the
butcher, is a landmark and below it spreads the Crusader
town, now partially below ground level. The most important
edifice of the Crusader town is the great refectory hall of the
Knights Hospitallers, one of the finest examples of Crusader
architecture of the 13th century. The entire old city of Acre
is basically Crusader. It is still possible to trace the quarters
of the Italian city-states and Crusader knights, to visit the
many inns, which, although rebuilt in the 18th century, are
Crusader in origin, and to walk streets lined with Crusader
private homes.

ADUMMIM – MA'ALE ADUMMIM

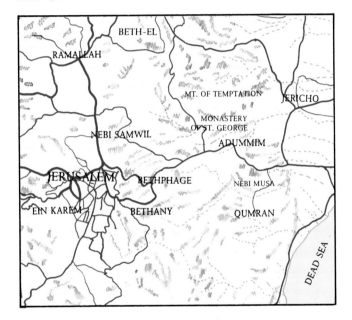

THE INN OF THE GOOD SAMARITAN

Adummim or Ma'ale Adummim (the red, or bloody, ascent)
is a site located halfway on the main road between Jerusalem
and Jericho. Its strange name probably derives from the
exposed patches of red limestone, tinted by iron oxide, which
served to define the boundary between the territories of the
tribes of Judah and Benjamin (Joshua 15:7; 18:17).

Being located in the Judean Desert, Adummim never
developed into a settlement. It may, however, have been the
site of both an inn for travellers between Jerusalem and Jericho
and a fortress to guard the road. The ruins of a police station
and an inn built in 1903 by the Turks are visible south of
the road.

The fact that this location is so suitable as a stopping place
for travellers on the road has led to its identification with the

Ma'ale Adummim.

Inn of the Good Samaritan which serves as the backdrop to the well-known parable in Luke 10:25-37. The good Samaritan found a man who had been robbed and badly wounded on the Jerusalem-Jericho road and brought him to an inn; he gave the innkeeper instructions and money to take care of the man. No remnants from the time of Jesus or of earlier days have as yet been found on the site. The mosaic floors and fragmentary walls unearthed in the courtyard of the police station probably belong to a Byzantine monastery, which, it seems, was built on the traditional site of the Inn of the Good Samaritan.

Another interesting feature of Adummim is a castle built by the Knights Templars of the Crusader Kingdom of Jerusalem on the north side of the road. The castle was called Maldouin, a corruption of the Hebrew name Ma'ale Adummim, or simply Chastel Rouge.

It is here at Adummim that the traveller from Jericho gets his first glimpse of Jerusalem. Further up the road towards Jerusalem is the new suburb of Ma'ale Adummim.

AWARTA

An Arab village in the mountains of Samaria, about 6km (4 miles) south-east of SHECHEM (Nablus). In the village are three sites connected with the priestly family of Aaron, Moses' brother. In the centre of the village is a tombstone believed to be that of Ithamar, Aaron's son, and brother of Eleazar who became the High Priest after Aaron died. On the western side of the village, on top of a hill, is a fenced enclosure and in it is another tomb which the Moslems attribute to Ezra the scribe, and the Jews, to Eleazar son of Aaron who *died and they buried him in a hill that pertained to Phinehas his son, which was given him in Mount Ephraim* (Joshua 24:33). Phinehas himself is believed to be buried next to his son Abishua, in the cemetery on the eastern hill of the village. The site is marked by a domed structure. Abishua is particularly revered by the Samaritans, who believe that he wrote their ancient Torah scroll which is kept to this day in their synagogue at Shechem.

The 70 elders who received some of the spirit of God and helped Moses bear the burden of the people (Numbers 11:16-17) are said to be buried in a cave next to the tomb of Abishua.

The site of the village of Awarta was inhabited in the First Temple period, the Byzantine and Early Moslem periods and again from the Ottoman period. It was a very important Samaritan centre between the 4th and 12th centuries and contained one of their main synagogues.

BANIAS-CAESAREA PHILIPPI

The river Hermon at the site of Caesarea Philippi.

The spring at Banias.

An ancient city at the foot of Mount Hermon in the north of Israel, on the road leading from Kiryat Shmona to the Golan Heights. It is located near the spring of the river Hermon, one of the three rivers which join to form the Jordan River. The name Banias is the Arabic pronunciation of Paneas or Pamias – the city of Pan, the god of springs and shepherds of ancient Greece, who was worshipped here in the first centuries A.D. The cult of Pan seems to have flourished on the rock escarpment above the town, where several caves and niches can be seen including the one from which the spring feeding the Hermon River issues. One elaborate rock-cut niche surmounted by a decorative conch may have contained the statue of the god Pan. Under it is a Greek inscription which mentions the nymph Echo and Diopan, the Greek god, "lover of music."

The city of Panias was given to King Herod by the Roman emperor, Augustus. In gratitude Herod built an elaborate palace here in honour of Augustus (Josephus Flavius, *Wars I, 21:3*). Fragments of walls found some 70m (215 ft) southwest of the rock escarpment, built in the Roman technique of *Opus reticulatum* , i.e., in a herring-bone pattern, may be remnants of this palace. After Herod's death, his son Philip became ruler of the region and made Panias his capital. He further beautified the city and renamed it Caesarea Philippi, a name by which it is mentioned in Matthew 16:13-20 and Mark 8:27-30 as the northernmost point visited by Jesus and his disciples. During this visit the true nature of Jesus "the Christ, the Son of the living God" was recognized by Simon Bar-Jonah. Jesus blessed Simon and changed his name to Peter ("The Rock") saying, *and upon this rock I will build my church* (Matthew 16:18). Jesus also gave Peter the keys to the kingdom of heaven saying, *whatsoever thou shalt bind on earth shall be bound in heaven: and whatsoever thou shalt loose on earth shall be loosed in heaven* (Matthew 16:19). The spot where Peter is believed to have

Rock-cut niche dedicated to the god Pan.

received the keys to the kingdom of heaven is shown above the rock escarpment.

The importance of Panias to Christianity grew with time. While in the first centuries it was still a pagan city where the small Christian community was persecuted and its churches burnt, in the 4th and 5th centuries it was already a episcopy and two of its bishops participated in church councils, one in 325, the other in 451.

Even after the Arab conquest in the 7th century, Panias, now called Banias, remained a prosperous city on the road to Damascus. Its importance increased in the Crusader and Mameluke periods, when it was surrounded by a strong wall and towers, which are well preserved, and can be seen on the west, south and east sides of the site.

Today Banias is a major tourist attraction, with pleasant surroundings, important remnants of the past, and many local amenities.

BEER-SHEBA

Abraham's Well in Beersheba.

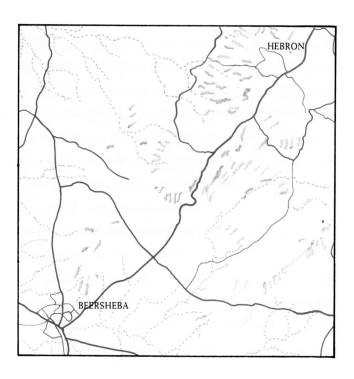

Capital of the Negev region in the southern part of Israel, Beer-sheba was an important town in biblical times, and was connected in particular with the Patriarchs. The meaning of Beer-sheba – "Well of the Oath" – refers to the oath sworn by Abraham and Abimelech ruler of the region, proclaiming Abraham's ownership over *a well of water, which Abimelech's servants had violently taken away* (Genesis 21:25). Thus the name evokes the semi-arid character of the northern Negev, where people and animals alike are dependent solely on water wells. Abraham then planted a terebinth tree (or a grove according to the King James translation) in Beer-sheba *and called there the name of the Lord, the everlasting God* (Genesis 21:33). The dispute over water wells continued in the time of Isaac, Abraham's son (Genesis 26:15-33). Because of the dispute Isaac retreated from the coastal plain to Beer-sheba, where he received God's blessing and built an altar thus adding to the sanctity established in the days of Abraham. Here also the covenant with Abimelech was renewed. Jacob departed twice from Beer-sheba, first when he left for Haran (Genesis 28:10), and then, much later in his life, when he went down to Egypt (Genesis 46:1-5).

From the days of the Judges, Beer-sheba was the southern limit of the Promised Land (I Samuel 3:20; I Kings 4:25) and its sanctity was recognized.

Of the many wells in and around Beer-sheba, one, near the Bedouin market, is known as the Well of Abraham. The ancient biblical period settlement was located at Tell Beer-sheba, some 4km (2.5 miles) east of the town. Excavations carried out on the tell between 1969 and 1976 have revealed a series of settlements from the time of the Judges to the destruction of the Kingdom of Judah (12th-6th centuries B.C.) In those days Beer-sheba was a well-planned town with strong defences, an impressive gateway, a storage building and private residences. These well-preserved remnants can be seen on the tell. After the fall of the Kingdom of Judah the settlement left the tell and moved to a new site within the limits of modern Beer-sheba. Here traces of the Roman-Byzantine periods (3rd-6th centuries A.D.) have been found. On both sides of the Wadi Beer-sheba, south of the town, were found interesting villages of the 4th millennium B.C. The ancient inhabitants of these villages were master-craftsmen in copper and ivory, and their products are among the most sophisticated found in the entire Near East. Some of these are exhibited at the Israel Museum in Jerusalem.

The modern town of Beersheba began its development in 1900 when it became the regional headquarters of the Turkish army. It grew under the British mandate (1971-1948) but its major expansion started in the early 1950s. Nowadays, Beersheba is a fast-growing town with a modern medical centre, a university, a symphony orchestra and other cultural and industrial institutions.

View of the excavations at Tell Beer-sheba. (below left) Krater from Tell Beer-sheba. (below right) Egg of an ostrich from the Persian period found at Tell Beer-sheba.

BETHANY

A village on the lower eastern slope of the MOUNT OF OLIVES, *nigh unto Jerusalem, about fifteen furlongs off* (John 11:18), on the Jerusalem-Jericho road. The name Bethany derives from the Greek form of the Hebrew Beth-Ananiah (The house of a person named Ananiah), or the shortened version Beth-Aniah. The site does not seem to have been inhabited prior to nor during the First Temple period. The earliest occupation dates to the 6th century B.C., the Persian period, to which time dates also the first literary mention of the place (Nehemiah 11:32). From that time on, Bethany has been continuously settled and was, as it is now, the last stop on the Jericho road before entering Jerusalem. The present Arab village is called Al-Azariyeh, an Arabic version of the name of Lazarus, the most famous inhabitant of the village.

It was the sojourn of Jesus in the village of Bethany which made the place significant and holy to the Christian world. Lazarus and his two sisters Martha and Mary, who were friends and admirers of Jesus, lived in Bethany and welcomed him in their home. Here Jesus preached, while Martha served him

View of Al-Azariyeh (Bethany).

food and Mary sat at his feet and listened to his words (Luke 10:38-42). The most famous event which occurred in Bethany was the resurrection of Lazarus, as narrated in the Gospel of John, chapter 11. Lazarus became sick and died, and was buried in the family sepulchre. Jesus, who was at that time staying east of the Jordan, came to Bethany four days after Lazarus was buried and was met by Martha and Mary. They both beseeched Jesus to bring their brother back to life, saying, *Lord, if thou hadst been here, my brother had not died* (John 11:21). Jesus went to the tomb of Lazarus and *cried with a loud voice, Lazarus, come forth. And he that was dead came forth, bound hand and foot with graveclothes...* (John 11:43-44). This was one of the greatest miracles performed by Jesus, and it caused many who were present to believe in him.

The last visit of Jesus to Bethany took place six days before the Passover, when he was a guest in the house of Simon the Leper, with the resurrected Lazarus and Martha and Mary being present. On this occasion the devoted Mary anointed Jesus with a very costly ointment and wiped his feet with her hair. When the disciples, and especially Judas Iscariot, complained of the waste of money which could have been given to the poor, Jesus explained Mary's act as a sign of his coming death (John 12:1-8). From Bethany Jesus proceeded to Jerusalem where the final episodes in his life took place leading to the Crucifixion.

CHURCH OF ST LAZARUS

A short distance to the east of the tomb stands the imposing Roman Catholic Church of St Lazarus, built in 1952-53. It has a silver dome and a modern mosaic floor depicting scenes from the story of Lazarus. Prior to the builing of the church the site was excavated and remnants of a 4th-century church were found. Its apse can be seen inside the new church, and part of its mosaic floor, which includes geometric designs, is in the courtyard. This early church was destroyed by an

Church of St Lazarus at Bethany.

earthquake and rebuilt in the 6th century on a larger scale. It was in use until the time of the Crusaders, who restored it and reinforced it with buttresses. The foundations of the 6th-century church were incorporated into the modern church.

The site of the village of Bethany itself was uphill, beyond the churches and the mosque. The remains of a Crusader-period Benedictine monastery mark the traditional place of the house of Mary and Martha. Beyond are the ruins of a Crusader tower built to defend the monastery.

The population of the village of Al-Azariyeh was predominantly Christian until the 20th century, when many Moslem residents, especially from Hebron were drawn to it.

TOMB OF LAZARUS

Bethany attracted believers from the very early days of Christianity. The place of the tomb of Lazarus, the most important and holy site in the village, was not forgotten, and as early as the 4th century a church stood at the site. Some parts of this church, including its apse, were uncovered by excavations in 1881 under a mosque named Al-Uzeir, another Arabic variation of the name of Lazarus. The excavations also exposed a rock-cut sepulchre believed to be the tomb of Lazarus. The sepulchre consists of a vestibule and burial chamber reached by descending 24 well-worn steps. When the mosque was built, Christians were not allowed to enter the tomb. In 1613 the Franciscan Custodian of the Holy Land was allowed to cut a new entrance to the tomb from the outside, which is used to this day. In 1883 a Greek Orthodox church and small convent were erected on the site. Inside the church is the Stone of Colloquy, marking the place where Jesus was met by Martha and Mary.

Entrance to the tomb of Lazarus in Bethany.

BETH-EL

View of Beth-el.

The Hebrew name Beth-el means "The House of God." It is here that God revealed himself to the Patriarch Jacob in the famous Vision of the Ladder (Genesis 28:11-22). The site must have been important even before the divine revelation, being situated on the main highway which runs along the watershed of the Judean Mountains, about 22.5km (14 miles) north of Jerusalem. It is along this highway that Abraham travelled when he first came to the Land of Canaan, and pitched his tent east of Beth-el (Genesis 12:8), at that time called Luz (Genesis 28:19). Abraham built an altar on the site where he camped, thus either sanctifying the place for the first time, or drawing upon earlier notions of holiness. Abraham returned to the same site after his sojourn in Egypt (Genesis 13:3-4). But it is Jacob who is most intimately associated with the place, having had there the vision of the ladder spanning heaven and earth on which angels ascended and descended and having there heard God's promise to give the land to his numerous descendants. Jacob named the place Beth-el and erected a pillar of stone there to commemorate his experience. Upon his return from his long sojourn in Haran, God summoned Jacob back to Beth-el, where he built an altar. God revealed himself again to Jacob and renewed his promise (Genesis 35:1-15).

The exact site of the divine revelation, of the pillar and of the altar has been forgotten over the ages, and no building or sign mark the significant events which took place there. The town of Beth-el is identified with the Arab village Beitin which preserves the sound of the biblical name. Remnants of this ancient town have come to light in archaeological excavations. It was established that the site was already inhabited in the Early Bronze age (3rd millennium B.C.) and that occupation continued almost without interruption for

View of Beitin, identified with Beth-el.

some 3,500 years until the Arab conquest in the 7th century. The town enjoyed a period of prosperity in the 2nd millennium B.C., spanning the Middle Bronze age – traditionally identified with the age of the Patriarchs – and the Late Bronze age, i.e., the time of the sojourn of the Children of Israel in Egypt. This fortified and well-built Canaanite town was sacked, perhaps by the tribes of Joseph (Judges 1:22-26) and Ephraim in whose territory it lay (I Chronicles 7:28). Next to the destroyed Canaanite town, the Israelites built a small, modest and unfortified village, now named Beth-el in memory of the vision of their ancestor Jacob. Soon Beth-el became a centre of religious life, and the Ark of the Covenant, the holiest object of Israelite worship, was placed there in a modest temple (Judges 20:18, 27; 21:2), presumably visited by Samuel (I Samuel 7:16; 10:3).

Archaeological excavations indicate that this Israelite settlement of the times of the Judges was sacked twice, perhaps by the Philistines, a fact not mentioned in the Bible.

Beth-el prospered again in the time of the United Monarchy, and with the division of the country between Judah and Israel it was on the southern border of Israel. For a while it was captured by the kings of Judah (II Chronicles 13:9) and perhaps even destroyed. The ancient sanctity of Beth-el was used by King Jeroboam who, in his attempt to draw his people away from Jerusalem, established a rival cult at Beth-el, and erected a temple with an altar and a golden calf. He set up a new order of priests, and even ordered a new feast to be celebrated at Beth-el (I Kings 12:27-33). The people of Israel accepted these innovations, not so the people of Judah whose condemnation is voiced by a man of God who came to Beth-el and reproached Jeroboam (I Kings 13:1-6).

Beth-el was visited by the prophets Elijah and Elisha, who met there *sons of the prophets that were at Beth-el* (II Kings 2:2-3). We do not hear from them a condemnation of the cult of the place, such as was voiced by Amos (4:4; 5:5-6), Hosea (10:15) and Jeremiah (48:13). It seems that the sanctuary at Beth-el was destroyed by Josiah (II Kings 23:15), who invaded Israel and sacked all its places of worship in his attempt to establish the centre of worship of God in Jerusalem. After Josiah's reform Beth-el was never again a place of worship.

Beth-el developed during the Hellenist period. In 160 B.C. it was fortified by Bacchides (I Maccabees 9:50), and in A.D. 69 it was captured by the Roman general, Vespasian. Shortly afterwards it was rebuilt as a Roman township. Beth-el grew to relative importance in the Byzantine period because of memories of the divine revelation, and a church was built over the site where Jacob was believed to have had his vision. Remnants of the main street of the settlement of that time were uncovered in excavations. The town flourished until the Arab conquest.

The stone on which Jacob is said to have rested his head while having his dream is interwoven in an interesting manner with legends of areas far removed from the hills of Judea. A popular Irish legend claims that the Stone of Tara is that same stone. It was later taken to Scone in Scotland where it was used as the coronation stone of the kings of Scotland. It was removed by Edward I (1272-1307) to Westminster Abbey in London, where it is to this day placed under the coronation throne of the kings of England.

BETH JAMAL

A complex comprising a monastery and an agricultural school situated on a hill about 2km (1.5 miles) south of Beth Shemesh, approached by a dirt road leading east from the Beth Shemesh-Valley of Elah road. The monastery was built in 1881 by the Salesian Order on the site believed to be that of the village of Gamala, the hometown of Rabban Gamaliel I, Paul's teacher (Acts 22:3). In 1915 the remnants of a Byzantine church were found on the site including a mosaic floor with the Greek inscription *the most famous and holy to God, Stephanus*. The tomb discovered under the Byzantine church was thus identified as the tomb of St Stephen. In 415 the body of the saint was transferred to the CHURCH OF ST STEPHEN in JERUSALEM. In honour of the discovery of the ancient church and tomb, a new church was built on the site following the plan of the Byzantine basilica. The school and dormitory were built in Italian style. The area around is rich in both natural and planted forests.

BETHLEHEM

A picturesque town, some 9km (5.5 miles) south of Jerusalem, of great historical and religious importance. It is a mountain town, some 770m (about 2,500 ft) above sea level, on the edge of the Judean Desert and very close to the main Beersheba-Hebron-Jerusalem-Bethel road known as the Way of the Patriarchs. The site of ancient Bethlehem, located in the vicinity of the CHURCH OF THE NATIVITY, has not been

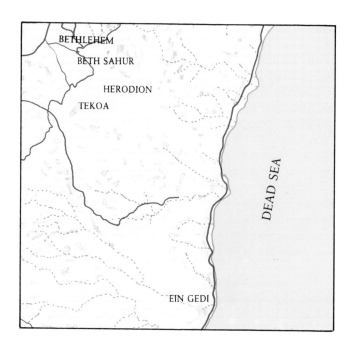

excavated, thus the ancient history of the town has not been archaeologically documented. It is not known when the site was first occupied, nor when it rose to prominence. Our knowledge is derived only from literary sources. Bethlehem seems to have had religious significance as early as the time of the prophet Samuel, who came to Bethlehem, *And he said, Peaceably: I am come to sacrifice unto the Lord: sanctify yourselves, and come with me to the sacrifice* (I Samuel 16:5). Those who took part in that sacrifice – Jesse and his sons, including David – have immortalized Bethlehem.

Sunrise over the belfreys and minarets of Bethlehem.

Aerial view of Bethlehem.

Bethlehem, where King David was born, was also the birthplace of Jesus a thousand years later. This latter event has sanctified Bethlehem for all Christendom, and important sites connected with the Nativity and events related to it abound in the town. Most important among these are the CHURCH OF THE NATIVITY, the MILK GROTTO and the SHEPHERDS' FIELDS. Since the 5th century the population of Bethlehem and its vicinity has been predominantly Christian. Bethlehem is flanked by two Christian villages – Beth Jala and Beth Sahur – which have today almost merged with the town.

Bethlehemite wearing traditional costume.

A visit to Bethlehem is a profound religious experience. It is also an encounter with a colorful, folkloristic environment. The market of Bethlehem, located west and uphill from Manger Square at the centre of town, is a meeting place for Bedouins from the Judean Desert, villagers from adjacent villages and townspeople, each wearing their special costumes and selling their specialized products. Occasionally one can still see an older woman in the street wearing a traditional everyday costume, but for a good look at the better quality garments, as well as at traditional household objects, one should visit the small, well-kept folklore museum in a tiny alley next to the main street of the old town. Watch for the sign on the left-hand side as you walk back from the market to Manger Square.

Bethlehem is also renowned for its traditional crafts in olive wood and mother-of-pearl. Statues, rosaries, jewellery and other objects worked in these materials make lovely souvenirs.

ARMENIAN MONASTERY

(left) St Jerome's lecture hall. (right) Painting of the Virgin and Child over the 17th-century altar in the church of the Armenian Monastery.

South of the main CHURCH OF THE NATIVITY lies the Armenian Monastery which actually closes the court in front of the church on its southern side. Inside the monastery are substantial segments of the Byzantine and Crusader period structures, the most notable of which is a large colonnaded hall with Byzanytine capitals, believed to be the hall where St Jerome taught his disciples.

The Church of the Nativity is thus a place of worship for Christians of different denominations, who unite in the commemoration of the events which occurred in the humble cave on the very first Christmas Eve.

CHURCH OF ST CATHERINE

North of the CHURCH OF THE NATIVITY lies the Franciscan Church of St Catherine. This is a relatively modern church,

built in 1882 over the ruins of a 12th-century Crusader church.
From the main hall, steps lead down to a series of five
subterranean chambers. In the first St Jerome lived and
worked, and in the second is his tomb and the joint tomb of
his pupils, Sts Paula and Eustochium. All the tombs are empty
(the bones of St Jerome are shown in the Church of St Mary
Major in Rome, alongside the silver manger which stood in the
Grotto of the Nativity in the Byzantine period). The adjacent
chambers contain the tomb of St Eusebius, St Jerome's
successor, the Chapel of the Innocent Children and the Chapel
of St Joseph. The last chamber is connected by a door to the
Grotto of the Nativity. All these caves were studied and
restored in 1962-64, and were found to have been
pre-Byzantine burial caves.

In front of the Church of St Catherine is a beautiful Crusader
cloister, restored in 1948-49. In the centre of the cloister is a
statue of St Jerome and next to it a skull, symbolical of the
strict hermetic life he led.

Church of St Catherine at Bethlehem.

CHURCH OF THE NATIVITY

This impressive church, standing in the centre of Bethlehem on the traditional site of the birth of Jesus, is one of the holiest places for the Christian world, perhaps "the earth's most sacred spot" as St Jerome wrote. The church, the surrounding area with its many other places of worship, and the entire town of Bethlehem are full of memories of the birth of Jesus and of the first days of his life.

According to the Gospels, the crucial events of Jesus' birth and early recognition took place in what was then a natural cave, used as a stable, on the outskirts of Bethlehem. Mary and Joseph, coming from Nazareth, had to stay here, as there was no room for them in the local inn. Here, in these humble surroundings, Mary gave birth to her firstborn son, whom she wrapped in swaddling clothes and placed in the manger (Luke 2:7). It was here that the humble local shepherds came in search of the newborn child, after an angel appeared to them (Luke 2:8-20). Wise men from the East, guided by a star, also came to adore the infant, and brought rich gifts of gold and incense (Matthew 2:1-12). When Jesus was a month old, the family left Bethlehem and went to Jerusalem to present its firstborn son in the Temple, in accordance with Jewish custom (Luke 2:22-24).

Bethlehem does not play any further role in the life of Jesus but the memory of the grotto where he was born lived in the hearts of the early Christians. The Roman authorities did what they could to wipe out this memory. They planted a grove dedicated to the pagan god Adonis, lover of Venus, in the immediate vicinity of the cave and established his cult in the grotto. The knowledge of the Nativity in that cave was

The fortress-like exterior of the Church of the Nativity (background) and the Armenian Monastery (right).

nevertheless not forgotten, and Origen, who visited Bethlehem in the year 220, relates that it was common knowledge among the inhabitants of the area including the heathens. It was only when Emperor Constantine of Byzantium made Christianity the official religion of the empire that the cave was cleared of the pagan ritual and a magnificent church erected over it. What had been until then a secluded cave at the edge of an obscure village, became the heart of the town of Bethlehem and a focal point of devotion for Christians throughout the world.

The Church of the Nativity, built in 326, was one of the three earliest official churches, built with public funds, commemorating the three principal events in the life of Jesus. The Grotto of the Nativity was enlarged and its shape adapted to the needs of worship. The ground above the cave was levelled to accommodate the altar and an octagonal structure built around it. From this octagon, the main body of the church, the basilica, stretched to the west. It was an imposing structure, with a wide central nave and four aisles, two on each side, divided by four rows of monolithic columns. In front of the facade of the church with its triple entrance was a square atrium (courtyard). The church was renowned for its beauty and splendour, and visitors of the 4th and 5th centuries marvelled at its mosaic floors, frescoed walls, and marble columns. The original humble manger was replaced by one made of silver. The church became a focus of pilgrimage from all over the Roman world. In 386 a most distinguished group of devotees, including the Roman patrician lady Paula, her daughter Eustochium and St Jerome, secretary to Pope Damasus, arrived in Bethlehem. Paula founded a convent near the church, and St Jerome secluded himself in a cave in the

Plan of the Church of the Nativity compound.

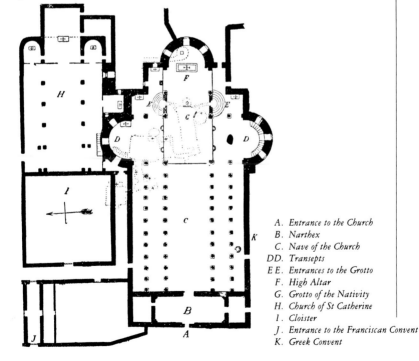

A. Entrance to the Church
B. Narthex
C. Nave of the Church
DD. Transepts
E E. Entrances to the Grotto
F. High Altar
G. Grotto of the Nativity
H. Church of St Catherine
I. Cloister
J. Entrance to the Franciscan Convent
K. Greek Convent

Roof of the Church of the Nativity. From this angle, the transepts and apse of Justinian's church can be seen.

vicinity, where he worked at the translation of the Bible from the original Hebrew into Latin, known as the Vulgate. This translation is still the official Bible of the Roman Catholic Church, and was instrumental in spreading knowledge of the Bible throughout the Christian world.

The church of Constantine was damaged with time, and during the reign of Emperor Justinian in the 6th century an ambitious rebuilding programme was undertaken. The old church was actually demolished, its floor was covered with about 520mm (20 inches) of soil and the new church was erected on a higher level. The church one visits today is basically Justinian's basilica. Like the previous one it is a five-aisled basilica, with a narthex added between the main hall and the atrium. The area surrounding the cave was enlarged, and a transept ending in an apse on each end replaced the octagon. There is a third apse in the eastern wall of the church. The facade of the church, with a large central entrance and two smaller side ones, was covered with a colourful mosaic depicting the Nativity and the Magi. When the Persians invaded Palestine in 614, they destroyed many of its churches, but this one was spared because, so the story goes, the invaders were surprised to see a representation of the Magi dressed as Persians. The church remained more or less unchanged in the

Interior of the Church of the Nativity. Remains of the mosaic of Constantine's ▷ church can be seen through the opening in the floor.

following centuries, although at some point a straight lintel replaced the arch of the main entrance.

With the arrival of the Crusaders the church was personally taken by the Norman noble, Tancred, and one hundred of his knights while the rest of the Crusader army was resting at Emmaus before marching on Jerusalem. On Christmas day 1100, six months after the fall of Jerusalem, Baldwin was crowned first king of the Latin Kingdom in the Church of the Nativity in Bethlehem.

The Crusaders fortified the church and built a monastery next to it with a beautiful cloister; both church and monastery were surrounded by a wall. The inside of the church was restored and embellished, but its basic shape was not changed. The lower part of the walls was panelled with white marble, the upper part covered with rich mosaics, and the limestone columns painted with images of the Apostles.

During the centuries following the fall of the Latin Kingdom in 1187 the Church of the Nativity changed hands frequently among the various Christian denominations active in Palestine. Very little was done to maintain it and it slowly fell into decay. The two major contenders for possession of the church were the Greek Orthodox and the Franciscans. The contest sometimes degenerated into violent clashes, pillaging and destruction of holy objects. Since 1873 there has been a

The star which marks the spot where Jesus was born.

policeman on duty day and night in the church to prevent such occurrences. An earthquake in 1834 and a fire in 1869 also added to the lamentably dangerous state of the church. Only in 1933 was a partial restoration undertaken by the British Mandate government and further repairs have been carried out since 1967 under the auspices of the Israeli government.

The visit to the church is a solemn and gratifying experience. The visitor approaches the entrance via a wide, paved courtyard, part of the old Byzantine atrium. Of the three original entrances to the church, the two side ones are walled up, while the central part is narrowed down to a small, low opening. This was done around the year 1500 to prevent horses from entering the church. Once inside, the visitor stands in the low but wide narthex, which is in almost total darkness. One door opens onto the main hall of the basilica, and then the magnificence of the church is fully revealed. The nave and aisles do no contain any furniture. Traces of the medieval drawings can be seen on the columns, as well as fragments of the mosaics on the upper walls, and sections of the Constantine mosaic floor under some wooden boards. The ceiling of exposed wooden beams dates to the 14th century, with 19th-century restorations.

The eastern part of the church, from the upraised choir, is richly embellished in Greek Orthodox style. The high wooden

The manger in the Grotto of the Nativity in which Mary laid the infant Jesus.

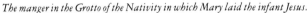

iconostasis (screen separating the altar from the main church) is covered with icons and rich geometric and floral decorations. The many hangings and standing lamps are also typical features of eastern churches.

North of the choir, in the northern arm of the transept, is the Chapel of the Kings, named after the Kings, or Magi, who are believed to have come here. This part of the church belongs to the Armenian Church.

From here a flight of steps leads down to the Grotto of the Nativity. On the white marble floor on one side of the cave is the fourteen-pointed silver star bearing the words *Hic de Virgine Maria Jesus Christus natus est* – "Here Jesus Christ was born to the Virgin Mary." In the north side of the cave is the Manger, and facing it, an altar dedicated to the Wise Men from the East. The grotto is illuminated by many oil lamps and its walls are covered with fireproof material, a precaution against fires which caused serious damage here in the past.

HOUSE OF JOSEPH

A small house east of the MILK GROTTO, built in 1890 by the Franciscans on the spot where, according to a 14th-century tradition, the house of Joseph, the husband of Mary, stood (Luke 2:4).

MILK GROTTO

A short distance south of the Church of the Nativity is this famous grotto. The site is sacred to Christians and Moslems alike and is frequented by many pilgrims, especially new mothers who collect the soft white chalk from the walls of the cave and mix it with their food, as it is believed to increase the milk of nursing mothers. There is a tradition that the white colour of the chalk was caused by a drop of milk which fell from Mary's breast when she took shelter here with her husband and new-born baby Jesus. The white stone of the grotto was also believed to have other therapeutic powers, and from the 7th century on fragments were sent from here to churches in Europe. When the Crusader king, Baldwin II, besieged Ashkelon in 1123, he had stones from the Milk Grotto brought to his camp, to ensure victory.

Today the grotto belongs to the Franciscans, who built a church over it in 1871.

(left) Entrance to the Milk Grotto. (right) The Flight of the Holy Family to Egypt depicted on one of the columns.

The Shepherds' Field.

At the time of Jesus' birth in Bethlehem, several shepherds were keeping watch over their sheep in a nearby field. *And lo, the angel of the Lord came upon them... Fear not: for, behold I bring you good tidings of great joy, which shall be to all people... unto you is born this day in the city of David a Saviour, which is Christ the Lord...* (Luke 2:9-11). The shepherds went to Bethlehem, found Mary, Joseph and the infant Jesus, and returned to their flocks glorifying and praising God. The place where the humble shepherds first received the message about the Nativity became one of the holiest Christian sites.

The exact spot where the angel appeared to the shepherds is not known, but tradition points to two sites, both on the outskirts of the Christian-Arab village of Bet Sahur, now an eastern suburb of the town of Bethlehem. One of the traditional sites of the Shepherds' Field, known locally as Deir el-Ranat (Convent of the Shepherds) is on the left-hand side of the road that leaves Bet Sahur to the east. The site, identified with biblical Tower of Edar (Tower of the Flock) where Jacob sojourned after his wife Rachel died (Genesis 35:21), is in the care of the Greek Orthodox church. Excavations on the site carried out in 1972 showed that it was indeed revered as early as the 4th century. Initially a natural cave was used as a place of worship. According to tradition, the shepherds received the good tidings in the cave, although no cave is mentioned in the biblical narrative. In the 5th century the cave was enlarged and a large, ornate church built inside it. Because the entire church was subterranean, it has been well preserved to this day and is one of the best examples of early Byzantine churches. It can be visited today near the new Greek Orthodox church.

Two churches were built in the 6th century over the subterranean church without damaging the older one, and in the 7th century a monastery was added on the site. Pilgrims who visited the monastery reported that they had been shown the tombs of the shepherds.

In the early 11th century the site was deserted but its significance was not forgotten. From the 12th century on pilgrims came to see the famous ruins and left detailed descriptions of them.

In the middle of the 19th century another site nearby, on the right-hand side of the road, was proposed as the Shepherds' Field. It was purchased by the Franciscans who in 1954 built a lovely, tent-shaped chapel designed by the renowned architect Barlozzi. It is decorated with panels depicting scenes from the early life of Jesus. Excavations conducted prior to the construction of this chapel revealed the ruins of a vast monastic agricultural establishment.

Further to the east of Bet Sahur is a plain known as the Field of Ruth. In these pastoral surroundings, the story of Ruth is said to have taken place.

TOMB OF RACHEL

The traditional burial place of Rachel, the beloved wife of the Patriarch Jacob. The small building with a sparkling white dome is located on the northern outskirts of the town of Bethlehem, south of Jerusalem. The biblical narrative tells that the family of Jacob was travelling on the main road of the mountain area of Canaan when Rachel was about to deliver her second child. On the way she went into difficult labour and gave birth to Benjamin, the youngest of the children of Jacob. *And Rachel died, and was buried in the way to Ephrath, which is Bethlehem. And Jacob set a pillar upon her grave: that is the pillar of Rachel's grave unto this day* (Genesis 35:19-20). The sad facts of Rachel's death and burial on the way to Bethlehem are recounted by Jacob to Joseph, Rachel's firstborn child (Genesis 48:7).

Rachel's tomb.

Another biblical tradition places the tomb of Rachel at Zelzah in the territory of Benjamin (I Samuel 10:2), and yet another, at Ramah – about 10km (6 miles) north of Jerusalem. It is at Ramah that Rachel stood watching her children being driven into exile by the Babylonians, and lamented and bitterly wept (Jeremiah 31:15). The same image, quoted from Jeremiah, was used by Matthew, when telling of the massacre of the Innocent Children of Bethlehem (Matthew 2:17-18). Rachel thus became the supreme Mother figure, watching over her children at all times. Of all the traditions about the location of the tomb of Rachel, the one near Bethlehem is the most favoured, and this is reflected in the writings of Josephus Flavius, the Talmud and the Church Fathers.

The earliest building over the place of the tomb was erected by the Crusaders, although previously it seems to have been marked by a small pyramid. The Crusader building was square with four open arches, and surmounted by a dome. The holiness of the place to Jews and Christians was accepted by the Moslems, who, however, allowed only people of their faith to enter the tomb after they had expelled the Crusaders. In 1841 Sir Moses Montefiore obtained the keys of the place for the Jews.

The building over the tomb has not changed much. The open arches were walled up in 1788, and in 1841 a square vestibule was added. The place of the tomb itself is marked by a large stone overlaid with velvet coverings.

Rachel's tomb is visited by numerous people of all faiths, especially by women who seek help from the gentle and beloved mother. Praying at the tomb is considered especially beneficial with regard to fertility and childbirth. According to popular belief a red thread measured against the tombstone is a good luck charm and a piece of such thread is often tied around the wrists of brides and newborn babies.

BETHPHAGE

An ancient village on the MOUNT OF OLIVES, the exact location of which is not known. It could not have been far from BETHANY from which Jesus sent two of his disciples to bring him a donkey on which he rode into Jerusalem (Matthew 21:1-16; Mark 11:1-11).

The name Bethphage means in Hebrew "house of the unripe figs," probably because of the many fig trees that grew around the village. Today the name Bethphage applies to a Franciscan church built next to the very steep road that descends from the Mount of Olives eastwards towards the village of El-Azariyeh (ancient Bethany) and the Jerusalem-Jericho highway. Here in the 4th century was a church commemorating the meeting of Martha and Mary with Jesus (John 11:20-32); during the Crusader period this was the site of a church from which the Palm Sunday Procession started. In 1887 the Franciscans purchased the ground and built the present church on it. It contains a most unusual cubical stone, accidentally discovered on the site in

View of Bethphage.

1875. The stone has on its sides various paintings – the resurrection of Lazarus, people holding palms, and a group of people with a donkey and its foal – which commemorate events that took place in the vicinity. On one side is a Latin inscription mentioning the name Bethphage. The paintings, which seem to be from the Crusader period, were badly damaged when first found and were restored. The work was completed in 1950 when the church was enlarged and adorned with frescoes.

Several Jewish burial caves from the Second Temple period were excavated in the church compound. They contained stone burial ossuaries with decorations and inscriptions.

BETHSAIDA – BET SAIDA

An ancient town of fishermen, as the name, which means "House of Fishing," implies. Although its exact site is not known, it is commonly accepted that Bethsaida was located on the north-eastern shore of the SEA OF GALILEE, in the Betekha valley, a marshy area where rivers coming down from the Golan Heights drain into the sea. No place of worship commemorates its importance as the native town of Peter, Andrew and Philip (John 1:43), and the place where Jesus performed many miracles. Because its inhabitants did not accept Jesus and his teachings, Jesus cursed Bethsaida as he

The Betekha Valley where Bethsaida may have been.

did CHORAZIN saying, *Woe to thee... Bethsaida! for if the mighty works which were done in you, had been done in Tyre and Sidon, they would have repented long ago in sackcloth and ashes* (Matthew 11:21). It is thought that the curse was so powerful that Bethsaida completely disappeared from memory.

CAESAREA

A most important port city on the Mediterranean coast of the Holy Land, in the Northern Sharon. It was established during the Hellenistic period (3rd century B.C.) as a Phoenician port town named Straton's Tower and served as a harbour for ships sailing between Syria and Egypt. The town was captured in 96 B.C. by the Hasmonean king, Alexander Jannaeus, who opened it to Jewish settlement. The mixed character of its population was the source of much trouble in later years. Straton's Tower rose to prominence in the days of King Herod. In 22 B.C. Herod undertook one of his most ambitious enterprises – the construction of a new city and harbour. Herod named it Caesarea Maritima, in honour of his benefactor Caesar Augustus. The harbour, and especially its arc-shaped wave breaker, was an enormous project. It was built according to Roman design with piers, many storage buildings, hostels for seamen and temples to Augustus. The entrance to the harbour was adorned with huge statues. The city was well planned with markets, public baths and a theatre

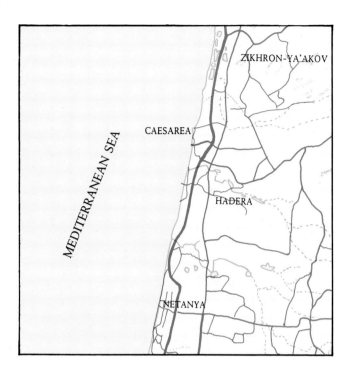

which has been excavated and restored and is used today for concerts and theatrical performances. The city also boasted of a stadium and hippodrome. Another enormous construction project of that time was the aqueduct for the transportation of water to the city from the Shuni springs on the Carmel mountain range. The system is some 12km (8 miles) long and is known as the Upper Aqueduct.

The city of Caesarea flourished in the years after Herod's death. When the Romans took over the country, Caesarea was made its administrative capital, the seat of the Roman procurators. While the Greek-Syrian population of Caesarea supported Roman policy, the large Jewish community opposed it and clashes were inevitable. In A.D. 66 20,000 Jews

Roman aqueduct near Caesarea.

Aerial view of the theatre and other Roman remains at Caesarea.

were killed in one day in Caesarea. In those troubled times Paul was preaching in Jerusalem. He was arrested and, being a Roman citizen, was sent to Caesarea where he was detained for 20 years, before going to Rome (Acts 23:23; 26:32).

During the war against the Romans, Caesarea was the headquarters of the Roman army. From here the Roman legions of Titus set forth to besiege Jerusalem, and it was to Caesarea that the captives were brought to be paraded in triumphal processions as well as to fight against wild beasts in its theatres.

Christianity was accepted in Caesarea very early, and by the end of the 2nd century it already had a bishop. Several of the best-known Church Fathers were active in Caesarea, among

Hall of the Crusader Main Gate and detail of vault.

them Origenes who headed its famous library in the 3rd century and Eusebius who compiled the *Onomasticon* – a book of place names in the Holy Land – in the 4th century. The city flourished in the Byzantine period, encompassing its largest area. In those days it covered 200 acres (800 dunams) and its city wall was 2.5km (1.6 miles) long.

Another time of glory for Caesarea was the Crusader period. The Crusaders actually built a new well-fortified city here, much smaller than the previous cities. The most striking remnants to be seen in Caesarea today are from this period; they include the walls, glacis and protective ditch around the city, and towers and gates with secret passages. Also to be seen are restored halls, a church that was never finished, and the Crusader harbour with its fortress.

After the Crusaders left Caesarea it was reduced to a heap of ruins. Today there is a suburban settlement east of the ruins of the ancient city and kibbutz Sdot Yam to the south. The harbour area has been made into a pleasant tourist attraction with a lovely beach, restaurants and artists' galleries.

CANA

A small village known today as Kafr Kana, about 8km (5 miles) northeast of Nazareth. Nestling in a small valley surrounded by pomegranate trees and cacti, it is inhabited by Christian and Moslem Arabs. Kafr Kana has been identified with Cana of Galilee since at least the Byzantine period. This is the village where Jesus performed his first miracle, as related in John 2:1-11. Jesus, his mother and his disciples attended a marriage ceremony in Cana, but there was no wine for the service. Mary urged her son to do something about it, but Jesus was reluctant saying *Woman, what have I to do with thee? mine hour is not yet come.* Despite his initial refusal, however, Jesus eventually caused the water in six stone jars to turn to

General view of Kafr Kana (Cana).

The two churches of Cana.

wine, to the amazement of the host and the guests. *This beginning of miracles did Jesus in Cana of Galilee, and manifested forth his glory, and his disciples believed on him.*

Cana was already a place of pilgrimage in the 3rd century. It was visited by St Paula and St Eustochium, disciples of St Jerome, who reported in a letter: "Not far from Nazareth they saw Cana, where the water was changed into wine." In the 6th century a church was built over a crypt believed to be the actual hall where the wedding took place. It seems that this was the site of the village synagogue as a stone bench carrying a Hebrew inscription was found there. The inscription reads: "Honoured be the memory of Joseph, son of Tanhum, son of Buta, and his sons, who made this mosaic. May it be a blessing for them, Amen." The stone dates to the 4th century.

Today a Franciscan church built in 1879 in the middle of the village marks the site of the miracle. Displayed in the crypt is a replica of what is believed to be one of the original waterpots now housed in the Cathedral of Cologne in Germany. Next to the Franciscan church stands the Greek Orthodox church which boasts of two large stone jars claimed to be two of the original vessels of the miracle. However, they seem to be old baptismal fonts.

Another place of worship in the village is the Chapel of St Bartholomew, honouring Bartholomew, the Nathanael of the Gospel of John (1:45-51), one of the first disciples of Jesus.

CAPERNAUM

An ancient fishing town on the northwestern shore of the SEA OF GALILEE uninhabited since the 8th century. Jesus settled here after he left NAZARETH (Matthew 4:13), and it was the place where he made his first disciples from among the humble local fishermen – Simon who was called Peter and his brother Andrew, as well as James and his brother John (Matthew

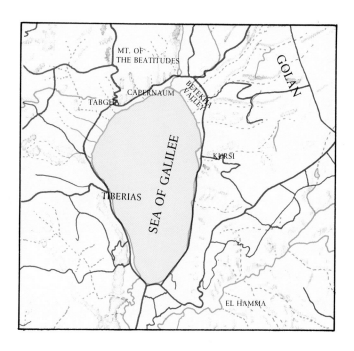

4:18- 22). Jesus returned many times to Capernaum from his preaching tours in the Galilee, making the town so closely connected with him that it was referred to as "his own city" (Matthew 9:1). He preached at the synagogue of Capernaum, and here he healed various people: a man possessed by the devil, Simon's mother-in-law, a paralytic, and eventually many of the sick and possessed of the town (Mark 1:21-34; 2:1-12). It was also in Capernaum that Jesus raised from the dead the daughter of Jairus, an official of the synagogue (Mark 5:21-43). Among the recorded teachings of Jesus at Capernaum were many parables, such as that of the sower, of

Excavations at the village of Capernaum.

tares among the wheat, of a grain of mustard seed, of leaven, of the treasure hidden in the field and of the fishing net (Matthew chapter 13). Because of his preaching and the many miracles which he performed, large crowds of people from Capernaum and the vicinity flocked around Jesus and formed the nucleus of one of the earliest congregations of converts to the new religion. The town of Capernaum thus played a major role at the very beginnings of Christianity, and is of the utmost importance and interest to pilgrims.

Since Capernaum was a place of such significance, the early explorers of Palestine attempted to trace its past, and in 1838 the American explorer Edward Robinson succeeded in identifying its location. The first archaeological excavations were conducted by Charles Wilson in 1866, but only after the entire area had been purchased by the Franciscan order was work carried out on a larger scale. In 1905 two German archaeologists, Kohl and Watzinger, found and cleared the impressive synagogue. Work in it and nearby has been carried out until recently.

It has been established that settlement on the site began in the 2nd century B.C., and that from that time on it was a small, unfortified town that did not take part in the first and second wars against the Romans, and remained peaceful and unscathed. Capernaum grew in the 4th century, but declined after the Arab invasion in the 7th century. The site was abandoned and its ruins were covered over and forgotten.

The most conspicuous structure in the town was a magnificent synagogue, built around A.D. 300, of white limestone brought from a distant quarry to this region of black basalt. Entrance to the synagogue was from the south, the direction of Jerusalem, through three doorways in a very ornate façade, one large central one and two smaller ones flanking it. The central hall was rectangular, with three rows

The synagogue at Capernaum.

Detail of columns at the synagogue of Capernaum.

of columns parallel to the side and back walls. The columns supported the ceiling and there was an elaborately decorated upper gallery which was entered from the outside by a flight of stairs. Adjacent to the main hall was a colonnaded courtyard. The rich carvings which adorned the synagogue, some of which have been restored to their original position while others have been left lying on the ground, testify to the wealth of the local Jewish population. Above the main entrance carved in the stone are the figures of an eagle and of cupids holding wreaths. This unusual combination of motifs indicates that when the synagogue was built the commandment forbidding the creation of images was interpreted in a rather liberal fashion. Later on, however, with the change of mood to a stricter interpretation, these carvings were disfigured, and replaced by ornamental motifs more in keeping with Jewish norms. They included leaf, flower and fruit elements, and geometric patterns as well as objects of ritual significance, such as the portable Ark of the Covenant. Two of the columns bear donors' inscriptions. The synagogue at Capernaum is the best example of the lavishly decorated Galilean synagogues.

Alongside the Jewish community, there existed in Capernaum a Judeo-Christian community, the "Sectarians" as they are referred to in the Talmud. This community was there perhaps as early as the 2nd century A.D. It seems that most of the time the two communities lived in relative harmony, as reported by the nun Egeria who visited Capernaum between 381 and 384 and saw both a church and a synagogue. The pilgrim of Piacenza, writing in 579, mentions "the house of Peter which is now a basilica" but does not mention a synagogue.

Several dwellings dating from the 1st century B.C., have been excavated around the synagogue. Of special significance is the so called House of Peter, the architectural history of which can be traced over a period of about 600 years. Between the 1st century B.C. and the beginning of the 4th century A.D. this was a common, poor residence, with several rooms grouped around an irregular courtyard. One of the rooms was distinguished by a better floor, or rather a succession of floors of crushed limestone, and a painted plaster coating on the walls. In the second stage, in the first half of the 4th century, this room became the centre of a building surrounded by a wall and thus secluded from the town. The room now had a roof supported by an arch. This may have been the church seen by the nun Egeria. In the middle of the 5th century this building was levelled and an octagonal church built on the site. It had a mosaic floor, part of which – including a peacock centerpiece – can still be seen. The octagonal plan for churches was quite common at the time in Italy, Syria and Palestine. Although there is nothing in the early house to identify its owner, its development into a fully recognized church indicates a strong tradition connecting it with Peter and with the activities of Jesus in Capernaum.

On the shore of the Sea of Galilee, a short distance from the ancient town of Capernaum, stands a Greek Orthodox monastery. This delightful white structure with glittering red domes was constructed in 1931 on the site of a Byzantine church dedicated to St John the Theologian.

CHORAZIN – KORAZIM

Remains at the site of the synagogue of Chorazin.

A town situated on a low basalt hill north of CAPERNAUM above the SEA OF GALILEE, on both sides of the road leading from the Tiberias-Rosh Pina road to Almagor. Chorazin, one of the largest Jewish settlements in the eastern Lower Galilee, is first mentioned in Matthew 11:21 and Luke 10:13 as a city where Jesus preached and which he later cursed because its inhabitants did not accept his teachings. A medieval tradition, first mentioned in the writings of a French pilgrim who visited the Holy Land in 1130, mentions Chorazin as the birthplace of the Antichrist. This tradition was affirmed by several pilgrims in later generations.

Archaeological investigations have not yet yielded much evidence from the time of Jesus. They have proven, however, that Chorazin was a thriving city in the 3rd-4th centuries A.D., when an elaborate synagogue was erected. Built of local black basalt stones, the synagogue stood on an elevated area in the centre of town and was approached by two flights of steps. It had one large hall with a row of pillars parallel to the back and the two side walls. Around these walls were stone benches on which the community sat during services. Carved stones, many fragments of which have been found in the vicinity, used to adorn the synagogue. The carvings included Jewish motifs such as the Ark of the Law, alongside Greek pagan motifs such as the head of Medusa (see CAPERNAUM). Next to the synagogue was another large public building, and, on a lower terrace, was a residential quarter with crowded houses.

Chorazin was in ruins by the end of the 4th century but was rebuilt and survived the Arab conquest of the 7th century. It was destroyed at the beginning of the 8th century.

DEIR HAJLA – ST GERASIMUS

Monastery of St Gerasimus.

The Arabic name of this monastery – "Monastery of the Partridge" – preserves the name of the ancient town Bet Hoglah, in the territory of the tribe of Judah. The monastery is located in the lower Jordan Valley, about 3km (2 miles) north of the Jerusalem-Amman highway, and some 7km (4.5 miles) southeast of Jericho. This is one of the traditional sites of the baptism of Jesus, despite the fact that it is not located on the Jordan River itself. The monastery was founded at the end of the 4th century by St Jerome (Hieronimus), the Bethlehem monk who first translated the Bible into Latin, a translation known as the Vulgate (see CHURCH OF ST CATHERINE, Bethlehem). In the Byzantine period the monastery was known as the Laura of Calamon, but was later given the name St Gerasimus after the head monk of a nearby monastery, now completely destroyed. This last name was retained by the present Greek Orthodox monastery built in 1882 on medieval foundations. Remnants of the Byzantine period monastery, including a 6th-century mosaic, have been incorporated into the church. Only a few monks now occupy the monastery.

EIN KAREM

A picturesque village west of Jerusalem, nestled in a deep valley surrounded by high, steep mountains and adorned with many olive and cypress trees. In its centre is a sweet water spring (*ein*), used since time immemorial to water the gardens and vineyards (*karem*) of the village. There is evidence that the site was already inhabited in the Bronze Age. It is thought to be the Beth Haccerem mentioned in Jeremiah 6:1, and has been identified with the "city of Juda" mentioned in Luke 1:39-40 as the native town of John the Baptist. Luke relates that after the Annunciation: *Mary arose in those days, and went into the hill country with haste, into a city of Juda; and entered into the house of Zacharias, and saluted Elisabeth.* The identification of "the city of Juda" with Ein Karem dates back to the Byzantine period. In the Middle Ages the village was known as St John in the Mountains. The home of Zacharias where John was born and the place where Mary visited

General view of Ein Karem.

Elisabeth, were already venerated. The tradition has been preserved to this day and the two churches – the Church of the Visitation and the Church of St John – commemorating these events are the principal edifices in the village, which abounds in other churches and convents.

Now a green and attractive suburb of Jerusalem, the village is inhabited by many artists who enjoy its old domed houses and beautiful scenery.

CHURCH OF ST JOHN THE BAPTIST

An interesting building combining remnants of many periods, in the village of Ein Karem, where John the Baptist is believed to have been born. A statue of the goddess Venus found on the site and now displayed in the courtyard in front of the church, as well as a wine press and two tombs, indicate that the site was inhabited, and probably venerated, in the Roman period. The earliest church on the site dates to the 5th-6th centuries and was built over the Roman tombs.

Church of St John the Baptist at Ein Karem.

A mosaic fragment of the Byzantine church decorated with peacocks, partridges and flowers has survived, along with a Greek inscription which reads: "Hail martyrs of God." This Byzantine church was destroyed in the 7th century, restored by the Crusaders, and then destroyed again after the Crusaders left the country. Fragments of the Crusader edifice may be seen on the southern side of the church compound. The main church one can visit today was built in 1674. Six square pillars divide the hall into three aisles, the central one ending in an apse in front of which is the high altar dedicated to John the Baptist. On the right is Elisabeth's altar, and on the left are steps leading down a natural cave – identified as the Grotto of the Nativity of St John. This grotto may well have been part of the house of Zacharias and Elisabeth, John's parents. The church is adorned with 17th-century paintings.

CHURCH OF THE VISITATION

Church of the Visitation at Ein Karem.

One of the most beautiful and most artistically decorated churches in the Holy Land, it commemmorates the meeting of Elisabeth and Mary. It is situated on the lower slope of the hill south of the village of Ein Karem, beyond its main spring – the Fountain of the Virgin. The church, incorporating remnants of many periods, was finished in 1955. In it is a natural grotto which once contained a small spring, and remnants of houses in front of the grotto. Some of these houses were inhabited in the Roman period, the period in which the Visitation took place. The Byzantines converted the grotto into a place of worship, and the Crusaders actually built churches over it – a large two-storied church above the grotto and a smaller one in front of the grotto, over the houses. Around the churches was a compound which contained towers and dwellings for the church personnel. After the Crusaders left the Holy Land, the compound fell into disuse and eventually collapsed. The area around the church was bought by the Franciscans in 1679, but the permit to rebuild the lower church was granted only 200 years later.

Among the art works adorning the lower church are three large frescoes, one depicting the Visitation, one Elisabeth hiding St John, and the third, Zacharias burning incense at the altar of the Lord. In the upper church are numerous frescoes and a painted ceiling in the Tuscan style of the 14th century. Its façade is adorned with a large mosaic showing Mary on her way from Nazareth to visit Elisabeth. The peaceful courtyard, with an arcade on one side, is decorated with ceramic plaques carrying in 42 languages the words of the Magnificat, Mary's hymn of thanksgiving beginning with the words "My soul doth magnify the Lord" (Luke 1:46-55).

CONVENT OF THE DESERT OF ST JOHN

Some distance west of Ein Karem, near the modern village of Even Sapir, is another holy place connected with John the Baptist – the Franciscan Convent of the Desert of St John. This convent commemorates the way of life of the young John as reported by Luke: *And the child grew, and waxed strong in spirit, and was in the desert till the day of his shewing unto Israel* (Luke 1:80), "desert" here meaning an uninhabited place of wilderness. The compound is small and simple, secluded in the mountains and surrounded by a wall. The grotto in which John is said to have lived is now a humble place of worship and the church, with its remnants of the Crusader period, is inspiring in its simplicity. In the small terraced garden is a spring, appropriately called in Arabic Ain el-Habis (The Spring of the Hermit).

MAR ZAKARIYA

Next to the CHURCH OF THE VISITATION, on a hill south of the village of Ein Karem, is a Russian compound noted for its beautiful grove of cypress trees. A handful of Russian nuns live in the compound and take care of the church of Mar Zakariya (St Zacharias) and of an unfinished church and tower, the construction of which stopped when the Russian Revolution broke out in 1917.

EIN KUNIYE

A Druze village on the southern slopes of Mount Hermon, north of the road leading from BANIAS to the northern Golan Heights. In the village is a tomb where, according to Druze tradition, Sit Shahwana, the sister of Jethro, Moses' father-in-law, is buried. Nothing is known of Sit Shahwana nor how she became identified as Jethro's sister. Perhaps because of the importance of Jethro in Druze tradition and the veneration of his burial place at NEBI SHUWEIB a famous local woman was elevated to the status of Jethro's sister, and a minor holy place became associated with him in this region of concentrated Druze population.

The village of Ein Kuniye is one of the most picturesque in the country. It is built on a high hill and is surrounded by orchards, olive groves, and poplar lanes, all watered from five springs that issue in the vicinity of the village.

EMMAUS

Remains outside the house where Jesus met two of his disciples.

An old town on the eastern edge of the AJALON VALLEY on the road leading from the coastal plain to Jerusalem. The name Emmaus is a Greek mispronunciation of the word *hamat* – hot spring, a reference to the one that issued there.

The Seleucid (2nd century B.C.) and Roman armies camped at Emmaus on their way to Jerusalem and there Judas Maccabee defeated the Seleucid army in 165 B.C. The site was fortified by the Hasmonean kings and was the scene of a short-lived mutiny against Rome in A.D. 4. It is believed that here the resurrected Jesus appeared and dined in the house of Cleopas (Luke chapter 24). Although this is the most accepted site for that event, its name having been preserved in the adjacent Arab village 'Amwas, there are two other possible locations – the village of 'Abu Ghosh, identified by the Crusaders as the scene of the appearance of Jesus, and the village of EL QUBEIBA where the Franciscans believe it occurred.

Emmaus was also important after Jerusalem had been destroyed by the Romans. In the Roman period its name was changed to Nicopolis – city of Nike, goddess of victory. It was a resort town and its hot spring, over which a public bath was built, became quite popular. The population of Emmaus-Nicopolis in the first centuries A.D. included Samaritans, whose synagogue has been excavated, and Christians who built churches there in commemoration of the appearance of Jesus. The importance of Emmaus continued until the Mameluke period, when it became a village.

Today the ruins of Emmaus are a part of Canada Park. One of its church sites is in the courtyard of Beth Shalom, a hostel north of the LATRUN MONASTERY. In the courtyard of the hostel a succession of churches has been discovered and excavated. The earliest was a church, built in the 5th century, following a basilical plan. It was constructed over a Roman villa which is believed to have been a meeting house for the early Christian community of the town. North of the church, part of the mosaic floors of which has survived, was a baptistry with a baptismal font cut in the rock. It, too, had mosaic floors, the best preserved parts of which can be seen next to the Crusader church. The designs used in the mosaics included animals, plants and geometric patterns.

In the 12th century the Crusaders built a small, Romanesque style church with massive walls over the ruins of the Byzantine basilica. The apse of the Byzantine church was incorporated into this Crusader church.

GALILEE

Landscape in Galilee.

The mountainous northern part of the Holy Land, bounded by the coastal plain on the west, the Jordan Valley on the east, the Jezreel Valley on the south and the Israel-Lebanon border on the north. Galilee is divided into two distinct regions – Upper Galilee and Lower Galilee – which differ not only in their

View of Meron in Upper Galilee.

elevation, but also in their climate, vegetation and history. The southern region, Lower Galilee, rises to elevations of up to 500-600m (1640-1970 ft), while the northern region, Upper Galilee, has peaks rising to 1000-1200m (3280-3940 ft). The highest mountain in Upper Galilee is Mount Meron which rises to 1208m (3963 ft). Lying between the two regions is the narrow Beth Hakerem Valley which extends from east to west. The northern side of this valley is an almost vertical escarpment, caused by a geological fault line. Upper Galilee receives more rain than any other region in the country and still has many tracts of natural forest. The largest settlement is Safed, which became a centre of Jewish mysticism at the end of the 15th century. Lower Galilee is drier, its eastern part in fact sometimes suffers from droughts. Its largest settlement is NAZARETH, one of the oldest cities in the Holy Land.

Galilee has been inhabited since prehistoric times and throughout all historic periods. Lower Galilee, however, has always attracted more settlements because of its topography and its proximity to the major routes of the Jezreel and Jordan Valleys. Galilee was most densely populated in the Second Temple, Roman and Byzantine periods, the very days in which Christianity was born and made its first steps there. Places like Nazareth, Jesus' hometown, have won world renown and drawn many pilgrims. In those same periods Galilee was the location of the major centres of Jewish life. The main politico-religious institutions of Judaism moved from one Galilean town to another and many famous rabbis lived and died there. Numerous tombs of these post-Biblical sages are scattered throughout Galilee and are revered to this day.

Nowadays the population of Galilee is mixed. Jews, Arabs, Druze and Christians of various denominations live in the many towns and villages of the area. The region offers a variety of beautiful landscapes, historic places and holy sites.

GATH-HEPHER – MASH'HAD

An Arab village in the centre of the Lower Galilee, northeast of Nazareth on the road to Tiberias. The place is identified with biblical Gath-Hepher, the birthplace of the Prophet Jonah son of Amittai (II Kings 14:25). His tomb is traditionally located in a cave under the mosque of the village. The shrine, known as Nebi Jonas, the Prophet Jonah, is revered by Jews and Moslems alike, who still visit the holy tomb today. Jewish pilgrims of the Middle Ages mentioned the tomb, and the Arabic name of the village Mash'had, which means the "burial place of the Shahid" (or the holy man), echoes this ancient tradition.

The village is renowned for its many olive and pomegranate orchards.

GILGAL

The first place where the Children of Israel encamped after crossing the Jordan River and where the twelve stones on which the priests stood during the crossing were pitched. These stones, placed perhaps in a circle – *gilgal* in Hebrew – were to serve as a reminder for future generations of the miracle of the crossing of the Jordan and of the mighty hand of God (Joshua 4:19-24). At Gilgal the Children of Israel who had been born in the desert were circumcised and there they celebrated the first Passover in the Land of Canaan eating of the fruit of the land, the manna having ceased to fall (Joshua 5:2-12).

Despite the importance of the place and of the events that occurred there, the site of Gilgal has been forgotten. A possible candidate is a place with several small mounds by the road leading from the Jordan River to Jericho, about 4km (3 miles) southeast of the town. Excavations carried out in 1950 revealed several walls of the Byzantine and early Moslem period, and a church first built in the 4th century which survived until the 9th century. It may have been the Byzantine church known

View in the region of Jericho where Gilgal is said to have been.

from literary sources as the Dodekalithon – Twelve Stones.
South of the mounds is a barely visible water reservoir known
locallly as Birket el-Jiljuleh, the Arabic name preserving the
ancient name Gilgal. Another possible location is Tel Jaljul,
some 8km (5 miles) north of Jericho. The Arabic name
preserves the biblical name, but again no relevant remnants
were found on the site. The new settlement nearby has been
named Gilgal.

HEBRON

City of the Patriarchs, holy to Jews, Moslems and Christians
alike, and today the most important city of the Judean
Mountains.

View of Hebron with the Cave of Machpelah in the centre.

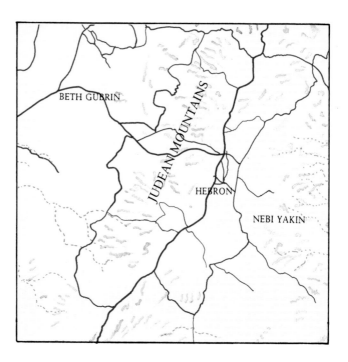

Hebron is one of the oldest towns in the Holy Land; excavations have shown that it was inhabited in the 3rd millennium B.C. The Bible also refers to its antiquity when mentioning its foundation, seven years before Zoan in Egypt (Numbers 13:22). Abraham roamed in the neighbourhood of the town, and when his wife Sarah died he bought the CAVE OF MACHPELAH from Ephron the Hittite (Genesis chapter 23) *and Abraham buried Sarah his wife in the cave of the field of Machpelah before Mamre: the same is in Hebron in the land of Canaan* (Genesis 23:19). That cave is the holiest site in Hebron.

Hebron was of significance also in the days of King David who ruled from it for seven years before he conquered JERUSALEM and transferred his capital there (II Samuel 2:1-11). Since those ancient times Hebron has remained a small town, centered around the Cave of Machpelah.

Hebron is the highest town in the Holy Land, being some 950m (3000 ft) above sea level. It has preserved the traditional character of a hill town, with stone houses and steep, narrow winding alleys. Its population consists mostly of Moslems.

Hebron and its surrounding countryside are renowned for their fine grapes. As the Moslems are forbidden to drink wine, they grow table grapes which are also dried as raisins. If you visit the area between July and October, you should sample the large green grapes sold along the roads. Hebron also boasts of many traditional crafts, notably glassblowing and pottery, and many workshops are scattered along the road leading to Hebron and in the town itself. In the market you can come across the iron-smiths, makers of agricultural tools, woodcarvers and other craftsmen working in their small, dark, shops.

ABRAHAM'S TEREBINTH

A Russian-Pravoslav church west of Hebron, close to the Hebron-Beersheba road. The church was built in 1871 and served as a hostel for Russian pilgrims who visited the Holy Land before the Second World War. In the courtyard of the church is a huge old terebinth tree, believed by some to be the tree planted by Abraham in Beersheba (Genesis 21:33). The tree is slowly dying and is supported by iron scaffolding.

CAVE OF MACHPELAH

The Cave of Machpelah, one of the most sacred places in the Holy Land, is the burial place of the three pairs of Patriarchs and Matriarchs of the Book of Genesis. It is situated in the heart of the town of Hebron, about 31km (19 miles) south of Jerusalem. The purchase of the Cave by Abraham is described in detail in the Book of Genesis, chapter 23. When Sarah died, Abraham looked for a place to bury her, and purchased the Cave of Machpelah from its owner, Ephron the Hittite. He himself was buried there and after him his son Isaac and his wife Rebekah and Isaac's son Jacob and his wife Leah.

The place is sacred to Jews, Christians and Moslems because of its association with Abraham, patriarch of the Jewish and Arab nations, the first of the genealogical line from which Jesus descended: *The book of the generation of Jesus Christ, the son of David, the son of Abraham* (Matthew 1:1).

Later traditions held that other biblical personalities were also buried in the Cave – Adam and Eve, the sons of Jacob, Moses and his wife Zipporah. According to the *Kabbalah*, the

The Cave of Machpelah: Herodian wall with flat pilasters. The upper part of the wall and minaret are later additions.

Interior of the mosque over the Cave of Machpelah. Cenotaphs of Isaac (right) and Rebekah (left).

cave leads to the Garden of Eden. The Cave of Machpelah thus became the traditional mausoleum of some of the most revered biblical figures and a place of worship for the three monotheistic religions.

Nothing is known about the original configuration of the burial cave. The meaning of the ancient name "Machpelah" is unknown. The word may be related to the Hebrew word for "double," and tradition explains it as meaning "the double cave" – one cave above, or next to, the other, or "the cave for doubles," or pairs.

The structure which now stands over the traditional site of the cave was originally built by King Herod (37 B.C.-A.D. 4). An earlier structure may however have stood there, as there are written references to the traditional place of the six cenotaphs of the Patriarchs and Matriarchs dating from at least one hundred and fifty years before Herod, in the days of the early Hasmonean kings. The cenotaphs now revered in the edifice are not the actual tombs, but only structures marking the site of the subterranean burial cave.

The superstructure of the Cave of Machpelah is a large rectangle measuring approximately 60×32m (200×106 ft) surrounded by thick, well-built walls. The flat pilasters which decorate the upper part of the walls, the well-fitting stones and the manner of dressing the stones are all typical of the Herodian style of construction. In those days the site was an

(left) Decorative grille in the Cave of Machpelah. (right) Corner of the main hall of the mosque at Machpelah.

open-air *temenos* (sacred enclosure) with six cenotaphs standing in the same places as those today, although no doubt shaped differently. Since then the site has undergone many changes. A pilgrim in the 6th century described a church with four rows of columns, forming a basilica structure. A Greek inscription in the corner of the left aisle of the present structure may be from that church. After the Moslem conquest in the 7th century the church was converted into a mosque. The Crusaders re-converted the structure into a church and gave it the general features it now has. During that period monks entered the subterranean caverns and left a description. They found a circular chamber and in it bones, which they believed to be those of Abraham and Isaac. Behind it was another chamber with the bones of Jacob, as well as fifteen jars containing the bones of Jacob's sons. The monks ceremoniously washed the bones and then built a stairway for pilgrims who visited the chambers. One of those pilgrims was the famous medieval Jewish traveller, Rabbi Benjamin of Tudela, who entered the cave in the year 1170.

After the Mameluke conquest of 1250 and re-conversion of the structure into a mosque, the passage leading to the subterranean chambers was blocked up and entrance strictly prohibited. Jews and Christians were not permitted to enter the edifice, though Jews were allowed to ascend the outer staircase as far as the seventh step and pray there. The Mameluke rulers repaired the structure, added the crenellation on top of the outer, Herodian walls and two minarets. Their additions are easily recognized by the characteristic alternating red and white stones used in their construction.

The visitor to the Haram el Khalil (the Shrine of the Beloved of God i.e., Abraham), as the site is called in Arabic, enters the compound from the east. The first pair of cenotaphs are those of Abraham and Sarah. To the right are those of Leah and Jacob, and to the left, within the main mosque, those of Rebekah and Isaac. All the cenotaphs are covered with gold-embroidered silk hangings – green for the Patriarchs, purple for their wives – and surmounted by red and white stone tent-like structures. The praying niche (*mihrab*) and pulpit (*minbar*) inside the mosque are very ornate.

PLAIN OF MAMRE – RAMAT EL KHALIL

An ancient enclosure, located on a high hill east of the main Jerusalem-Hebron road, some 3km (2 miles) north of HEBRON, on the road leading to Kiryat Arba. It comprises a ruined well and the remains of a church, surrounded by a wall. This is traditionally the place where Abraham pitched his tent and where he received the three angels of God who told him that he was to have a son by his aged wife Sarah (Genesis 18:1-16). Another tradition claims that the important Convenant of the Pieces between God and Abraham, in the course of which Abraham sacrificed animals and cut them into pieces, took place here (Genesis 15:5-21). (Another claimant to the place where this convenant occurred is the MOUNTAIN OF THE PIECES in the Hermon mountain range.) The site seems to have been venerated over a long period of time, and substantial remnants of a First Temple period (9th-7th centuries B.C.) holy place came to light during excavations carried out at the site in 1926-1928. King Herod (1st century B.C.) began building a large enclusure wall around the site, using a design concept similar to the one at the CAVE OF MACHPELAH in Hebron and the TEMPLE MOUNT in Jerusalem. There is no indication that the wall was completed or that any structure was built inside the enclosure. In A.D. 68 the Roman legions captured Hebron and destroyed the unfinished enclosure wall. It was the Roman emperor, Hadrian, who, around 130, restored the site and gave it its present-day shape. The walls seen today date to that

Enclosure wall and ruins at the Plain of Mamre.

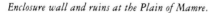

period. Hadrian also had a temple built to the god Hermes on the eastern side of the enclosure. Hermes was god of caravans, commerce and slave markets, and indeed one of the largest slave markets in the eastern provinces of the Roman Empire operated here. From the Roman period and until the Middle Ages there was a large tree growing in the enclosure identified with the terebinth, or oak, planted by Abraham, and the site was called Oak of Mamre.

No specific Christian tradition is associated with this site, but the Church Father, Eusebius, relates that Emperor Constantine's mother-in-law visited it and was shocked to see idols being worshipped under Abraham's tree. She informed Constantine, who had the area cleared and ordered a church to be built there. This was one of the four churches Constantine erected in the Holy Land, and it seems to have been the first, preceding the CHURCH OF THE HOLY SEPULCHRE, the CHURCH OF MOUNT ZION and the CHURCH OF ELEONA in Jerusalem. The remains of this church, which was very large and occupied the entire eastern third of the enclosure, include inscriptions, capitals of columns and building stones. Abraham's tree stood in the atrium (courtyard) of the church, and this is the way it is depicted in the 6th-century Medeba mosaic map.

In the southwestern corner of the enclosure is a well. According to a Christian legend, Abraham saw the face of his descendant Jesus in its water.

HORNS OF HITTIN

They comprise an extinct volcano in the eastern Lower Galilee, about 10km (6 miles) west-northwest of Tiberias, with two summits flanking a deep crater. Here the Crusader army was defeated on July 4, 1187 by the Moslem army of Saladin in a

The Horns of Hittin.

decisive battle that marked the end of the Latin Kingdom of Jerusalem. The claim of the Horns of Hittin to holiness lies in its identification by a small Protestant sect as the place where Jesus proclaimed his Sermon on the Mount, rather than on the commonly accepted site of the MOUNTAIN OF THE BEATITUDES. Members of the sect have erected a monument at the foot of the mountain.

The Horns of Hittin is a wonderful vantage point in the region, overlooking the road from the Sea of Galilee to the Galilee Mountains.

JAFFA – JOPPA

An ancient port city on a small promontory that juts into the Mediterranean Sea south of Tel Aviv-Jaffa. Established in the Canaanite period, it was an Egyptian stronghold until the 12th century B.C. Although allocated by Joshua to the tribe of Dan (Joshua 19:46), it was never conquered by the Israelites but remained in foreign hands throughout the First Temple period and the Persian period. In the days of the Ptolemies Joppa was granted autonomy with the right to mint coins. In 144 B.C. Simon Maccabee conquered Joppa and brought it under Jewish rule for the first time. Being a port city it became very important for the economy of Judah, and Alexander Jannaeus struck a series of coins to commemorate the conquest. Joppa was detached from Judah by Pompey in 64 B.C. but returned to it by Augustus in 30 B.C. In those days it was a prosperous port town, inhabited by Jews and gentiles alike, and was the scene of various activities of Peter. Here Tabitha was restored to life (Acts 9:36-41) and here Peter, while staying in the HOUSE OF SIMON THE TANNER, had the vision of the beasts (Acts 10:5-16).

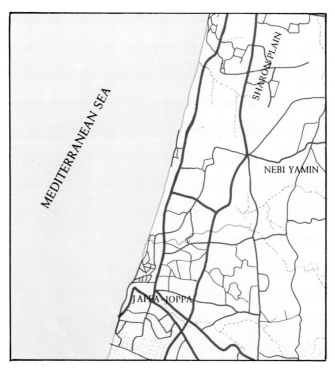

A view of Jaffa from the sea.

Joppa has retained its position as an important port throughout history. With time the town spread. New suburbs were built north, south and east of the old and crowded town. In the 1950-1970s the old town was cleared of most of its private buildings and those that remained were renovated. Archaeological excavations in the area revealed various layers of the ancient town.

Today the area of Old Jaffa is a pleasant tourist attraction with galleries, restaurants and studios of well-known artists.

HOUSE OF SIMON THE TANNER

The traditional site of the house of *one Simon a tanner, whose house is by the sea side* (Acts 10:6) and where St Peter lodged on his visit to Joppa (Jaffa). Here Peter fell into a trance and was commanded to slaughter and eat unclean animals, as *What God hath cleansed, that call not thou common* (Acts 10:15). This vision encouraged Peter to carry his message to non-Jews and to baptize many who were not circumcised (Acts 10:19-48).

The house of Simon the Tanner at Jaffa.

The house identified as the house of Simon is an inconspicuous 19th-century residence in Simon-the-Tanner Street, near the lighthouse in the area of the old fortress that guarded the harbour. Part of it is now a mosque.

ST PETER'S CHURCH OF THE PRAVOSLAVS

Built on the site of an old Jewish cemetery at Giv'at Herzl between Jaffa and Tel Aviv, it is said that here, in 1835, Father Nurov discovered the tomb of Tabitha who was raised from the dead by Peter (Acts 9:36-42). The site was purchased in 1874 by the Russian Pravoslav church which built a church and a hostel here between 1888 and 1894. The church compound, surrounded by a high wall, became the first station in the Holy Land for many Russian pilgrims before 1914. Today the compound can be visited only at Easter, when services are held for the Orthodox community.

The Franciscan church of St Peter at Jaffa.

ST PETER'S CHURCH AND FRANCISCAN MONASTERY

A Franciscan church and monastery erected to commemorate the resurrection of Tabitha by Peter (Acts 9:36-42).

The compound, the construction of which began in 1642, is located on the summit of the tell of ancient Joppa (Jaffa), on the site of the fortress that guarded the harbour. Excavations carried out in the open plaza in front of the compound revealed traces of habitation from the Hasmonean to the Byzantine period.

The current buildings, however, date from the 19th century. In the courtyard of the monastery is a statue of St Louis, king of France, who led the 9th Crusade and fortified Joppa.

JERICHO

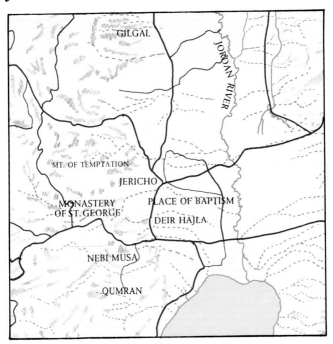

One of the oldest cities in history, centered around a large perennial spring that waters its surroundings and turns the area into a fertile oasis in the midst of a desert. The spring, source of life for the area, was no doubt sanctified by the early inhabitants of Jericho. In biblical times it was associated with the prophet Elisha who purified its water by throwing salt into it (II Kings 2:19-22) and hence its name ever since – the Spring of Elisha. Jews, Christians and Moslems alike attributed therapeutic qualities to the water of the spring. It was also believed that one could foretell catastrophes such as floods and earthquakes in the movement of its water. John the Baptist was active in the region, making Jericho one of the most important Christian centres in the Holy Land.

In the area around Jericho are many important holy sites such as QUARANTAL MONASTERY, DEIR HAJLA and the PLACE OF BAPTISM.

Excavations showing the fortifications of ancient Jericho.

A visit to Jericho should start with the ancient site, known as Tell Sultan, where remnants of thousands of years of habitation have been unearthed. The tell, about 2km (1.4 miles) north of the centre of modern Jericho, is situated next to the Spring of Elisha which was no doubt the most essential resource of the settlement. An impressive stone tower built some 10,000 years ago, can be seen on the tell.

Jericho figures prominently in the stories of the conquest of Canaan in the days of Joshua. Its miraculous capture (Joshua 6:1-21) opened the way to Canaan to the Children of Israel. In later generations Jericho was of minor importance and major construction was carried out only in the days of King Ahab (I Kings 16:34).

Around the 4th century B.C. the ancient tell was deserted, and a new site in the oasis, where modern Jericho stands today, was chosen for settlement. The most prosperous times in the history of Jericho were during the Hasmonean-Herodian period. In those days the special combination of hot climate and a plentiful supply of water were put to use and large tracts of the oasis were planted with rare and medicinal plants, including that called "balsam" in the Bible, which has not yet been identified. In those days the nobility of Jerusalem, headed by the royal houses, built winter homes in the Jericho oasis. The Hasmonean and Herodian palaces have been thoroughly excavated on both sides of Wadi Kelt, southwest of modern Jericho, and can be approached by a dirt road branching westwards from the police station in the centre of the town. Herod added to the attractions of the resort by building a hippodrome and a theatre.

Jericho fell to the Romans in A.D. 70 after a fierce battle in which the defenders tried to destroy the valuable balsam

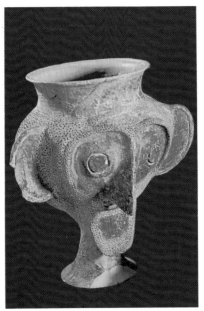

(left) Middle Bronze Age clay anthropomorphic vessel from Jericho. (right) Neolithic stone tower.

plantations. "A battle raged over every tree," wrote the Roman historian Pliny. After this destruction, and more so after the Bar Kochba Revolt of 132-135, the Jewish population dwindled. In the Byzantine period several churches were built in what is today modern Jericho, and many monasteries were founded around it.

Early Moslem rulers of the Umayyad dynasty were also aware of the advantages of Jericho's climate and one of its rulers built an ornate winter palace for himself about 2.5km (1.5 miles) north of Jericho. This palace, renowned for its splendid floor mosaics and intricate stucco wall carvings, is well worth a visit. From the 9th century on, Jericho steadily declined. The extensive ancient irrigation system was neglected, and the desert with its nomadic Bedouins had the upper hand in the area. Only in the 20th century were the irrigation canals put back into use and today Jericho is a thriving centre of agricultural enterprise, well known for its delicious subtropical and tropical fruit.

Javelin heads of the 2nd millennium B.C. found at Jericho.

JERUSALEM

Perhaps the holiest place on earth, revered by the three great monotheistic religious – Judaism, Christianity and Islam. Although today a bustling modern city with about 500,000 inhabitants, Jerusalem still preserves its special atmosphere of a holy city and abounds in places of worship that incorporate memories of divine revelations and of world-changing events that occurred here.

The beginnings of Jerusalem were humble. People were first drawn to the site known today as the CITY OF DAVID because of the GIHON SPRING (Spring of the Virgin) that issues in the VALLEY OF JEHOSHAPHAT. The earliest remnants of occupation date to about 3500 B.C. and 3000 B.C., when part of the City of David was built up with houses. The site was first fortified in the 19th century B.C., at a time when Jerusalem enters history. It is then that Jerusalem is mentioned for the first time in Egyptian records by the name Rushalimum. To this period perhaps belongs Malchizedek king of Shalem, who was also "priest of the most high God" (Genesis 14:18-20). It would thus seem that even in those early days Jerusalem was a place of sanctity. Jerusalem figured prominently among the Canaanite city-states in the middle of the 14th century B.C., when its ruler, Abdi-Hebpa, corresponded with the Egyptian Pharaoh Akhenaton. To this time, or perhaps somewhat later, belong the massive terracing walls discovered on the eastern slope of the City of David, designed to protect the city from land-slides and add flat ground for construction. This Canaanite town was first taken by the tribe of Judah (Judges 1:8) who apparently could not hold it. It would seem that after its capture by Judah, Jerusalem was inhabited by the Jebusites, perhaps a tribe of Anatolian origin. They must have been a rather strong tribe as the tribe of Benjamin, in whose territory Jerusalem was, *could not drive out the Jebusites that inhabited Jerusalem* (Judges 1:21). The Jebusites remained in Jerusalem until it was conquered by David around 1000 B.C. (II Samuel 5:6-9; I Chronicles 11:4-7). This was the turning point in the life of the city. David transferred his seat from HEBRON to the

Inscription in a tomb chamber of the early 6th century B.C. This is the only known inscription from the First Temple period mentioning Jerusalem by name.

General view of Jerusalem. ▷

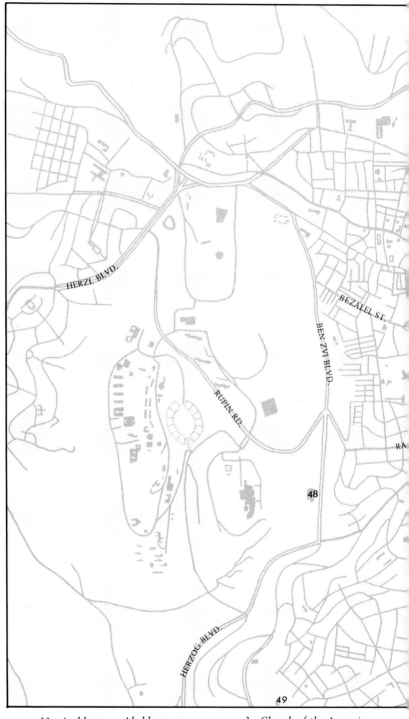

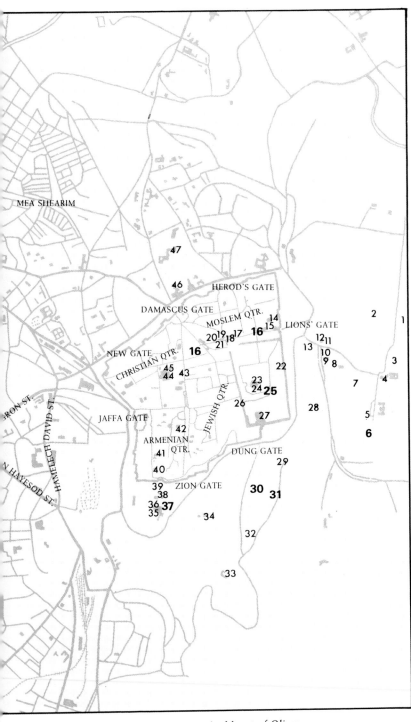

MEA SHEARIM

47

46 HEROD'S GATE

DAMASCUS GATE

MOSLEM QTR. 14
15 LIONS' GATE
2 1

20 19 18 17 16
21

NEW GATE 16 12 11
CHRISTIAN QTR. 13 3
10
45 43 9 8
44 22 7 4
23
24 25
26 5
27 28 6

JAFFA GATE

42
ARMENIAN QTR.
41
40

39 ZION GATE
38 DUNG GATE
36 37 29
35
34 30 31

32

33

JEWISH QTR.

CRON ST.

HAMELECH DAVID ST.

N HAYESOD ST.

fortress of Zion which he renamed City of David, thus making Jerusalem his capital. But David did more. He made of Jerusalem a place of holiness by transferring to it the Ark of the Covenant, symbol of the Divine presence. Since then Jerusalem has been intimately tied with the name and personality of David. Here he lived and here he died and was buried (see TOMB OF DAVID), and here his dynasty created the special relationship between God, city and king.

David's son, Solomon, was the one who actually built the Temple of God on the threshing floor which David had bought from Araunah the Jebusite (II Samuel 24:21-24). The site was later known as the TEMPLE MOUNT. Solomon's temple was a small but lavishly decorated building, surrounded by courtyards. South of the Temple Mount, Solomon built a palace, and several administrative buildings. He repaired the city walls and turned Jerusalem into a city worthy of his affluent kingdom: *And the king made silver to be in Jerusalem as stones, and cedars made he to be as sycomore trees that are in the vale, for abundance* (I Kings 10:27). Very few traces of Solomon's time have as yet been unearthed. One impressive remnant, however, is a huge retaining wall which must have supported a monumental building, discovered in the City of David.

When the kingdom was divided after the death of Solomon, Jerusalem remained capital of Judah. While Judah knew periods of expansion and contraction, Jerusalem continued to grow and expand to the west. In the time of King Hezekiah the western hill where the Jewish and Armenian Quarters stand today was surrounded by a massive wall in preparation for the siege of Sennacherib. At the same time HEZEKIAH'S TUNNEL was dug under the City of David to convey water to the protected POOL OF SILOAM. The city continued to

Excavations at the foot of the southern wall of the Temple Mount; the Second Temple period staircase leads up to the Temple.

expand to the north, and reached more or less the vicinity of present-day Damascus Gate. Jerusalem was surrounded by cemeteries on all four sides. The end of Jerusalem of the First Temple period came in 586 B.C., when the Babylonians besieged it, sacked it and exiled most of its inhabitants.

About fifty years after the Babylonian exile, in 538 B.C., King Cyrus of Persia allowed the exiled Jews to return to Jerusalem and rebuild the Temple. This was the beginning of what is known as the Second Temple period, which lasted until Jerusalem fell to the Romans in A.D. 70.

The Jerusalem of this period was small and confined to the City of David, where remnants of the wall built by Nehemiah after the Babylonian exile were found. The Temple at this time was also small and modest, but served the purpose of uniting the nation around the Law of God. Jerusalem passed from Persian to Hellenistic rule with the conquests of Alexander the Great in 332 B.C. Under the Ptolemies of Egypt, Jerusalem knew relative peace, but under the Seleucids of Syria it entered a period of advanced hellenization which eventually brought about the Hasmonean revolt of 165 B.C. In 164 B.C. Judah Maccabee seized Jerusalem and restored the worship in the Temple. Under the Hasmonean dynasty Jerusalem expanded again to the western hill and was surrounded with what Josephus Flavius calls the First Wall. Jerusalem entered a period of glory in the days of King Herod (37 B.C.-4 B.C.). Herod redesigned the Temple Mount and gave it the shape it has to this day. He also rebuilt the Temple itself and constructed the fortress Antonia, as the PRAETORIUM north of the Temple Mount. Herod built for himself a palace where the police station and the Armenian Seminary now stand, and constructed three towers on the site of the Citadel popularly called today "David's Tower." In the north the Second Wall was added. The line of this wall has not yet been found, but there is no doubt that GOLGOTHA, the place of execution, was outside the city.

After Herod's death Jerusalem was ruled by Roman procurators. Those were troubled times for the people of Jerusalem who fought for their independence. In those days Jesus was active in Jerusalem, preaching his new ideas and converting people, until he was arrested, tried and executed. Jerusalem abounds in memories connected with the life and death of Jesus, that have made it holy to Christianity. Despite the difficult times, Jerusalem continued to expand until it reached its northernmost limit in the Third Wall, a wall begun by Herod Agrippa in A.D. 44, but completed only on the eve of the great Roman siege. Jerusalem in those days was an important centre of pilgrimage, with hundreds of thousands of Jews flocking there on the three pilgrimage festivals – Passover, Pentecost and Tabernacles.

Jerusalem was completely destroyed by the Roman army led by Titus in A.D. 70. Visible remnants of this destruction can be seen to this day in the so-called Burnt House excavated in the Jewish Quarter of the Old City, while the WESTERN WALL of the Temple Mount which escaped the destruction became the Jewish symbol of the fall of Jerusalem. At first the Romans,

The so-called Burnt House in the Old City of Jerusalem during excavations.

who established an army camp in the ruined city, did little to revive Jerusalem. Only after the Bar Kochba Revolt of 132-135, a heroic Jewish attempt to regain independence, did the Roman emperor Hadrian take interest in the city. He had it built as a Roman colony which he named Aelia Capitolina. He made a deliberate attempt to erase any trace of Jewish and Christian memories in the city, and built pagan temples over the holy sites. Public buildings such as triumphal arches, agoras and public baths were added to the city from which Jews and Christians alike were barred. The character of Jerusalem changed completely when Constantine, emperor of Byzantium, declared Christianity the state religion in 332. He sent his mother Helena on a relic-finding mission, after which he ordered the building of three imperial basilicas – the CHURCH OF THE HOLY SEPULCHRE, the CHURCH OF MOUNT ZION and Eleona Church on the MOUNT OF OLIVES. Jerusalem entered its first Christian phase marked by intensive church building. This phase came to an end with the Persian invasion of 614 during which most of the churches were devastated.

This short-lived invasion was followed by the Arab conquest of Palestine in 638, which initiated the long period of Moslem domination of Jerusalem. The Moslems sanctified the Temple Mount and built on it the magnificent DOME OF THE ROCK and EL AQSA MOSQUE. Thus Jerusalem became holy to yet another religion. Moslem domination was interrupted by the Crusaders who conquered Jerusalem in 1099. The Crusaders rebuilt most of the churches and left their imprint on the basic network of streets and bazaars of the Old City of today. They left Jerusalem in 1187 after their defeat at the HORNS OF HITTIN, and the Moslem ruler Saladin restored Islamic rule in Jerusalem. This lasted for some 750 years, under Ayyubid, Mameluke and Ottoman Turkish rule who turned the Old City of Jerusalem into a typical oriental town. The present day walls were constructed by the Ottoman sultan, Suleiman the Magnificent, in the middle of the 16th century.

Thereafter Jerusalem slowly deteriorated and lost its importance.

The second half of the 19th century brought new life to Jerusalem with the growing interest of imperial European nations, mainly France, Germany, England and Russia. At that time people started to leave the protection of the city walls and build new neibourhoods which grew to become the New City. The 20th century saw the capture of Jerusalem by the British led by General Allenby (1917), the 1948 war between Jews and Arabs which ended in the division of the city, and its re-unification in Israeli hands in 1967.

Jerusalem nowadays has spread much beyond its historic boundaries. It enjoys complete religious freedom and the sanctuaries of all religions are well maintained and open to everyone. A visit to Jerusalem is a profound spiritual experience, especially for those who seek the roots of their faith and their history.

ACELDAMA – AKELDAMA

A site on the southern bank of the Hinnom Valley, above a cave-studded rocky escarpment, outside the built-up area of Jerusalem. Its original name was Potters' Field, indicating the activity carried out in the fields and caves in the vicinity. Some of the caves were used in the time of the Second Temple as Jewish burial places, for which niches were cut in the rock.

According to Matthew 27:3-8, this was the site purchased by the high priests of Jerusalem for thirty pieces of silver – the price of Judas' betrayal of Jesus. Since then the name of the site was changed to Aceldama (or Akeldama; Acts 1:19) an Aramaic word meaning "Field of Blood." It was perhaps here that the Apostles hid during and immediately after Jesus' trial. The Christian community of Jerusalem buried its dead in and around the caves, and later the caves were used as cells by hermits. The site was again used as a cemetery in the Crusader period when the Knights of St John buried poor pilgrims there. They constructed a large vaulted hall, still partially preserved, for this purpose.

In 1874 the Greek Orthodox church erected a monastery on the site and named it after St Onuphrius, an Egyptian hermit.

The Monastery of St Onuphrius at the site of Aceldama in the Hinnom Valley.

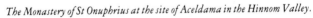

ALEXANDER NIEVSKY CHURCH

A Russian church and monastery east of the CHURCH OF THE HOLY SEPULCHRE. When built, the site revealed dramatic finds – the easternmost parts of the original, Constantine (4th century) Church of the Holy Sepulchre. The staircase that led to that earlier church and the southern entrance from the atrium (courtyard) to the church can be seen in the basement of the Alexander Nievsky Church. Also in the basement is an earlier structure, an arch which is believed to have been part of one of the gates leading to the main forum (city square) of Roman Jerusalem. This forum was part of the new city plan introduced in the 2nd century A.D. by the emperor Hadrian who rebuilt Jerusalem as a Roman colony under the name Aelia Capitolina.

The land on which Alexander Nievsky Church stands was purchased in 1857 by the Imperial Pravoslav Society for the construction of the Russian consulate and a hostel for pilgrims. But when the important remnants were found, work was delayed, and the consulate and hostel were built in the Russian Compound in western Jerusalem. The church was finally finished in 1887.

EL AQSA MOSQUE

The largest mosque in Jerusalem, on the southern side of the TEMPLE MOUNT. The name el Aqsa means "the farthest," i.e., from Mecca. It refers to the place, not determined geographically, to which the prophet Mohammed, mounted on his steed al-Burak, flew in a night journey. From this place he ascended to heaven to receive the Koran, the Holy Book, from the angel Gabriel. Shortly after the conquest of Jerusalem by the Moslems in 638 the unspecified place called el Aqsa came to be identified with the Temple Mount in Jerusalem, thus making it particularly holy to Islam.

El Aqsa Mosque (right) and the Dome of the Rock (left) on the Temple Mount.

The first mosque on the Temple Mount was a temporary, wooden structure built by Omar, the Moslem conqueror of Jerusalem. The present structure was built by the Umayyad caliph, el-Walid, at the beginning of the 8th century. Little remains of the original structure, which, owing to the position of the mosque over Herod's artificial addition to the Temple Mount, was in constant danger of collapse. In 747 it was badly damaged by an earthquake and then rebuilt on a much larger scale. It was destroyed again in 1033 and reconstructed once more. In 1099, with the Crusader conquest of Jerusalem, it was identified as Templum Solomonis. At first it was used as the palace of the Crusader kings, and then it was handed over to a newly created order of knights which became known as the Templars, dwellers of the temple. When Saladin took Jerusalem in 1187 he reconverted El Aqsa into a mosque which it has remained to this day. Damage from earthquakes in 1927 and 1936 necessitated an almost complete rebuilding of the mosque, in the process of which ancient sections of the original mosque were brought to light.

Today the El Aqsa Mosque is a huge hall 82 × 55m (269 × 180 ft), with seven rows of columns supporting the roof. Over the southern part is an 11th-century dome. In the southern wall is a *mihrab* (niche) oriented towards Mecca, the holy city of Islam. This wall, which is decorated with mosaics, is one of the few remnants of the original mosque. Near the *mihrab* are a preacher's platform and another elevated one for the leader of the service. There is no other furniture in the spacious hall; the congregation sits and prostrates on the carpet-covered floor. East of the main hall are three rooms. One of them-the Mihrab of Zachariah-is a small Crusader chapel with a typical medieval rose window and other architectural features of that period. West of the main hall is a smaller one of the Crusader period, used today as a women's prayer hall.

Entrance to El Aqsa Mosque.

Under the mosque is a large subterranean hall divided in two by a row of seven pillars. Although it is called El Aqsa el Kadima – "the ancient El Aqsa" – it has nothing to do with the mosque but was one of the original entrance passages to the Temple Mount in the Second Temple period. It is usually closed to the public.

CATHEDRAL OF ST JAMES

Embroidered drape depicting Mary holding James's head at the Cathedral of St James.

The largest and holiest place of worship of the Armenian community in Jerusalem. The cathedral is located inside the Armenian Convent in the Armenian Quarter – the southwestern part of the Old City of Jerusalem. The cathedral is believed to stand on the spot where James was beheaded by order of Herod Agrippa I, grandson of Herod the Great, in the year A.D. 44, as related in Acts 12:1-2: *Now about that time Herod the king stretched forth his hands... And he killed James the brother of John with the sword.* There was already a monastery dedicated to St James there by the 7th century, but the present one dates to the Crusader period.

The cathedral is entered through the convent, from the road encircling the western side of the Old City. At the entrance to the Convent is an ornate fountain erected at the turn of the 20th century to commemorate the 25th anniversary of the accession to the throne of the Ottoman sultan, Abd el Hamid. One crosses an open courtyard, in the floor of which are tombstones. In the walls surrounding the courtyard are small stone plaques, known in Armenian as *Katchkars*, placed there, in accordance with Armenian custom, by pilgrims. In the vestibule in front of the church are two unusual instruments

– an old wooden board and a piece of iron. They were used until 1840 instead of bells, these having been forbidden by the Moslem authorities.

The doors of the church are covered with heavy leather sheets. The church hall is divided by four pillars into three aisles. Above the pillars are eight arches which support an impressive cupola of intricate structure. The pillars are panelled with blue Spanish tiles. In the northern nave is a small, richly decorated chapel, where St James is believed to have been beheaded. While his head is said to have remained here, his body, so tradition claims, reached Santiago de Compostella in northern Spain. The walls of the chapel are lined with glazed ceramic tiles painted in the Armenian style. Some of the tiles depict scenes from the Old and New Testament, based on medieval manuscript illuminations. Next to the Chapel of the Beheading is the sacristy, in which the treasures of the Armenian Patriarchate are kept. These treasures, collected over many centuries, include exquisite amber scepters and richly embroidered vestments, among them a mitre fashioned in 1740 for the patriarch Gregory the Chainwearer which is elaborately embroidered with gold thread and studded with precious stones. These and other treasures are displayed to the public on a sumptuous altar on St James' Day, the 10th of January. On the southern wall of the church is a door leading into the narrow Chapel of Echmiadzin, named after the holy city in Armenia. In the chapel, next to the altar, are three stones – one from the Jordan River, one from Mount Sinai, and one from Mount Tabor.

The convent has a famous library with 30,000 volumes, many printed in the Armenian printshop of the convent, the oldest in Jerusalem. It also has a marvellous collection of ancient illuminated manuscripts, kept separately in a building behind the Cathedral. In the late 1970s a most interesting Armenian Museum was opened in the compound, south of the Cathedral. The Armenian Patriarch lives on the second floor of the building next to the Cathedral.

(left) Armenian ceramics decorated with scenes from the Bible. (right) Mitre of Patriarch Gregory the Chainbearer.

CHURCH OF MARY MAGDALENE

A church and monastery on the western slope of the MOUNT OF OLIVES, above the CHURCH OF THE AGONY, built in 1885-1888 by the Russian Czar Alexander III in memory of his mother Maria Alexandrova. The church is dedicated to Mary Magdalene, name-saint of the Czar's mother. The church was designed in the 17th-century Russian style with distinct gilded onion-shaped domes, and is one of the more spectacular views Jerusalem has to offer. The church is especially impressive at night, when its lit domes seem to be floating above the dark trees. The interior of the church is rather plain, but it houses paintings by Vereshaguine and Ivanoff, two famous Russian painters of the 19th century. In the crypt of the church is buried Princess Elizabeth Feodorovna, sister of the Czar. She, together with her husband Duke Serge of Moscow, was the founder of the Imperial

Church of Mary Magdalene.

The Church of Mary Magdalene at night.

Orthodox Society of Palestine which carried out the building of the church. The princess met a violent death during the Russian Revolution of 1917 and her body was smuggled out of Russia through China.

In the church compound archaeological excavations have unearthed an ancient flight of steps. This is perhaps a section of the 537 steps that lead from the summit of the Mount of Olives to the VALLEY OF JEHOSHAPHAT mentioned in 9th-century Latin documents.

CHURCH OF ST ANNAS

A church in the southern part of the Armenian Quarter, not far from Zion Gate. The Armenians believe that this is the site of the house of Annas, father-in-law of the high priest Caiaphas, to which Jesus was first led after his arrest (John 18:13). The church was built around 1300 in the style of a classic Byzantine basilica and was first called Church of the Angels, but in 1350 it became known as the Church of Annas. In the vestibule is a well, and in the left nave of the church hall is a small chapel where Jesus is believed to have been detained.

Outside the church grows an olive tree which, according to Armenian tradition, is an offshoot of the tree to which the Romans tied Jesus. The Arab name of the church is Deir ez-Zeituna (House of the Olive Tree).

CHURCH OF ST ANNE

The church stands in a large compound on the northern side of Lions' Gate Street, just inside the Lions' – or St Stephen's – Gate in the eastern wall of the Old City of Jerusalem. It is the most characteristic and best preserved Crusader church in Jerusalem.

The church marks the traditional site of the house of Anne and Joachim, Mary's parents. Though various traditions claim Mary was born in Nazareth or Bethlehem, remnants of a small oratory found near the church show that the site was revered for its association with Mary as early as the 3rd century. The Byzantine empress, Eudoxia (438-460), built a basilica in

116

Church of St Anne.

honor of St Mary over this oratory, thus officially giving the Jerusalem tradition supremacy. Eudoxia's basilica, like many Christian shrines in Jerusalem, was destroyed by the Persians in 618. It was rebuilt soon afterward and was in use throughout the early Moslem period as a nunnery and place of refuge for poor Christian women.

The Crusaders completely rebuilt the church in 1140, and gave it the name of St Anne, by which it is known to this day. Of the old Byzantine church only the crypt venerated as the birthplace of Mary was preserved. The new church was built in austere Romanesque style, with thick walls giving it a fortress-like appearance. The structure leans very slightly to one side, thereby – so the pious claim – representing Christ on the Cross. The interior space of the church is divided by massive pillars into three aisles, each ending in an apse. During the Crusader period the nunnery next to the church became rich and famous, and benefited much when prominent

Inscription in Arabic from the time of Saladin above the entrance of the Church of St Anne.

members of the royal house of the Latin Kingdom joined it.

Following the Moslem victory over the Crusaders in 1187, the compound was converted into an Islamic theological school, named Salahiyeh, in honour of the conqueror Saladin The site remained in Moslem hands until 1856 when, following the Crimean War, it was presented to the French government which had the church restored.

Today the compound around the church is run by the White Fathers. It includes, besides the church, a convent, a museum (entrance on request) and a seminary.

CHURCH OF ST ETIENNE

This church, part of the extensive Dominican compound north of the Damascus Gate, stands on the place where, according to a tradition dating from the Byzantine period, Stephen was stoned (Acts 7:58-60). In the 5th century a very ornate basilica was built here by the Byzantine empress, Eudoxia, and she herself was buried nearby. This basilica was destroyed during the Persian invasion of 614; it was rebuilt in the 8th century and, after falling into disuse, restored by the Crusaders who called the adjacent city gate, the Gate of St Stephen. Once again in 1187, when Jerusalem fell to Saladin, the basilica was razed. The site was purchased in 1881 by the Dominican order. The monks conducted large scale archaeological excavations, discovered the ruins of Eudoxia's basilica and built the Church of St Etienne over the ruins. They also exposed a series of burial caves, part of the extensive cemetery of Jerusalem in the First Temple period.

The Greek Orthodox church believes that the stoning took place in the VALLEY OF JEHOSHAPHAT, where they built their CHURCH OF ST STEPHEN.

There is a tradition that the body of Stephen was discovered in 415 at Kfar Gamala, identified with BETH JAMAL south of Beth Shemesh. The body is said to have been transported to Jerusalem and deposited in the Church of Mount zion, where the CHURCH OF THE DORMITION now stands.

One of the burial chambers of the First Temple period in the grounds of the Church of St Etienne.

CHURCH OF ST MARK

A Syrian Orthodox church and small convent, centre of the small, ancient Syrian Orthodox, or Jacobite, community in Jerusalem. The church stands in a narrow alley which branches off from St Mark's Street, parallel to David Street, between the Armenian and the Jewish Quarters in the Old City of Jerusalem. Many traditions surround this site. St Mark's mother, Mary, is believed to have had her house here. Peter escaped from his Roman guards and hid here after he was arrested by King Herod Agrippa I (Acts 12:3-17). Another tradition holds that this was the place where Mary, Jesus' mother, was baptized, and the baptismal font used on that occasion is shown inside the church. The picture of Mary above the font is believed to have been painted by St Luke.

Entrance to the Syrian Orthodox Church of St Mark.

The Syrians also believe that here was the Upper Room where Jesus and his disciples ate the Last Supper.

The Church of St Mark is a 12th-century Crusader building standing over the ruins of a Byzantine church. The entrance to the church and convent is clearly marked with a sign in English, Arabic and Syriac. The archbishop of the community lives next to the church.

A former archbishop, Mar Athanasius Samuel, was the person to whom the Bedouins of the Qumran area brought the famous Dead Sea Scrolls which they had found in the desert caves. He recognized their antiquity and importance, and thanks to him several scrolls were purchased by Israeli archaeologists and are on display at the Shrine of the Book in the Israel Museum in Jerusalem.

CHURCH OF ST PETER'S IN GALLICANTU

Church of St Peter in Gallicantu.

A modern church, built in 1931, about halfway down the eastern slope of MOUNT ZION. According to the Assumptionist Fathers – owners of the church and the surrounding property – it stands on the site of the house of the high priest Caiaphas where Jesus was arrested. This then is an alternative to the Armenian Church of the HOUSE OF CAIAPHAS on the summit of Mount Zion. Under the church is a cave thought to be where Jesus was detained for the night following his arrest.

On the grounds stood a Byzantine church, which seems to have been the one dedicated to the triple denial and repentance of Peter (Matthew 26:34). The church was destroyed by the invading Persians in 614 and rebuilt by the Crusaders. Saewulf, the English pilgrim who visited the Holy Land in 1102, was the first to give the church the name St Peter's Gallicantu ("cock-crow") taken from Luke 22:60-61: *And immediately, while he yet spake, the cock crew... And Peter remembered the words of the Lord... Before the cock crow, thou shalt deny me thrice.* Archaeological excavations were carried out prior to the construction of the new church and uncovered many objects of the First Temple period, including inscribed stone weights and a Hebrew inscription. Sections of a terraced street from the time of the Second Temple were also found.

CHURCH OF ST SIMEON

A small Greek Orthodox church built in 1890 at the top of a hill in the new city of Jerusalem, overlooking the residential neighbourhoods of Katamon and of the so-called Greek and German colonies. According to a tradition that developed in the 16th century, here stood the house of Simeon who witnessed Jesus' presentation at the Temple – the old man who *was just and devout, waiting for the consolation of Israel... And it was revealed unto him... that he could not see death, before he had seen the Lord's Christ* (Luke 2:25-26). After seeing the infant Jesus brought to the Temple by Mary, Simeon knew he could depart in peace.

The small church is surrounded by a lovely pine grove and a park which serves the residential neighbourhoods in the vicinity.

CHURCH OF ST STEPHEN

A church, built in the late 1960s, in the VALLEY OF JEHOSHAPHAT next to the bridge that crosses the valley between the Old City of Jerusalem and the MOUNT OF OLIVES. This Greek Orthodox church stands on the place "out of the city" where Stephen, the first Christian martyr is believed to have been stoned (Acts 7:58-60). The adjacent eastern gate of the Old City, commonly called Lions' Gate, is known in Christian tradition as St Stephen's Gate.

Another tradition points to a site north of the Damascus Gate as the place of the stoning of Stephen, and on it stand the CHURCH OF ST ETIENNE in the great Dominican compound.

CHURCH OF THE AGONY

The Church of the Agony standing at the foot of the MOUNT OF OLIVES was built on the traditional site of the GARDEN OF GETHSEMANE, over the rock where Jesus is believed to have prayed for the last time before being turned over to the Romans (Mark 14:32-35).

The church was designed by the Italian architect Barlozzi and built in 1919-1924 with donations from all over the world, hence the other name by which the church is sometimes known – Church of All Nations. The design of the church follows that of the Byzantine basilica over which it is built, and parts of the mosaic floor of the ancient church are incorporated into the new floor. In the centre of the church is the rock on which Jesus prayed. The church has very harmonious proportions, and is noted for the special light that filters through the purple and brown stained windows. On the outside, the gable facing the main Jerusalem-Jericho road is adorned with a spectacular mosaic depicting Jesus as a link between man and God, with the whole of humanity raising their eyes to him in hope. Above the head of Jesus appear the

Mosaic in the gable of the Church of the Agony.

Greek letters Alpha and Omega, as it is said in Revelation 1:8: *I am Alpha and Omega, the Beginning and the Ending, saith the Lord...* On the pillars stand statues of the four Evangelists: Mathew, Mark, Luke and John. The two deer which face the cross surmounting the facade symbolise David's verse: *As the hart panteth after the water brooks, so panteth my soul after Thee, O God* (Psalms 42:1).

CHURCH OF THE ASCENSION

Ruins of a church mark one of the sites most holy to Christianity; the spot from which Jesus ascended to heaven (Luke 24:50-51). It is located east of the main road which runs on top of the MOUNT OF OLIVES, next to the CHURCH OF THE PATER NOSTER. The original church was built on this spot in the 4th century. It was a rotunda with a double row of columns surmounted by arches, surrounding the rock from which Jesus is said to have ascended and on which he is believed to have left his foot print. There is no evidence that this Byzantine edifice ever had a roof. This church was not destroyed until the 10th century.

In the 12th century the Crusaders built a new church on the site. Like its predecessor the Byzantine church, it was designed as a concentric structure surrounding the rock. Its shape, however, was now octagonal and with columns supporting a dome. Over the rock was a small edicule. In the courtyard of this church was a monastery, and the compound was surrounded by a thick wall with crenelations and watch towers. In those days, besides being a holy place, the compound also constituted a small fortress guarding the Jerusalem-Jericho road. While the church was destroyed at the end of the Crusader period, the edicule with its columns and very ornate capitals, bearing designs of vegetation and fabulous animals, has been well preserved. The walls between the columns, however, are a post-Crusader addition.

In the days of Saladin (1187) the ruined church was in Moslem hands and never rebuilt. Every year, on August 15, a celebration in honour of the Assumption is held here by the

Church of the Ascension.

various Christian communities. Each community has an allocated space in the courtyard, marked by some stones referred to as "altars." Above these altars in the wall surrounding the compound, are hooks to which coloured ribbons and flags are tied during the celebration, lending it a carnival atmosphere.

(RUSSIAN) CHURCH OF THE ASCENSION

At the very summit of the MOUNT OF OLIVES stands one of the landmarks of Jerusalem – the belfry of the Russian Church of the Ascension. While most Christians believe that the place of the Ascension of Jesus occurred further to the south, where the remains of the Byzantine and Crusader CHURCH OF THE ASCENSION have been preserved, the Russian Pravoslav church had its own tradition, and in 1870-1880 the church, the bell tower and a hospice were built on the summit of the mountain. The Russians believe that the Ascension took place at the very spot where the tower stands, and that during the event Mary stood on a stone which is shown inside the church. The huge bell in the tower was made in Russia in 1885 and brought by boat to Jaffa. From there it was taken on foot to Jerusalem as an act of devotion by Russian women. Since 1907, when it was turned into a nunnery, the compound has been inhabited by Russian nuns. Although only a few live

The tower of the Russian Church of the Ascension. ▷

there nowadays, they are renowned for their icon-painting in the best Russian-Byzantine tradition and for their beautiful singing of the Vespers every afternoon.

East of the Russian compound are remnants of a 4th-century Armenian church where an exquisite mosaic floor has been well preserved. It is told that the head of John the Baptist was found in a hollow part of the mosaic floor, and indeed, under the floor is a burial chamber. At the edge of the mosaic is an Armenian inscription: "This is the tomb of Blessed Susana, the mother of Artavan, September 18." This inscription was inserted in the 5th or 6th century into the earlier floor, and from it one can conclude that there was an important Armenian community in Jerusalem in those days.

CHURCH OF THE ASSUMPTION

A most interesting and unusual church in the Kidron Valley at the foot of the MOUNT OF OLIVES stands partially below the level of the road. It is believed that Mary, Jesus' mother, is buried there. It is not known how the legend concerning the tomb of Mary developed, since according to Christian dogma Mary did not die but "fell asleep" and was then assumed to heaven in body and soul.

The tradition, however, is very old and the earliest church on the site was built in the 4th century. The valley bed was then deeper than it is today, having filled-up over the centuries. The church was constructed according to a cruciform plan at what was then the level of the valley bed. The shrine attributed to Mary, perhaps in a cave, was in the centre. The remnants of this early Byzantine church are now deep down at the very bottom of the present church and are reached by a wide flight of steps. In the 6th century an upper floor was

Crusader façade of the Church of the Assumption.

Edicule over Mary's tomb in the Church of the Assumption.

added over the 4th-century church, but it was destroyed during the Persian invasion in 618.

The church got its present shape in the Crusader period when the site was handed over to the Benedictine Order, who built a large basilica over the ruins of the old church. The exquisite façade of this basilica has been preserved intact and is one of the best examples of Crusader architecture in Jerusalem. Next to the church the Benedictines built the Monastery of St Mary of the Valley of Jehoshaphat and a

Plan of the Church of the Assumption.

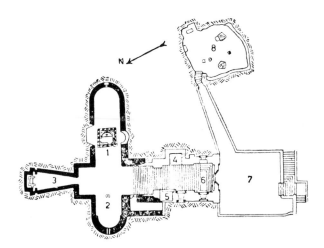

1. *Tomb of Mary*	5. *Chapel of Joseph*
2. *Coptic Altar*	6. *Entrance*
3. *Closed corridor*	7. *Courtyard*
4. *Chapel of Anne and Joachin*	8. *Grotto of Gethsemane*

hostel, both of which, along with much of the basilica, were destroyed when Saladin conquered Jerusalem in 1187. Since the 18th century the church has belonged to both the Greek Orthodox and the Armenians, who share it also with the Coptic and Syrian churches.

The Church of the Assumption is reached by a stairway leading down from the main Jerusalem-Jericho road into an open courtyard. To the right of this courtyard is a passage which leads to the GROTTO OF GETHSEMANE. On the north side is the well-proportioned Crusader church. It takes a minute or two to adjust to the darkness and to the heavy smell of incense that fills the church. Upon descending the wide, Crusader period steps that in fact fill up the entire space of the church one sees, on the right, in a niche, the Chapel of Anne and Joachim, Mary's parents. In this niche the Crusader queen, Melisand, was buried in 1161. On the left is another niche with a chapel dedicated to Joseph, Mary's husband. At the bottom of the steps is a wide hall, a remnant of the 4th-

The bells at the Church of the Assumption.

century Byzantine church. To the left is an apse with a Coptic altar and to the right stands the most important structure in the church – a small edicule alledgedly housing the tomb of Mary. The edicule is richly decorated with icons, candlesticks and flowers while the interior of the tomb is quite bare, with a stone bench on which lay Mary's body. Numerous hanging lamps fill the space in front of the tomb. They are lit on holidays and special occasions and give the church an air of mystery. Next to the edicule is an altar shared by the Armenians and the Syrians.

CHURCH OF THE DORMITION

A relatively modern church and monastery, built between 1906 and 1910, on the site where, according to tradition, Mary died, or rather "fell asleep," as Christian dogma refers to the event, hence the full name of the church: Dormitio Beatae Mariae Virginis. During the Byzantine period the Church of Mount Zion, one of the three earliest churches in Jerusalem, stood on the same spot. The church was built by Emperor Constantine and was Mother of all Churches. The land on which the modern church and monastery stand was given as a gift by the Ottoman sultan, Abdul Hamid II, to Kaiser Wilhelm II of Germany when the latter visited Jerusalem in 1898. The Kaiser laid the foundation stone for the church, and handed the land over to the Union of German

A narrow street leads to the Church of the Dormition on Mount Zion.

Catholics for the Holy Land. Monks of the Benedictine Order live in the monastery and run the church.

The church of the Dormition is a stout, circular building, surmounted by a distinct conical grey roof. Both the church and the nearby belfry are among the notable landmarks of Jerusalem. Entrance to the church, which is renowned for its works of art, is from the west. The spacious circular prayer hall is adorned with colourful wall mosaics depicting events from Christian and Benedictine history. High up in the Byzantine style apse is a mosaic picture of Mary and the infant Jesus. Below it is a mosaic inscription in Latin of the verse, *Behold, a virgin shall conceive, and bear a son, and shall call his name Immanuel* (Isaiah 7:14). Further down the wall, between the windows, are depicted in mosaic seven prophets of the Old Testament. The floor of the hall is decorated with an interesting design made of concentric circles in which are symbols of the zodiac and the names of 16 prophets and the 12 Apostles.

In the centre of the circular crypt under the hall lies a life-size statue of the sleeping Mary made of cherry wood and ivory. The dome above the statue is adorned with artistic mosaic pictures of famous biblical women. Six chapels surround the crypt, three of them dedicated to Austria, Hungary, and the Ivory Coast who donated funds to the church.

The church of the Dormition has a fine organ and well-attended concerts of liturgical and chamber music are held in

Statue of Mary in the crypt of the Church of the Dormition.

the church. It is interesting to note that there are other Christian traditions which claim that Mary left the Holy Land after the crucifixion and lived and died elsewhere. One widely held tradition places her house at EPHESUS in Turkey.

CHURCH OF THE FLAGELLATION

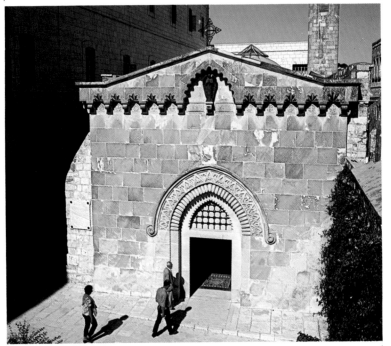

Church of the Flagellation.

A Franciscan church in the compound of the Studium Biblicum Franciscanum in the eastern part of the Old City of Jerusalem, next to the CHURCH OF THE CONDEMNATION, on the spot where, according to tradition, Jesus was flogged by the Roman soldiers. The church was built in 1839 over a medieval predecessor, and in 1927-29 it was completely rebuilt in medieval style by the architect Barlozzi. Especially noteworthy are the three stained-glass windows of the church on which are depicted Pontius Pilate washing his hands, the Flagellation, and the triumph of Barabbas. The mosaic of the dome of the sanctuary is designed as a crown of thorns.

CHURCH OF THE HOLY SEPULCHRE

One of the holiest places for Christianity, the Church of the Holy Sepulchre houses the tomb where Jesus was laid after his crucifixion. The church includes under its roof "the place called GOLGOTHA, that is to say, a place of a skull" (Matthew 22:23), as well as the 10th, 11th and 12th stations of the VIA DOLOROSA. Within the compound are also the Church of St Helena and the Chapel of the Finding of the Cross. Each of these separate sections of the compound was built in a different period and in a different style, and together they form a large, sprawling, and rather confusing complex. The church is visited every year by hundreds of thousands of pilgrims.

Main entrance to the Church of the Holy Sepulchre. Three marble pillars standing on high bases flank the twin arched portals

While today the Church of the Holy Sepulchre is in the centre of the Christian Quarter of the Old City of Jerusalem, both the Golgotha and the Sepulchre were originally outside the walls of Jerusalem. Their extra-mural situation, hard to grasp today, was determined by Jewish custom, strictly adhered to in the days of Jesus, of total separation between activities of life and those connected with death – execution and burial – which were always performed outside the walls of a city. It would seem that not far from the northwestern section of the city wall of those days were two adjacent places – Golgotha, the place of execution, and a nameless hill where Joseph of Arimathea had bought for himself a sepulchre, as was the custom of wealthy Jewish families. This tomb, where Jesus was laid after the Crucifixion, was no doubt a normal

Jewish burial cave with a rock-cut open court from which an entrance led into the burial chamber. The entrance was closed by means of a large, heavy rolling stone which posed a problem to Mary Magdalene, mother of James and Salome, who asked, *Who shall roll us away the stone from the door of the sepulchre?* (Mark 16:3). In the typical burial chamber were niches cut into the wall into which the deceased were laid.

The natural configuration of both Golgotha and the hill of the Sepulchre was changed in the 4th century when most of the rock was removed to level the ground for the construction of a basilica. Today the natural rock can be seen only inside the tomb, behind the Rotunda and at the foot of Golgotha.

The holy places of Golgotha and of the Sepulchre lived on in Christian tradition despite the fact that in A.D. 135, when Jerusalem became the Roman colony Aelia Capitolina, the emperor, Hadrian, ordered a temple to Zeus to be built on Golgotha and an altar to Venus over the Sepulchre. These stood there until 326, when Helena, mother of Constantine, the first Christian Byzantine emperor, came to Jerusalem and found the remains of the Cross in an underground cistern. Constantine had a large basilica built on the site which encompassed under one roof all three adjacent holy sites – the Sepulchre, Golgotha-Calvary and the Cave of the Finding of the Cross. Remnants of Constantine's basilica have been preserved in various places in the present-day church and surrounding area, allowing a reconstruction of that enormous monument. Entrance was from the east, via steps, and three entrances that can be seen in the basement of the nearby ALEXANDER NIEVSKY CHURCH. These led to an atrium (open courtyard) that preceded the huge basilica which was divided by four rows of columns into five naves. The basilica was called Martyrium ("Witness"), and was 45m (150 ft) long and 26m (85 ft) wide. Behind the apse was a cloister, in the southeast corner of which was the square rock, all that was left of Golgotha. The westernmost part of the edifice was a circular church, the Anastasis ("Resurrection") with the Sepulchre – from around which all the rock was removed – in the centre. Constantine's basilica was destroyed in 614, immediately rebuilt, destroyed again in 1010, and again restored on a much reduced scale centering mostly on the Anastasis, with the other holy sites left outside. The deterioration of the Church of the Holy Sepulchre under Moslem rule was the rallying battle-cry of the armies of the Crusaders at the end of the 11th century, and once they conquered Jerusalem they set out to restore and beautify it. The church as we know it today is basically the work of the Crusaders. They reunited all the holy sites under one roof, built an edicule over the Sepulchre, restored the Rotunda of the Anastasis and built a church surrounded by an ambulatory over what was a cloister in the Constantine basilica. From the ambulatory they built a staircase leading down to the Chapel of St Helena and the Cave of the Finding of the Cross.

Since the end of the Crusader period the Church of the Holy Sepulchre suffered severe damage caused by fires, earthquakes, and general neglect. Furthermore, the edifice was

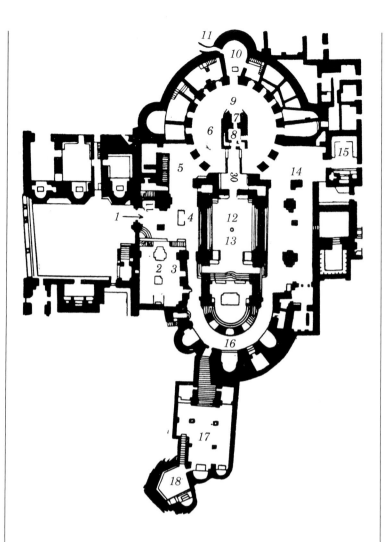

1. Main entrance
2. Latin chapel of Golgotha
3. Greek chapel of Golgotha; Chapel of Adam (underneath)
4. Stone of Anointing
5. Armenian sacristy
6. Rotunda
7. Tomb of Jesus
8. Chapel of the Angel
9. Chapels of the Copts
10. Chapel of the Syrians
11. Burial cave
12. Greek Orthodox choir
13. Omphalos
14. Place of the Apparition
15. Chapel of the Apparition
16. Ambulatory
17. Chapel of St Helena
18. Chapel of the Finding of the Cross

Plan of the Church of the Holy Sepulchre.

divided between six Christian communities – Greek Orthodox, Armenians, Franciscans, Ethiopians, Copts and Syrian Jacobites – each zealously protecting its rights and, if possible, trying to extend them. The different communities did not usually cooperate on matters of repair and restoration which became particularly acute after the disastrous fire of 1808 which almost completely destroyed the Rotunda. Only in 1957 did the various communities manage to unite and initiate a program of restoration which should be completed within the next few years.

Entrance to the Church of the Holy Sepulchre is from the south, through an open courtyard with three chapels on the left and three on the right. Noteworthy is the belfry on the left, built between 1160 and 1180. Originally it had another storey, which collapsed in the 16th century. The facade of the church is in typical style, composed of a double arched gateway and corresponding windows above, flanked by small pillars and capitals. The sculptured lintels of the gates were moved to the Rockefeller Museum in 1935 to protect them from the elements. To the right of the double gate is a flight of steps leading to a Crusader edicule that once served as a separate entrance to Calvary. Entrance to the church is through the left gateway.

Once inside, Golgotha is on the right-hand side and is reached by ascending a steep flight of steps. The sanctuary at the top of the steps is divided by two pillars: on the right is the Latin chapel and on the left, the Greek Orthodox. The Latin chapel, completely remodeled in 1937, has mosaics on the walls depicting Jesus being nailed to the cross and Jesus on the cross. These are the 10th and 11th stations of the Via Dolorosa. On the ceiling is a figure of Christ, a remnant of a Crusader mosaic.

The Greek Orthodox chapel is built over the rock of Calvary itself, and the place where the cross stood is marked by a silver disc beneath the altar table. This is the 12th station of the Via Dolorosa. To the right of the altar is a fissure in the rock, believed to have been caused by an earthquake at the time of the death of Jesus on the cross (Matthew 27:51). This fissure continues down to the Chapel of Adam under Calvary where, so the tradition goes, Adam was buried and where the blood of Jesus dripped onto his skull. Between the two chapels of Golgotha is the altar of Our Lady of Dolours, the 13th station where Mary received the body of her son.

The Stone of Anointing.

Edicule of the burial chamber of Jesus in the Rotunda.

Going down again to the level of the church, we find on the left the Stone of Anointing, a slab of polished stone surrounded by candelabra, on which the lifeless body of Jesus was washed and anointed before being placed in the tomb. Left of the passage that leads to the Rotunda is the Armenian sacristy. On the wall is a huge new mosaic picture showing the three Marys witnessing the last scenes of the Passion.

The Rotunda is an impressive space, surrounded by massive pillars and surmounted by a huge cupola. In its centre is the Holy Sepulchre in the form of a richly decorated edicule. Inside are two small chambers; the first is the Chapel of the Angel, with a rock bench on which the three women saw an angel who announced "he is risen" (Mark 16:5-6), and in the second is the Holy Sepulchre itself, a rock bench covered with a marble slab. Three masses are celebrated daily inside the

Sepulchre; the Greek Orthodox at 1 p.m., the Armenian at 2:30 p.m. and the Catholic at 4 p.m.

Behind the edicule over the Sepulchre is a tiny chapel belonging to the Copts, and behind it – beyond the pillars of the Rotunda – a chapel of the Syrians-Jacobites. From this chapel one can enter an anonymous burial cave in the rock, proving that this area was indeed a Jewish cemetery in the time of Jesus.

In front of the Sepulchre, in the very centre of the church, is the newly remodeled Greek Orthodox choir, with a lavishly decorated iconostasis. On the floor is a stone goblet which represents the Omphalos, the centre of the world, according to the words of the Psalmist: *For God is my king of old, working salvation in the midst of the earth* (Psalms 74:12). It is interesting to note that the earlier Jewish tradition points to the ROCK OF FOUNDATION on the TEMPLE MOUNT as the centre of the world.

On the northern side of the Rotunda is the Franciscan Chapel of the Apparition where, according to tradition, Jesus appeared before Mary Magdalene (John 20:13-17). Behind the chapel is the Convent of the Franciscans. From the chapel one proceeds through a long gallery in which can be seen architectural fragments of the earlier phases of the church. Along the ambulatory are two Greek-Orthodox and one Armenian chapels. From here one goes down to the Armenian Chapel of St Helena. On the walls flanking the steps are numerous small crosses cut in the stone by generations of pilgrims. The chapel was completely renovated in 1950, and its floor mosaic has pictures of churches in Armenia. Steps lead further down from this chapel to the Chapel of the Finding of the Cross. This was originally a cistern hewn in the rock

Crosses engraved in the wall by medieval pilgrims at the Church of the Holy Sepulchre.

on the side of Golgotha, and it was here that Helena, Constantine's mother, found the True Cross.

Going up the steps one continues along the ambulatory to the above-mentioned Chapel of Adam at the foot of Golgotha-Calvary, and then back to the entrance.

CHURCH OF THE PATER NOSTER – ELEONA

Located on the MOUNT OF OLIVES, this church, belonging to the Carmelite Sisters, is believed to have been built over the grotto in which Jesus assembled his disciples and taught them the Pater Noster prayer – The Lord's Prayer (Luke 11:1-4). This was the site in the 4th century of the elaborate church of Eleona, one of the four churches Emperor Constantine ordered to be built in the Holy Land. Although nothing of this church can be seen above ground, excavations carried out in 1910 and 1918 clearly revealed its plan. The church had a basilical shape and was about 30m (100 ft) long and about 18.6m (60 ft) wide. The present Pater Noster grotto was the crypt of that church. In front of the church was a wide atrium (courtyard) surrounded by an ornate portico. It was destroyed in the 7th century, rebuilt by the Crusaders, and destroyed again by Saladin. The grounds were purchased in 1868 by the Princess de la Tour d'Auvergne and handed over to the Carmelite Sisters who have their headquarters in the MONASTERY OF THE CARMELITE ORDER in Haifa. The present-day church was built in 1875, its most renowned feature being the plaques which carry the Pater Noster prayer in 60 languages on the walls of the cloister.

Over the grotto is the unfinished chapel of the Sacred Heart which was began in 1920.

Church of the Pater Noster.

CHURCH OF VIRI GALILAEI

A Greek Orthodox church on the top of the MOUNT OF OLIVES, in the village of A-Tur. Its name means "men of Galilee," a reference to the description of the ascension of Jesus to heaven (Acts 1:11). In the courtyard of the church are remnants of a Byzantine chapel where, according to legend, Mary was told by the angel Gabriel that she was about to die. Many Second Temple period burial caves were found near the church.

CITY OF DAVID - OPHEL

The oldest inhabited part of Jerusalem, today outside and south of the city wall of the Old City. It is a relatively low and narrow spur of a hill, between the VALLEY OF JEHOSHAPHAT on the east and the Tyropoeon Valley in the west. These two valleys join at the southern tip of the City of David, affording it natural protection on three sides. In the Valley of

General view of the excavations at the City of David, looking north.

Jehoshaphat the GIHON SPRING issues forth; it is the only perennial spring in the entire area, and the ultimate reason for the settlement of Jerusalem on this particular hill.

The earliest settlement on the hill, later known as the City of David, dates to around 3000 B.C. This makes Jerusalem one of the oldest and also continuously inhabited sites in the Holy Land. As early as the 19th century B.C., perhaps in the days of Melchizedek, king of Shalem (Genesis 14:18-20), Jerusalem was mentioned by name in Egyptian texts and was surrounded by a wall found in archaeological excavations. This is the wall that David took around 1000 B.C. when he conquered the stronghold of Zion. Following his victory, David *dwelt in the fort, and called it the city of David* (II Samuel 5:9), the name by which it has been known ever since. It was also sometimes called Ophel, a name of obscure origin, perhaps meaning "citadel." Here David built his house and here he was buried (1 Kings 2:10). The Temple, however, was not built in the City of David but on the TEMPLE MOUNT north of it, and between these two sections of the city was an area known as *Millo* – "the fill" – apparently because it was narrow and steep and had to be strengthened by filling and terracing.

From the days of King Solomon the city of Jerusalem expanded northwards and westwards. Private buildings were erected in the new areas, and the City of David remained a residential quarter. Its proximity to the Gihon Spring, however, made it a focal point for various water supply systems which provided water in times of siege. The earliest is the so-called "Warren's Shaft," named after Sir Charles Warren who discovered it in the 1860s. This is a system of vertical shafts and sloping tunnels leading down to the spring from half-way up the eastern slope of the City of David. The shaft has been cleaned and restored and is open to the public. The second is Hezekiah's Tunnel, cut just before 700 B.C. in preparation for the siege of Sennacherib. Hezekiah's tunnel conveys the water from the spring to the POOL OF SILOAM on the south western corner of the City of David. When the tunnel was cleaned at the beginning of the 20th century a Hebrew inscription, in the script used in the First Temple period, was found on the wall of the tunnel. The inscription tells how the tunnel was dug from both ends – a tremendous feat of engineering, even though it may have followed a natural fissure in the rock. Armed with torchlights and plastic sandals, one can walk inside the tunnel, which still carries water, from the spring to the pool. The inscription was cut out of the rock and taken to Istanbul where it is displayed in the Archaeological Museum.

Archaeological excavations have been carried out in the City of David since the 1860s. They revealed not only the water supply systems, but also city walls of various periods, from the 19th-century B.C. Canaanite wall to that destroyed by the Romans in A.D. 70. Enormous Canaanite-period terraces that supported the eastern slope of the city were also revealed, as well as a stepped terrace wall, perhaps of the time of King Solomon. This terrace wall, preserved to the height of some 16.5m (55 ft), may have supported a public structure that

Excavations at the City of David with First Temple period houses built over Solomonic stepped structure.

once stood on top. Among the interesting discoveries at the City of David, are private houses of various periods, elongated cuttings in the rock once thought to be the royal necropolis of the Davidic dynasty, stone quarries, tombs and many small objects.

Today a suburban Arab neighbourhood stands on the City of David.

COENACULUM

The upper floor of a building on MOUNT ZION, in whose lower floor is the TOMB OF KING DAVID. In this hall, according to Christian tradition, Jesus and his disciples ate the Last Supper, as related in Matthew 26:17-29 and Mark 14:12-25. This was also the site of the miracle of Pentecost, when the spirit of God descended on the Apostles who began to speak in many different languages (Acts 2:1-4).

The hall, restored in the mid-1980s, is part of the 12th-century Crusader Church of Our Lady of Mount Zion, and many architectural details of that period have been preserved. Notable are the arched windows and in particular the capitals of the columns in a small, domed, arched structure over the flight of steps in the southwestern corner of the hall. Sculptured on the capitals are three pelicans, the two on the sides plucking at the breast of the one in the middle – a motif used in Christian symbolism to typify the atonement. This capital is one of the best examples of Crusader art in Jerusalem. Other interesting details of that period are two painted coats of arms; one of them is of the German city of Regensburg.

When the building was taken over by the Moslems in the 15th century, they turned the Coenaculum into a mosque by

The Coenaculum.

adding a prayer niche (*mihrab*) in its southern wall. A large Arabic inscription on the wall dating to 1524, commemorates this event and mentions the Ottoman Sultan Suleiman the Magnificent who built the walls of the Old City of Jerusalem.

In a small room east of the main hall is a cenotaph, a copy of the tombstone in the room below attributed to King David.

CONVENT OF THE SISTERS OF ZION

A convent north of the ECCE HOMO, built in the 1860s by the French Father Ratisbonne next to the site of the PRAETORIUM. The convent is one of the most interesting sites in Jerusalem because of its location and the finds uncovered during its construction. While the convent was being built, substantial parts of the LITHOSTROTOS, the ancient pavement which until recently was believed to have been the courtyard of the Praetorium were discovered. This pavement is now known to have been part of a 2nd-century A.D. forum built by the Roman emperor, Hadrian. The northern of the three arches of a triple

Roman triumphal arch, formerly believed to have been the
Ecce Homo, also came to light. The entire compound
underwent substantial renovations in 1985-6 and all these
important remnants are incorporated into various parts of the
convent. The arch was used in a most ingenious way. The
monastic church was built in such a way that the altar is
framed by the intact, ancient arch. At the western end of the
church the bare rock of the hill appears, dotted with grottoes
believed to have been the guard rooms of the prisoners' cells
of the Roman barracks of the Praetorium. East of the church
is the Lithostrotos, on the stones of which the Roman soldiers
incised gaming boards. From here several steps lead down to
the Struthion Pools.

On still lower level, under part of the Lithostrotos pavement,
were found two huge water reservoirs fed by rain water. This
double cistern dates to the Second Temple period, when it was
called the Struthion Pools, and was part of a chain of reservoirs
providing water for the citizens of Jerusalem. In those days
the pools were open but were covered over in the Roman
period as part of the new urban design of Aelia Capitolina.

A visit to the convent is one of the most rewarding
experiences for the visitor to Jerusalem who can join a free
guided tour conducted by one of the Sisters.

Altar framed by part of the triumphal arch built by Hadrian.

DOME OF THE ROCK

A spectacular structure at the centre of the TEMPLE MOUNT. It stands on an elevated platform, and with its unusual colour scheme of gold and blue can be seen from a great distance. It is one of the most striking landmarks of Jerusalem. The Dome of the Rock is the oldest completely preserved relic of the early Moslem period in the world. It was built in 691 by the Umayyad caliph, Abd el-Malik, to protect the rock which is at the summit of the Temple Mount believed in Jewish tradition to be the ROCK OF FOUNDATION, a belief which was adopted by the Moslems. This is also thought to be the rock on which Abraham was to sacrifice Isaac. The contrast between the stark grey rock and the glittering ornamental dome surrounding it is remarkable.

The Dome of the Rock.

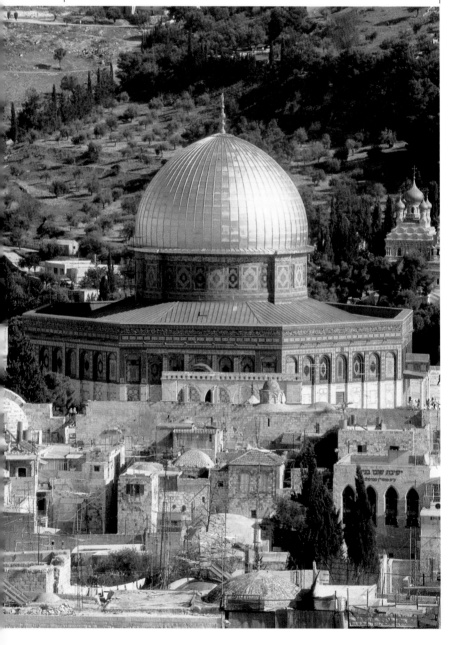

The Dome of the Rock, which is sometimes erroneously referred to as the Mosque of Omar, was not built as a mosque. Its function was commemorative. The plan of the building is a circle within an octagon itself within an outer octagon. The inner circle and octagon are formed by pillars and columns and the outer octagon – by the walls of the building, each wall being some 20m (65 ft) long. Thus two concentric circular passages or corridors are formed inside the building. The inner circle of pillars and columns supports the high dome, its height corresponding to the diameter of the building. The proportions of the edifice are considered perfect. The Dome of the Rock is highly ornate. On the outside, the lower part of the walls are panelled with marble slabs, and above them are glazed blue tiles which also cover the exterior of the drum below the dome. These tiles were made locally by Armenian

Ceiling of the Dome, with chain falling to the centre of the world.

craftsmen who used Turkish designs and techniques. In 1966 the dome was covered with sheets of gold-coloured anodized aluminium.

The interior of the Dome of the Rock is also richly ornamented. The mosaics that cover the drum and the band over the columns and pillars of the inner circle are the most striking of the interior decorations. These superb mosaics date to the time of the construction of the building, at the end of the 7th century. They are made of cubes of glass, mother-of-pearl and gold sheet, and their predominant colours are green and gold. The designs include amphoras, stylized vegetation and jewellery forms, motifs taken from Byzantine and

The southern entrance to the Dome of the Rock.

Part of the row of pillars supporting the decorated arches.

Sassanian-Persian art. Along the walls of the outer corridor runs a band bearing an Arabic inscription composed of verses from the Koran. This is the oldest extant inscription in the Arabic script. The date of mosque's construction is worked into the inscription. The decorations on the interior of the dome and the ceiling of the two circular passages are of a different nature. The motifs are abstract and the red colour predominates. They are relatively late, dating to the 14th century.

Part of decorative band with a palmetto and grape motif.

Decorated interior arches. Note 7th-century Arabic inscription on the back wall.

The rock in the centre of the building is surrounded by a high sculptured wooden screen. In the southwestern corner of the screen is a tower-like wooden structure protecting a depression in the rock believed to have been left by the hoof of Al Burak, the winged horse that flew Mohammed up to heaven from here. On the southern side of the rock is a decorated entrance leading down to a cave under the rock.

DOMINUS FLEVIT

A Franciscan church on the western slope of the MOUNT OF
OLIVES, on the spot where – according to Christian tradition
– Jesus contemplated the city of Jerusalem and lamented its
future destruction (Luke 19:41, 44), hence the name of the
church which means "the Lord wept." The modern church,
designed by the Italian architect Barlozzi in the shape of a tear,
stands on the site of a 5th-century Byzantine monastery with
mosaic floors.

Dominus Flevit on the slope of the Mount of Olives.

ECCE HOMO

Part of an arch spanning the beginning of the VIA DOLOROSA,
between the location of the PRAETORIUM and the CONVENT OF
THE SISTERS OF ZION in the eastern part of the Old City. The
meaning of the name is "Behold the man," words by which
Jesus was shown to the people by the Roman procurator,
Pontius Pilate (John 19:5); the arch was believed to have been
the one under which those words were uttered. In 1857 the
arch and a plot of land north of it were purchased by the
French priest, Ratisbonne, to construct the Convent of the
Sisters of Zion. When the ruins were cleared the entire arch
was exposed, and turned out to be a triple arch. The northern
of the three arches was incorporated into the chapel of the
convent.

Excavations at the base of the arch proved that the Ecce
Homo and the LITHOSTROTOS pavement connected to it were
constructed together in the 2nd century A.D. as part of the

Roman colony Aelia Capitolina built in Jerusalem. The Ecce Homo was, in fact, the centre span of a typical Roman triple triumphal arch that stood in the forum (central plaza) of the town; it was thus built some 100 years after the time of Jesus.

Ecce Homo Arch.

GARDEN OF GETHSEMANE

In the days of Jesus there was an orchard at the foot of the MOUNT OF OLIVES, known as Gethsemane. The meaning of the word *gethsemane* in Hebrew is olive-oil press, indicating that the slopes of the Mount of Olives were indeed covered with olive trees, and that agricultural activities were performed here, very close to the city of Jerusalem. To this garden Jesus and his disciples retired, to meditate and pray. The caves and rocks of the garden were well known to the small group of Jesus' disciples, who passed them regularly on their way in and out of Jerusalem. In the Garden of Gethsemane Jesus spent the last night before he was arrested (Matthew 26:36). Not much has been left of the original garden, most of the area is now the site of various churches – The CHURCH OF THE AGONY, the CHURCH OF MARY MAGDALENE and the GROTTO OF GETHSEMANE. Nevertheless, in the garden next to the Church of the Agony grow eight very ancient olive trees with twisted

An ancient olive tree in the Garden of Gethsemane.

and bent trunks. It is said that they were in the Garden of Gethsemane in the days of Jesus.

GARDEN TOMB

A site north of the Old City of Jerusalem, believed by some Protestants, mainly Anglicans, to be the authentic Tomb in the Garden where Jesus was buried. This suggested location runs contrary to the belief of the majority of the Christian world which sees in the CHURCH OF THE HOLY SEPULCHRE inside the Old City the true site of the tomb of Jesus. Doubts concerning the traditional site of the tomb have arisen now and again in the Christian world, mainly on the grounds that Jewish burial customs prohibited intra-mural burial. The tomb where Jesus was laid had, therefore, to be located outside the city. For those who believed that the Old City as it stands today and as it stood for many centuries reflects the configuration of Jerusalem in the time of Jesus, the location of the Church of the Holy Sepulchre presents a serious problem. Standing as it does in the centre of a crowded city, it could not, some argued, have been a religiously suitable burial ground.

Thus, during the 18th and the 19th centuries alternatives to the site of the tomb of Jesus and to the adjacent GOLGOTHA - CALVARY were suggested. The best known of these is the site known as the Garden Tomb. The suggestion was made by the British general, Charles George Gordon, who came to Jerusalem in 1883. His gaze rested on a hill north of Damascus Gate which seemed to him to resemble a skull and which he immediately identified as Golgotha – in Aramaic, "skull." As it happened, someone had dug in the area several

Entrance to the Garden Tomb.

years before and discovered a rock-cut tomb; later an ancient cistern was cleared nearby, proving that the place had been a garden in antiquity. The shape of the hill, the burial cave, and the garden seemed to fit the New Testament description. The place was purchased by the newly founded Garden Tomb Association which to this day keeps it open for visitors and conducts guided tours (free) on the site.

The premises of the Garden Tomb include a lovely garden, an observation point on what is believed to be the Hill of the Skull, and the rock-cut tomb. Recent research has shown that the tomb is of the First Temple period, rather than of the Second Temple period – the time of Jesus.

GIHON SPRING - SPRING OF THE VIRGIN

The only perennial spring in the entire area of Jerusalem, issuing in the VALLEY OF JEHOSHAPHAT at the foot of the eastern slope of the CITY OF DAVID. The water of the spring gushes periodically and fills a subterranaen pool in a cave reached by a flight of 32 steps. These steps are the origin of the Arabic name of the spring – Umm el-Daraj (Mother of the Steps). It may be assumed that the spring, a source of life-giving water,

The Gihon Spring. This is the oldest known water source in Jerusalem. It gushes out in the Kidron Valley.

was holy to the early inhabitants of Jerusalem. This perhaps explains why the ceremony of the anointing of Solomon as King of Israel took place at the Gihon Spring (I Kings 1:38).

During the First Temple period, when Jerusalem was capital of the Kingdom of Judah, several water systems were devised to better utilize the water of the spring. The so-called Warren's Shaft comprised vertical shafts and sloping tunnels which enabled the inhabitants of Jerusalem to reach the spring-water safely from behind the protection of the city wall. The date of its construction is difficult to determine, but it predates the tunnel, which was dug in the days of King Hezekiah in the second half of the 8th century B.C. to divert the water of the Gihon Spring to the POOL OF SILOAM. Access to the spring from outside the walls was no doubt closed and hidden from the enemy. The tunnel, which is 533m (about 1760 ft) long, is an engineering feat, in light of the technology of those days. It was dug from both ends, following a natural fissure in the rock. A third system runs along the eastern slope of the City of David. It was partially rock-hewn and partially built and had "windows" through which the water could be diverted to spill out and be used for irrigation.

The name Pool of the Virgin derives from the tradition that here the prophet Isaiah uttered his famous prophecy: *Behold, a virgin shall conceive and bear a son: and his name shall be called Immanuel* (Isaiah 7:14).

Today the water of the spring of Gihon is used mainly for irrigation. Women and children go there in the heat of summer to cool themselves in the fresh water.

GOLDEN GATE

A general name for a blocked-up double gate in the centre of the eastern wall of the TEMPLE MOUNT. The southern of the two gates is called the Gate of Mercy and the northern one, the Gate of Repentance. Behind them on the Temple Mount is an elaborate gate-house surmounted by two domes and supported by columns with decorated capitals. The rooms in the gatehouse are now empty and closed, but until the 15th century they were used as Moslem prayer and study rooms.

The Golden Gate seen today is thought to have been constructed in the late Byzantine period. It stands on the site of the Gate of Shushan or the Beautiful Gate built by the returnees from Babylon. The Shushan Gate is believed to be the one through which Jesus entered Jerusalem on Palm Sunday, being the gate opposite the MOUNT OF OLIVES (Mark 11:11; John 12:13). It must have been through the present gate that the Byzantine emperor, Heraclius, entered Jerusalem on March 6, 631, carrying the True Cross which had been taken by the Persians who invaded Jerusalem in 614. A festival commemorating the return of the Cross was celebrated by Christian communities until the end of the Crusader period. During that festival, as well as on Palm Sunday, the gates were opened. They were blocked up once and for all after Saladin conquered Jerusalem in 1187.

The twin portals of the Golden Gate; they were blocked after Saladin conquered Jerusalem in 1187.

The Golden Gate is holy to the Jews as well, because of the tradition that the Messiah will come to the Mount of Olives and enter Jerusalem through it. This tradition is expressed in an interesting way in the area close to the gate. The Messiah will be announced by the Prophet Elijah who, Jewish tradition holds, is of a priestly family. As priests are not allowed to enter cemeteries for fear of becoming ritually unclean, the Moslems established a cemetery on the slope outside the gate to prevent the entry of the Messiah. This cemetery is still in use.

GOLGOTHA – CALVARY

The place where Jesus was crucified, perhaps the commonly used site for such executions in the days when the Roman procurators ruled Jerusalem. The Scriptures refer to it as *a place called the place of a skull, which is called in the Hebrew Golgotha* (John 19:17). The word *golgotha* is an Aramaic form of the Hebrew *gulgoleth* meaning "skull," and most probably refers to the shape of the place, being rounded and bald as a skull. In the days of Jesus, Aramaic rather than Hebrew was the common language spoken in Judea hence the Aramaic form of the Hebrew word. The Latin *calva* has the same meaning, hence the name Calvary is used in European languages for the place of crucifixion.

The most accepted location of Golgotha is in the CHURCH OF THE HOLY SEPULCHRE. Golgotha being inside a building, it is very difficult to imagine the original configuration of the site, which was a sinister place outside the city. What has

The two chapels at Calvary: Latin on the right, Greek Orthodox on the left.

remained is an elevation, and the chapels of Calvary are indeed reached by a flight of steps. Also indicative of the original setting are a natural grotto under Golgotha known as the Chapel of Adam and a cistern further to the east known as the Chapel of the Finding of the Cross where, as the name implies, Helena, mother of Emperor Constantine, found the True Cross some 200 years after the Crucifixion.

An alternative location for Calvary was proposed in the 19th century, that of hill outside the northern wall of the Old City near the Damascus Gate. This hill, which some say resembles a skull, can be seen from the GARDEN TOMB, and is believed by some to be the true place of the Crucifixion.

GROTTO OF GETHSEMANE

The Grotto of Gethsemane.

A natural cave next to the CHURCH OF THE ASSUMPTION reached through a passage from the courtyard of the church. Here, according to tradition, Jesus prayed for the last time before he was arrested (Matthew 26:36). In the 4th century the cave was turned into a chapel. In the 12th century its walls were adorned with frescoes which are still partially preserved. Since 1392 the grotto has belonged to the Franciscans. Its natural features have been retained. It has simple benches and an altar, and is used frequently as a place for meditation.

HOUSE OF CAIAPHAS

An Armenian church on the summit of Mount Zion, close to Zion Gate of the Old City. According to an Armenian tradition this is the site of the house of the high priest Caiaphas, where Jesus was taken after his arrest. The church is part of the Armenian compound on Mount Zion, which also includes the cemetery of the Armenian community of Jerusalem. In the early 1970s, prior to the construction of a new Armenian church in the compound, archaeological excavations were undertaken. They unearthed a residence from the end of the First Temple period, residences from the Second Temple period with frescoes on the walls and a paved street from the Byzantine period.

THE LITHOSTROTOS

A large stone pavement, found under the CONVENT OF THE SISTERS OF ZION, the CHURCH OF THE FLAGELLATION and the CHURCH OF CONDEMNATION at the First and Second Stations of the VIA DOLOROSA. For many years the lithostrotos was believed to have been the pavement of the PRAETORIUM, where the Roman procurators and their soldiers stayed when they came to Jerusalem and where Pontius Pilate conducted the trial of Jesus. In various parts of the flagstones of the pavement – particularly in the section now in the Convent of the Sisters of Zion – gameboards were incised in the stones. These boards were no doubt used by idle soldiers to while away the time. Other sections of the pavement have parallel grooves to prevent horses from slipping.

(left) Stones of the Lithostrotos. (right) Game incised in the stone by Roman soldiers.

The Lithostrotos was sanctified in Christian tradition because of its association with the trial of Jesus. Lately, however, it was proven by archaeological excavations not to be connected with the Praetorium but rather to be the pavement of a forum (central plaza). In this forum was a triumphal arch, part of which is known as ECCE HOMO. Both forum and arch were found to be from the time of Emperor Hadrian (2nd century A.D.), when Jerusalem was turned into a Roman colony named Aelia Capitolina. The Lithostrotos is thus about 100 years later than the time of Jesus.

MONASTERY OF THE HOLY CROSS

A lonely monastery, once standing isolated among olive tree groves at a distance from the Old City of Jerusalem, but now in the heart of the new city which has spread westwards. Its closest neighbour is the Israel Museum, and near its ancient walls passes one of the main traffic arteries of modern-day Jerusalem. The monastery stands on the spot where, according to an ancient tradition, the tree from which the cross of Jesus was made grew. In fact, it is said, that this same tree was an offshoot of the Tree of Life that grew in the Garden of Eden through a twig that Seth, son of Adam, took and planted at the head of Adam's tomb. The monastery was built in the 5th century by King Tatian of Georgia. It was destroyed in 614 by the Persians, was rebuilt in the Crusader period and has been standing more or less intact since then. Because of its isolated location the monastery was sacked many times and has often been repaired. The structure looks more like a fortress than a monastery. The Monastery of the Holy Cross was in the possession of the Georgians until, burdened with

The Monastery of the Holy Cross in the heart of Jerusalem, stands on the spot where it is said that the tree of which the Cross was made grew.

heavy debts, they sold it to the Greek Orthodox Church which in 1858 opened a theological seminary there. Today it is inhabited by a few monks and is open to the public. Entrance is through a very narrow, low door to an inner courtyard. The walls of the monastic church are covered with frescoes that have been treated to reveal paintings of the Middle Ages.

MONASTERY OF THE PRISON OF CHRIST

A Greek Orthodox monastery, next to the CONVENT OF THE SISTERS OF ZION at the beginning of the VIA DOLOROSA. The monastery was built in 1906 over several artificial caves cut into the natural rock escarpment. These caves are on the same line as the caves in the basilica at the adjacent convent and together they form one complex. Some of them may have been used as stables and others as prison cells or guard rooms. In one cave there is a stone seat with two holes large enough to hold a man's legs. This is believed to have been Jesus' prison cell, or, according to another tradition, that of Barabbas.

MONUMENT OF ABSALOM

A large, ornate monument, half rock-hewn and half built, at the bottom of the VALLEY OF JEHOSHAPHAT between the MOUNT OF OLIVES and the TEMPLE MOUNT. The traditional name, Monument of Absalom, expresses the popular belief that this is the memorial mentioned in II Samuel 18:18: *Now Absalom in his lifetime had taken and reared up for himself a pillar, which is in the king's dale; for he said, "I have no son to keep my name ..." and it is called unto this day, Absalom's place.* Because Absalom revolted against his father David, Jewish, Christian and Moslems passers-by used to throw stones at the monument, and parents were accustomed to bring their rebellious children here to impress upon them the consequences of filial misconduct.

The Monument of Absalom is in a row of funerary monuments, facing the Temple Mount. While popular tradition attributes them respectively to Absalom, King Jehoshaphat, St James and the prophet Zechariah, archaeological investigation has revealed that in reality they are all Second Temple period tombs of prominent, yet mostly anonymous, citizens of Jerusalem. Only the monument wrongly attributed to St James bears an original Hebrew inscription on the architrave, naming the deceased – three generations of the priestly family of Hezir (mentioned in I Chronicles 24:15; Nehemiah 10:20). On the same row are two burial caves and two free standing burial monuments of which Absalom's memorial is one. The lower part of the the monument is square-cut out of the solid rock, adorned with half pillars in Ionic style supporting a Doric frieze. The upper

The Monument of Absalom in the Valley of Jehoshaphat.

part, built of well-cut stones, is a square surmounted by a circular drum and crowned with rather unusual conical pyramid that makes it a striking sight. The pyramid is topped with a palm leaf design. A similar monument, but smaller in size, is the adjacent, so-called Tomb of Zechariah. The row of monuments, and in particular the Monument of Absalom, attest to the high standard of the architects and the skill of the masons in Jerusalem in the Second Temple period and to the wealth of the city's population.

MOUNT OF OLIVES

The middle summit 815m (2,574 ft) above sea level, of a short mountain range closing the Jerusalem basin on the east, the other summits being Mount Scopus (829m, 2,720 ft), on which the Hebrew University is built, and the Mount of Offense (747m, 2,450 ft). The range is a pronounced climatic boundary between the wet Mediterranean climate region to the west and the arid desert climate area to the east. On its western slope facing Jerusalem, the Mount of Olives still bears remnants of the olive groves which gave it its name, while its eastern slope descends steeply to the Judean Desert. Thus the Mount of Olives has always been and is still the eastern boundary of Jerusalem, and the city has never spread beyond its foot.

In antiquity fires were lit on the mountain's summit to announce the appearance of the new moon and special sacrifices took place there. Since the Canaanite period, its slopes have been used for burial. In the First and Second Temple periods the upper classes of Jerusalem built elaborate tombs, sometimes with free standing memorials such as the MONUMENT OF ABSALOM. The slopes are used for burial to this day, and are especially favoured by Jews who believe that the Messiah will descend upon the Mount of Olives and proceed from there to Jerusalem. Thus those buried on the mount will be the first to be resurrected and to follow the Messiah.

The Mount of Olives has great prominence in the New Testament as it was the scene of many of Jesus' activities. Jesus and his disciples used to stay in the caves of the mountain and study there. Jesus was arrested by the Romans in the GARDEN OF GETHSEMANE, and from the summit of the mountain ascended to heaven. These and other events are commemorated by many churches, and a visit to them is an essential part of any pilgrimage to the Holy Land.

From the Mount of Olives, from just below the Intercontinental Hotel, one can see one of the most beautiful, breathtaking views in the world – the city of Jerusalem: the entire Old City, sections of the New, and the surrounding hills and valley.

MOUNT ZION

The southern part of the western hill of old Jerusalem. The designation "Mount" is rather misleading. Although on the east, south and west it is bounded by steep slopes that give it the appearance of a mountain, on the north it slopes gradually to the relatively flat ground on which the Armenian

The Church of the Dormition on the top of Mount Zion.

quarter is built. Indeed, until the construction at the beginning of the 16th century of the Turkish wall which surrounds the Old City today, Mount Zion was an integral part of the city and traces of the city walls of many periods have been found on it western and southern slopes. A local tradition pointing to the peculiar situation of Mount Zion in relation to the city tells that the two Ottoman builders responsible for the reconstruction of the city walls ordered by Suleiman the Magnificent were beheaded because they had not included Mount Zion and King David's tomb within the walls. Thier tombs are shown next to the Jaffa Gate.

In the days of the Old Testament the name Mount Zion was applied to the TEMPLE MOUNT. By the Second Temple period the name was given, for unknown reasons, to the present Mount Zion, and the tradition that the TOMB OF DAVID was on this mountain was born. This tradition sanctified the mount in the eyes of the Jews and, later, of the Christians and the Moslems as well.

According to the Gospels, various important events occurred on Mount Zion. The high priest Caiaphas lived on Mount Zion, which in his days was a prosperous residential neighbourhood, and Jesus was detained in his house after his arrest. In the COENACULUM Jesus and his disciples ate the Last Supper. On top of the Mount, the CHURCH OF THE DORMITION marks the place where it is said Mary "fell asleep." The spot on which this church stands is traditionally accepted as the place where the Apostles gathered for the first time. Here, at their meeting place, the Church of Mount Zion, one of the four earliest churches in the Holy Land, was built by Emperor Constantine. That church has since been considered the Mother of all Churches. Meagre traces of it were unearthed when the Church of the Dormition was built.

Because of all these events Mount Zion became sacred to Christianity, and since the very beginning of the Byzantine period various churches have been built on it.

POOL OF BETHESDA

Now there is at Jerusalem by the sheep market a pool, which is called in the Hebrew tongue Bethesda, having five porches. In these lay a great multitude of impotent folk, of blind, halt, withered, waiting for the moving of the water. For an angel went down at a certain season into the pool, and troubled the water: whosoever then first after the troubling of the water stepped in was made whole of whatsoever disease he had. And a certain man was there, which had an infirmity thirty and eight years... Jesus saith unto him, Rise, take up thy bed, and walk. And immediately the man was made whole, and took up his bed, and walked...
(John 5:2-11)

The Pool of Bethesda is situated inside of St Stephen's Gate, also known as the Lions' Gate, in the eastern wall of the Old City of Jerusalem. It is now part of a large compound owned by the French government since 1865 and run by the White Fathers. The compound contains the Pool, the Crusader CHURCH OF ST ANNE, a museum and a Greek-Catholic seminary.

The pool was one of several open-air reservoirs built during the Second Temple period in and around Jerusalem to provide

The Pool of Bethesda with remains of Byzantine and Crusader churches in and above it.

water for the growing population of the city. Its exact original name is not certain, as the New Testament gives three versions: Betsaide – meaning the house of fishing; Bethzeta – meaning the house of olive oil; and Bethesda – meaning the house of mercy. The last name is the one most commonly used.

The Pool of Bethesda lay in a small valley, which ran from the area of Damascus Gate to the northeastern corner of the Temple Mount and is now silted up. The water stored in the pool was mostly rain water, although there may have been a spring which later dried up. Possibly this spring gave the water of the pool its supposed curative powers (see also POOL OF SILOAM). Further down the same valley adjacent to the northern wall of the TEMPLE MOUNT, lay the Pool of Probatica – the Sheep Pool, where the sheep brought to the Temple to be sacrificed were washed. Today it is known as Birket Israel. Extensive excavations carried out on the site since 1956 revealed the impressive remnants of the Pool of Bethesda. In the Second Temple period the pool was very large and had

Plan of the Pool of Bethesda compound.

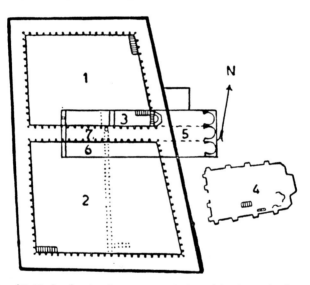

1. and 2. *North and south pools*
3. *North nave of the 5th-cent. church.*
   and Crusader chapel of the Paralytic
4. *Crusader church of St Anne*

5. *Apses of the 5th-cent. church*
6. *South nave of the 5th-cent. church*
7. *Central nave of church and central*
   portico of the pool

an elongated trapezoid shape, 100-110m (300-330 ft) long, 62-80m (180-240 ft) wide and 7-8m (21-24 ft) deep. The pool was carved out of the rock and divided into two basins by an uncut rock ledge. It was surrounded by four porticos, with a fifth built on the dividing ledge. It was here that the sick were laid, waiting to be cured. The belief in the therapeutic qualities of the water of the pool was accepted by the pagan inhabitants of Aelia Capitolina, the Roman colony established on the ruins of Jerusalem after its destruction in A.D. 70. Remains of a temple to Aesculapius, Greek god of healing, were discovered next to the pool, and in it were found marble representations of the healed organs, such as feet and ears, gifts of thanksgiving to the god.

The holiness of the site to Christendom was enhanced by the Byzantine empress, Eudoxia, who, in the 5th century, had an enormous basilica constructed over the pool. High supporting vaults were built inside the pool to create a platform on which the basilica was constructed. Many of them were uncovered in the excavations, and can be seen on the site today. The basilica was destroyed during the Persian invasion of 614 and its ruins collapsed into the pool. When the Crusaders arrived all they found on the site was the crypt of the Byzantine basilica, which was being used as a water cistern. The Crusaders built a small chapel, the Church of the Paralytic, north of the dividing ledge of the pools, over what was the northern nave of the Byzantine basilica. The façade, main entrance and apse of the Crusader chapel can be seen on the site, perched high over the pool.

POOL OF SILOAM

The Pool of Siloam.

A water reservoir on the southwestern corner of the CITY OF DAVID. To this pool the water of the GIHON SPRING is diverted by means of Hezekiah's Tunnel. The water of the Pool of Siloam, being spring water, was considered pure and was used in the ceremonies in the Temple. It was also thought to have curative qualities. Here Jesus restored sight to a blind man by making clay with his spittle and spreading it on the man's eyes. The man was then ordered, *Go wash in the pool of Siloam. He went his way therefore, and washed, and came seeing* (John 9:7). It is interesting that in the days of Jesus the Pool of Siloam was actually considered to be a spring, as attested by the contemporary historian Josephus Flavius. This is, no doubt, because by the 1st century A.D. Hezekiah's Tunnel was silted up and forgotten, although the water of the Gihon Spring continued to seep into the pool.

In the 5th century a church was built over the Pool of Siloam, and named "Our Saviour, the Illuminator." The pool was inside the church and surrounded by porticoes. The sick bathed in it in the hope of being cured. The church was destroyed in 614 and never rebuilt. The pool on the site today is cut into the ruins of the smaller Byzantine pool, architectural fragments of which are scattered in the water. A small mosque stands next to the site of the pool.

ROCK OF FOUNDATION

The Rock of Foundation in the centre of the Dome of the Rock.

An exposed rock in the centre of the DOME OF THE ROCK built on the summit of the TEMPLE MOUNT in the 7th century A.D. The rock has special significance in Jewish tradition as it is believed to be the site of the Binding (Sacrifice) of Isaac (Genesis 22:2-18). Many other events are said to have occurred on it. It is believed to be the place from which the creation of the world began and whence it spread to the entire universe, hence its name – the Rock of Foundation. Another legend connected with the idea that creation started here, is that the tomb of Adam is under the rock. The Moslems believe that Mohammed ascended to heaven from this rock to receive the Koran from the angel Gabriel on the night of his miraculous flight to EL AQSA.

Beneath the rock is a cave which is reached by descending seven steps. The Moslems call this cave the "Well of the Spirits" and point out four places in which Abraham, David, Solomon and the angel Gabriel are believed to have prayed.

It is commonly agreed that the two Jewish Temples stood in some specific relation to the rock, either on it or next to it. As neither the Bible nor sources of the Second Temple period mention the rock, the exact relation of the Temple to the rock remains unknown. The rock is first mentioned by a 4th-century A.D. pilgrim who called it the "perforated rock" and wrote that Jews used to wail over it and anoint it.

THE TEMPLE MOUNT – MOUNT MORIAH

A large trapezoid-shaped enclosure in the southeastern section of the Old City of Jerusalem, identified as biblical Mount Moriah where Abraham was to have sacrificed Isaac. In Arabic it is known as Haram esh Sharif – the "Noble Enclosure." The natural configuration of the mountain has been changed by numerous building alterations especially those of King Herod in the 1st century B.C. The area of the enclosure is 135 acres (140 dunams), about one sixth of the area of the Old City. It is surrounded by walls, the lower part of which are from the time of King Herod who gave the enclosure its current shape. The upper parts are from different periods and represent various stages of repair of the basic Herodian walls. On the Temple Mount are about one hundred structures, the most important of which are the DOME OF THE ROCK, built on the summit of the mountain over the sacred ROCK OF FOUNDATION, and the EL AQSA MOSQUE next to the southern wall of the enclosure. Beneath the pavement of the Temple Mount are several underground halls and many water cisterns. Nine gates lead into the enclosure – three in the northern wall and six in the western. In the eastern wall is the bricked up GOLDEN GATE. Two Second Temple period gates, now blocked up, have survived: the Huldah Gate in the southern wall and Barclay's Gate in the western wall.

The Temple Mount has been holy perhaps since the days of the Canaanites. Although, as said, tradition places the Binding of Isaac there, the first direct reference to it belongs to the time of King David. David purchased the site which had been a threshing floor belonging to Araunah the last Jebusite king of Jerusalem and built an altar on it (II Samuel

24:16-25). It was here that King Solomon built the First Temple around 950 B.C. The Temple, the centre of religious life of the Jewish nation, was divided into three parts, in the innermost and holiest of which stood the Ark of the Covenant. The Temple functioned until the destruction of Jerusalem by the Babylonians in 586 B.C. It stood in ruins until Cyrus, king of Persia, allowed the exiles of Judah to return to Jerusalem and build the Second Temple over the ruins of the first. This Second Temple was simple, but in time it was enlarged and beautified. Religious services in the Temple ceased only in the days of the Seleucid king, Antiochus IV, who defiled the Temple, which act provoked the Maccabean revolt in 167 B.C.

The great change in the configuration of the Temple Mount occurred in the time of King Herod. Until his days the Temple Mount was a natural, narrow hilly spur, extending southwards towards the City of David. Herod doubled the size of the

An aerial view of the Temple Mount from north to south. The Dome of the Rock appears in the centre of the photograph, the El Aqsa Mosque at the top. The large open space in front of the Western Wall can be seen on the right.

natural plateau of the summit by constructing enormous encasing walls on the south, southeastern, and southwestern sides of the hill. The area behind these walls was filled by means of tiers of vaults over which the platform was laid. Similar work was carried out in the northeastern corner, and the final result is the Temple Mount as we know it today. The southern part of the Mount is thus artificial, and under the filled up parts are various subterranean halls known as el-Kadima and Solomon's Stables, traditional names that do not reflect their true Herodian origin. These halls are usually closed to visitors. Herod also rebuilt the Temple itself, its modest dimensions and decorations not matching his taste for grandeur. The new temple was built on the same plan as its predecessors but with double their height.

From the time of Herod until its destruction by the Romans in A.D. 70, the Temple Mount was thronged with worshippers flocking into its spacious courtyards. It was especially crowded during the three festivals of Passover, Pentecost and Tabernacles, when pilgrims from the entire country as well as from abroad would come to worship. Among the multitudes was the family of the boy Jesus, and later Jesus the adolescent (Luke 2:41-47).

On the 9th day of the month of Ab (July) A.D. 70, the Second Temple was burnt by the Romans after ferocious fighting. After the short episode of the Bar Kochba Revolt of A.D. 132-135, when Jewish worship on the Temple Mount may have been resumed, the Romans erected on it a temple to Jupiter Capitolinus which stood until the 4th century, when Christianity became dominant. When the Moslems conquered Jerusalem in 638, the sacred character of the Mount for the Jews was accepted by the Moslems, who added their own belief that Mohammed had flown on his winged stallion Al-Burak from Mecca to the Temple Mount and from there up to heaven to receive the Koran from the angel Gabriel. The Moslems cleared the enclosure and built the Dome of the Rock and the El-Aqsa Mosque. The Crusaders appreciated the holiness of the Mount and transformed the Dome of the Rock into a church named Templum Domini, and the El-Aqsa Mosque into a church named Templum Solominis. Later the mosque was handed over to the Knights Templars who had their headquarters there and kept their horses in the underground hall known ever since as Solomon's Stables. Since the conquest of Jerusalem by Saladin in 1187 the Temple Mount has been in Moslem hands. Many additional small structures have been added in the enclosure – small domes, water fountains and places for rest and for prayer, some very ornate and beautiful.

Despite the destruction of the two Temples, the Temple Mount has retained its holiness for the Jews.

TOMB OF KING DAVID

The traditional burial place of King David on MOUNT ZION is one of the holiest sites for the Jews. The tradition that King David is buried on Mount Zion prevails despite the clear scriptural indication that he and his dynasty were buried "in the CITY OF DAVID" (I Kings 2:10), which modern research has proved to be the low spur east of Mount Zion and south of the TEMPLE MOUNT. It is interesting, however, that over a hundred years of archaeological excavations in the City of David have not yet revealed the royal necropolis. The transfer of the location of the Tomb of David from the City of David to Mount Zion is no doubt connected with the transfer of the very name Zion from the Temple Mount to what is now known as Mount Zion. It is not known why the name was changed, but it had definitely been changed by the lst century A.D. when the historian Josephus Flavius described Mount Zion in the location we know it today, with the Tomb of King David there.

Despite the description of Josephus, other alternatives for the burial place of King David have been popular at various times. One example is the Byzantine tradition that placed it

The traditional tomb of King David on Mount Zion.

in Bethlehem, because the City of David was believed in early Christianity to have been Bethlehem rather than Jerusalem (Luke 2:4). Only in the Middle Ages was the location of the Tomb of David on Mount Zion more generally accepted. The first to refer to it was the Moslem Jerusalemite historian el-Mukaddasi in 985. It was then cited by the Crusader historian Raymond d'Aguilers in 1100, and by the renowned Jewish traveller Benjamin of Tudela in 1165. After that it was noted by numerous pilgrims and became firmly entrenched in Jewish, Christian and Moslem belief. The Tomb of David acquired a reputation for super-human qualities over the ages, and many references to the tomb are embellished by fabulous stories of people entering the burial cave and finding great riches there, only to be struck by disaster. That there is indeed a cave under the building was established by the Italian engineer Pierotty, who in 1859 obtained permission to investigate the building. The shallow cave he discovered under the tombstone was empty. Further investigations were not encouraged.

The history of the building over the tomb is rather complicated. It was built mainly in the Crusader period, to which period the tombstone also seems to date. However, the thick northern, southern and eastern walls of the room where the tombstone stands are earlier, perhaps from the Roman period. The architect Pinkerfeld, who studied the building in 1949, suggested that those walls were the remains of an ancient synagogue. To the Crusader building was added in the 13th century a Franciscan monastery, the cloister of which has survived and serves as the inner courtyard through which one enters the building. In the 15th century a hostel (*khan*) was added. At that time, following fierce quarrels between Jews and Christians over the possession of the tomb, the entire compound was handed over by the Mameluke authorities to the Moslems, who added a low minaret.

Today the tomb complex includes the room with the cenotaph, another room in front of it, and a large room next to it. The three rooms are simple and without furniture except for wooden benches. The tombstone is covered with a velvet cloth, and over it stand Torah scrolls in ornate cases. During festivals – especially on Pentecost (Shavuot), the anniversary of David's death – the building fills up with Jewish worshippers and pilgrims.

Directly above David's tomb complex is the COENACULUM, the hall of the Last Supper, holy to the Christians.

TOMB OF THE PROPHETS

An interesting burial cave on the upper, western slope of the MOUNT OF OLIVES, inside the Jewish cemetery. Entrance to the cave leads into a semi-circular room cut by a straight central corridor perpendicular to the entrance from which two parallel circular corridors branch off. In the outer wall of the outer semi-circular corridors are the burial niches. Some of these niches have Greek inscriptions over them which relate that the deceased were brought from Transjordan. The inscriptions date the burial cave to the Byzantine period. A medieval tradition attributes the burial cave to the prophets Haggai and Malachi.

VALLEY OF JEHOSHAPHAT – KIDRON VALLEY

The valley that runs east of the Old City of Jerusalem and separates it from the MOUNT OF OLIVES. It has always been the eastern boundary of Jerusalem, and at no time in its history did the city expand beyond it. The valley has steep slopes at its start in the vicinity of Jerusalem and they become even more pronounced further on. As it ascends eastwards, the valley becomes a spectacular canyon with sheer cliffs continuing until it joins the Dead Sea not far from Qumran.

From the times of the Old Testament (e.g., I Kings 2:37) to this day the valley is known as the Kidron Valley. The prophet Joel, however, refers to it by its more poetic but less used name when he says: *I will also gather all nations, and will*

The Valley of Kidron.

bring them down into the valley of Jehoshaphat, and will plead with them there for my people and for my heritage Israel, whom they have scattered among the nations, and parted my land (Joel 3:2). The valley of Jehoshaphat, the meaning of which is "God Judges," will thus be the scene of the last judgement of all nations, where they will all assemble before God. Perhaps because of this prophecy the valley was a favoured burial site from the First Temple period on. Beautiful burial monuments from the Second Temple period, such as the MONUMENT OF ABSALOM, still stand at the bottom of the valley, opposite the TEMPLE MOUNT.

The valley is revered by Christians for the many events in the last days of Jesus which occurred here. Jesus used to cross the valley often when going from the Mount of Olives – where he spent much time-to the city of Jerusalem. On the lower slope of the Mount of Olives, close to the foot of the mountain, is the GARDEN OF GETHSEMANE where Jesus spent his last night of freedom. At the bottom of the valley is the CHURCH OF THE ASSUMPTION which contains the Tomb of Mary.

The tomb of Beni Hezir, on the left, and the so-called tomb of Zechariah, on the right, in the Valley of Jehoshaphat.

View of part of the Via Dolorosa.

The Via Dolorosa is among the holiest sites in Christendom. It is the path taken by Jesus when, bearing his cross on his back, he made his way to the place of his crucifixion. Following the Roman custom of the times, those who were condemned to death were obliged to walk through the city with their name and details of their conviction displayed.

The Via Dolorosa is a street no different from any other street in the northern part of the Old City, except for the nine stations which lie along it to commemorate the dramatic events of Jesus' last journey. It starts not far from Lions' Gate (St Stephen's Gate) and winds its way westward towards the CHURCH OF THE HOLY SEPULCHRE. This is the route followed by Jesus from the place of his trial – the Praetorium – to the place of crucifixion on GOLGOTHA.

(left) The traditional Friday procession along the Via Dolorosa. (right) The name of the street in three languages.

The exact route of the Via Dolorosa – as well as the location of the stations along it – is still disputed by scholars. Only some of the stations are mentioned in the New Testament, others are based on popular tradition. In the 4th-5th centuries processions from GETHSEMANE to Golgotha passed more or less along this route. In the Middle Ages there were other routes for the Via Dolorosa, some including Caiaphas' house on MOUNT ZION. The Way of the Cross was not finally fixed as it is today until the 15th century.

Of the 14 stations of the Via Dolorosa, nine are along the route and five inside the Church of the Holy Sepulchre. The nine stations are the PRAETORIUM, the CHAPEL OF THE CONDEMNATION where Jesus was given the cross to carry, the place where he fell for the first time, the CHURCH OF OUR LADY OF THE SPASM where Jesus met his mother, the place where Simon of Cyrene helped Jesus carry the cross, the house of Veronica who wiped his face with her veil, the place where Jesus fell the second time, the place where he talked to the women of Jerusalem, and the place where he fell for the third time. Every Friday at 3 p.m. the Franciscans hold a procession along the Via Dolorosa.

FIRST STATION – THE PRAETORIUM

The Praetorium is the First Station of the Via Dolorosa, the place of the Antonia fortress and of earlier fortresses that guarded the northern side of the Temple Mount during the Second Temple period. One of the fortresses was rebuilt by Herod in the 1st century B.C., and named in honor of his friend

Mark Antony, Julius Caesar's opponent. After Herod's death, when the country was ruled by procurators whose permanent seat was at CAESAREA, the Antonia Fortress was the headquarters of the Roman garrison stationed in Jerusalem and residence of the procurator when he visited Jerusalem. Thus it was to this stronghold, called by the Romans simply the Praetorium – "the fortress " – that Jesus was brought to trial before Pontius Pilate who stayed there during the fateful feast of Passover of the year A.D. 30.

Of the Praetorium itself little remains. The compound where it stood is now occupied by the Al'Omariyeh college and was formerly a Turkish barracks. The site is above street level and reached by a ramp. In the courtyard of the college, on a higher platform, is a small domed building which used

The Praetorium in the courtyard of the Al'Omariyeh college.

to be the Chapel of the Crowning with Thorns; it has now fallen into disuse. From the southern end of the courtyard there is a good view of the TEMPLE MOUNT, no doubt similar to that which the Roman soldiers stationed at the Praetorium saw in the days when the Temple was still standing.

SECOND STATION – CHURCH OF THE CONDEMNATION

The second station is commemorated by the Church of the Condemnation on the site of which, according to tradition, Jesus was condemned and the cross was given to him to carry. This small Franciscan church is part of the compound of the Studium Biblicum Franciscanum (Franciscan School for Biblical Studies) renowned for its library and archaeological museum which has a collection of about 10,000 coins and other antiques as well as a display of preserved specimens of the fauna and flora of the Holy Land.

The building of the church was originally a mosque. It was purchased by the Franciscan Order, restored and converted into a church in 1903-4. During restoration work the building was found to be standing over remnants of a Byzantine church, under which was the stone pavement of a 2nd-century A.D. Roman road, formerly believed to have been the LITHOSTROTOS of the PRAETORIUM.

THIRD STATION

A small chapel marks the spot where, according to tradition, Jesus fell for the first time under the weight of the cross. The site, which from the 15th century was the main entrance to the municipal public baths called Hamam es-Sultan, was purchased in 1856 by the Armenian Catholic church who built a chapel. In 1947-48 the chapel was renovated with donations from Polish soldiers stationed in Palestine during the Second World War. In the iron railing at the entrance to the chapel are two fragments of ancient columns.

Jesus falling under the weight of the cross depicted above the entrance to the Third Station. (below) Meeting of Jesus and Mary depicted in relief above the entrance to the Fourth Station.

FOURTH STATION-CHURCH OF OUR LADY OF THE SPASM

An Armenian-Catholic church, at the Fourth Station of the VIA DOLOROSA, marks the spot where Mary is believed to have spoken to Jesus on his way to the Crucifixion. The church, which was built in 1881, partially stands on the ruins of a Byzantine church. Large sections of the mosaic floor of the Byzantine church were found when the new church was built. They are now in the crypt. It was a square mosaic with a rich border and depicted in its centre is a pair of sandals, believed to represent the exact spot where the suffering Mary (Stabat Mater Dolorosa) was standing. Another part of the church was built over the ruins of a Mameluke-period public bath, known as Hamam es-Sultan.

FIFTH STATION

A small oratory built by the Franciscans in 1895, where, according to tradition, Simon of Cyrene, a pilgrim to Jerusalem who happened to be standing by, was compelled by the Roman soldiers to carry Jesus' cross (Matthew 27:32; Luke 23:26).

Entrance to the Fifth Station.

(left) Entrance to the Church of St Veronica – the Sixth Station. (right) The Seventh Station.

SIXTH STATION – CHURCH OF ST VERONICA

A Greek-Catholic church on the spot believed to be the Sixth Station of the VIA DOLOROSA on which stood the house of St Veronica. This pious and noble woman wiped the face of the suffering Jesus with her veil and the image of his face remained impressed up on it. This veil is said to have performed several miraculous healings, and since the year 707 has been kept at ST PETER'S BASILICA in Rome.

The church, part of which belongs to the Order of the Little Sisters of Jesus, was built in 1882 over remnants of a 6th-century monastery. In 1953 the church was restored by the Italian architect Barlozzi.

SEVENTH STATION

Two chapels built in 1875, one above the other connected by a flight of steps, on the site where, according to tradition, the weight of the cross caused Jesus to fall for the second time. Inside the lower chapel is a pillar, part of the colonnaded Cardo Maximus (the main street of Byzantine Jerusalem, which ran from north to south), of which substantial sections have been excavated and restored in the Old City.

Up to this point the Via Dolorosa wound its way inside the city of Jerusalem. Here, in the Second Temple period, was the Gate of Judgement through which Jesus is said to have left the city on his way to GOLGOTHA – CALVARY outside the city.

EIGHTH STATION

The Eighth Station is indicated by a cross engraved in a wall and the Greek word *Nika*. The inscription means "Jesus the Christian is victorious." Like the Seventh, this station is believed to have been located outside the city walls of Jerusalem in the Second Temple period.

The word Nika *and a Latin cross engraved in the stone mark the Eighth Station.*

NINTH STATION – THE COPTIC CHURCH

To reach this station, where Jesus is said to have fallen for the third time, one ascends a flight of 28 wide steps on Khan ez

Pillar marking the Ninth Station at the entrance of the Coptic Church.

Zeit street to the Coptic Church. Near its entrance is a stone column embedded in the wall to mark the Ninth Station. This is the last station outside the CHURCH OF THE HOLY SEPULCHRE. A door on the left of the Coptic Church leads to a terrace, which today is filled with mud hovels inhabited by a community of Ethiopian monks, reminding one of an African village. Nearby can be seen remnants of vaults that used to roof the refectory of the Crusader Canons of the Holy Sepulchre.

THE WESTERN WALL – WAILING WALL

A small section of the western butress-wall that surrounded the Temple compound built by King Herod in the 1st century B.C. It is the holy place most venerated by the Jews, as it is the only remnant of the Second Temple, which was destroyed by the Romans in A.D. 70. It is the focus of Jewish prayer, the place where – throughout the ages – Jews have expressed their grief over the destruction of the Temple and the long exile and their hope for their eventual return to the Holy Land. Because the wall was the scene of so much lamentation and weeping it became known by non-Jews as the Wailing Wall. Its holiness was already articulated immediately following the destruction of the Temple, in such sayings as, "The Presence of God (*Shechinah*) will never leave the Western Wall," or "God made an oath that this wall will never be destroyed." It only became an actual, central place of prayer for the Jews, however, some 700 years ago, when Jews moved into the southeastern section of the Old City, known since then as the Jewish Quarter. The Western Wall was officially recognized as holy to the Jews, and to them only, by the Ottoman Sultan Suleiman the Magnificent around the middle of the 16th century. The Sultan allocated a section of some 20m (70 ft) of the wall as a Jewish place of prayer and had 3m (10 ft) of ground in front of the wall paved, and a wall built on the west. Thus a small courtyard was formed accessible from the Jewish Quarter. Jews prayed for some 400 years within this limited area. Visitors would inscribe their names on the wall. Later this changed into the custom – practised to this day – of inserting notes with special requests to the Almighty between the stones.

In 1967 the space in front of the Western Wall was greatly enlarged and deepened, and became a place for private and communal prayer and for national celebrations. The exposed part of the wall today is some 60m (200 ft) long. The seven lowest courses of the wall are the original, Herodian section. Vertical shafts sunk near the wall showed that there are eight more courses of similar stones under the contemporary pavement, which go down to a paved street that in the Second Temple period ran along the Western Wall from north to south. Under this street there are nine more courses of foundation stones. The Herodian stones are easy to distinguish. They are usually large, very well cut, with straight lines and angles, and have a fine border. The face of the stone is flat and even. This high quality of stone craft can be seen in other special Herodian construction projects, such as the

The Western Wall.

TEMPLE MOUNT and the CAVE OF MACHPELAH in Hebron. Above the seven Herodian layers are four rows of large – almost square – stones, evidence of repairs made in the early Moslem period (7th century) and, above them, rows of small stones of various periods.

In the southern corner – today's women's prayer section – is a particularly wide stone spanning two courses of the Herodian wall. This is the lintel of one of the Second Temple period gates – most probably the Gate of Coponius – leading into the Temple esplanade. Today it is called Barclay's Gate after the 19th-century American who first discovered it. About half of the lintel is buried under the ramp that gives access to the Temple Mount today. South of this ramp is an excavated area in which the south western corner and entire southern wall of the Temple Mount enclosure have been exposed.

North of the Western Wall is a Mameluke period school, under which is a system of arches built against the Herodian wall. The most impressive is Wilson's Arch, named after one of the most important English explorers of Jerusalem. It once supported a bridge through which one could enter the Temple Mount area.

Today the paved plaza in front of the Western Wall is arranged in broad steps leading down to the prayer area which is divided into two sections, one for men and the other for women.

JORDAN RIVER

The largest river in the Holy Land, it flows in the Jordan Valley, which is part of the great Syro-African rift, a huge geological fault in the crust of the earth. Three streams that issue in the foothills of Mount Hermon join near Kibbutz Sede Nehemiah to form the united Jordan. The Jordan flows in a direct north-south course through the marshy area of the Hula Valley and on, till it falls into the SEA OF GALILEE in its north-eastern corner. The river leaves the Sea of Galilee at its southwestern tip and continues southwards in a very meandering course to the Dead Sea. All in all, the Jordan is some 500km (310 miles) long and descends some 900m (3000 ft) from 520m (1700 ft) above sea level at its place of issue to 207m (680 ft) below sea level at its entry into the Sea of Galilee, to 369m (1300 ft) below sea level when it enters the Dead Sea. It is a narrow river, not much more than a stream, and yet it played a most significant role in important events. Despite its narrowness, it presented an impassible barrier for the Children of Israel who had to cross it on their way to Canaan. Only a miracle that opened a path in the river, much like the miracle that occured during the Exodus, enabled them to cross (Joshua 3:15-17). The place of the crossing is shown near GILGAL. Curative qualities have been

View of the Jordan River.

attributed to the Jordan since at least the days of Elisha, who healed a leper in its waters (II Kings 5:10-14). In Christian history the Jordan River played a significant role as the PLACE OF THE BAPTISM (Matthew 3:13-17; Mark 1:9-11; Luke 3:21). The particular section of the Jordan where the baptism of Jesus is believed to have taken place is situated not far from JERICHO. It has been a favourite place of pilgrimage and bottles of water drawn there were sold all over the Christian world.

The northern part of the Jordan Valley is densely populated. Many villages and kibbutzim flourish thanks to the warm climate and abundant water. As one continues south, the climate becomes oppressively hot and arid and the valley had no settlements, except for Jericho which is an oasis. Lately, because of intensive irrigation, new settlements have been established on both sides of the river. The bridges over the Jordan are few; the best known is the Allenby Bridge near Jericho on which passes a lively traffic between Israel and the Kingdom of Jordan. In the summer when the water is low the Jordan can be forded in some places.

KURSI – COUNTRY OF THE GADARENES

Remains of the Byzantine church at Kursi.

Detail of the mosaic floor of the Byzantine church at Kursi.

Kursi, located on the eastern shore of the Sea of Galilee next to the road that leads up to the Golan Heights, is identified as the country of the Gergesenes (Matthew 8:28) or the country of the Gadarenes (Luke 8:26). The monastery is built on the site where, according to an early Christian tradition, Jesus miraculously caused the demons that had taken hold of a man to enter the bodies of pigs grazing on the nearby hill. The pigs ran wildly into the SEA OF GALILEE and were drowned (Matthew 8:28-32; Luke 8:26-33). The identification of the place of the miracle with the village of Kursi was established by early Christian writers and pilgrims, among them Mar Saba and his pupils, who prayed at the site in 491.

The church and monastery, which cover an area of some 4.5 acres (1.8 hectares), was built some time in the middle of the 5th century. The compound was surrounded by a wall and entered from the west, the direction of the Sea of Galilee, through the main gate which was flanked by a tower. In front of the church was an atrium (courtyard) paved with flagstones and surrounded by columns. The church was built as a basilica with a nave on each side of the central hall. Around the apse in the eastern wall were stone benches for the clergy. On both sides of the apse were rooms, the one on the south being used as a baptistry. The floor of the church was covered with colourful mosaics, some of which are well-preserved. Under the chapel, on the southern side of the main hall, was a crypt in which 30 skeletons, presumably of monks, were buried.

Near the northern wall of the monastery compound were houses in which the monks and pilgrims resided, as well as courtyards, ovens and drainage canals. The site was carefully excavated and restored in the 1970s and is now an important tourist attraction.

LATRUN MONASTERY

A large, prominent monastery on the eastern edge of the VALLEY OF AJALON, on the Tel Aviv-Jerusalem highway. It was built in 1890 by monks of the ascetic order founded at Soligny-la-

Trappe in France – hence known as the Trappists – whose strict rules of complete silence are followed here to this day. The name Latrun is an Arabic mispronunciation of Le Toron de Chevaliers (the Tower of the Knights), the name of the 12th-century Crusader castle that once stood on the site now occupied by the monastery. With time Le Toron was changed into el-Atrun and then to Latrun. This name gave rise in the 15th century to an erroneous identification of the ruined Crusader castle as the birthplace of the good thief (*boni latro* in Latin) who was crucified next to Jesus (Matthew 27:38-44), hence the place was called *Castrum boni Latronis* (Castle of the Good Thief).

The monastery is surrounded by agricultural land and is especially known for its vineyards and winery. It can be visited every morning and afternoon except Saturday and Sunday.

Latrun Monastery. (below) Remains of the Crusader castle.

LYDDA – LOD

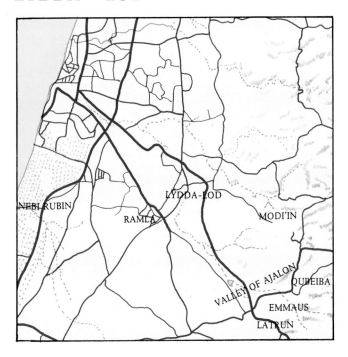

An ancient city situated on the eastern edge of the Coastal Plain, some 17km (11 miles) southwest of Tel Aviv, near the Ben-Gurion Airport (formerly called Lod, or Lydda, Airport). Lydda has been continuously inhabited since the New Stone Age, some 10,000 years ago, until the present day with few interruptions. Throughout much of its long history Lydda was neither an important nor a large city but in certain periods, however, it did attain prominence. One such period was between the destruction of Jerusalem by the Romans in A.D. 70 and the Bar Kochba revolt of 132-135, when many important rabbis lived and taught there. In those days Lydda prospered and was famous for its textiles and pottery. Despite the fact that after the Bar Kochba revolt the centre of Jewish life moved to the Galilee, Lydda maintained its position as a Jewish seat of learning for some 200 years more, after which it became an important Christian city.

Lydda's claim to holiness lies in the activities of Peter who healed a paralytic there (Acts 9:32-35). Equally important in the history of Lydda is St George who, according to Christian tradition, was a native of the city and a soldier in the Roman army in the 3rd century. While serving in a foreign country George died a martyr's death for his adherence to Christianity and his body was brought back to his hometown and buried there. In the Byzantine period a church was built over his tomb.

The Crusaders brought Lydda its second period of greatness. The church of St George, destroyed during the Arab conquest in the 7th century, was rebuilt as a fortified cathedral. St George was made patron-saint of the Crusading knights, being a soldier himself. The English Crusaders in particular favoured him and the king of England, Richard the

Lion-Heart who took part in the third Crusade, adopted him as patron-saint of England. St George's birthday has been celebrated in England since 1222 to this very day.

Lydda was in the hands of the Crusaders until 1260 when it fell to the Mamelukes who, in 1268, built a beautiful mosque over the destroyed Crusader cathedral, incorporating columns and other architectural fragments from it and even an inscription in Greek from the Byzantine church that had stood on the site. In 1870 the Greek Orthodox obtained permission to build a church next to the mosque, over part of the destroyed Crusader cathedral. The tomb of St George is now in the crypt of this church. Fragments of the Crusader cathedral are incorporated in the crypt, while remnants of the Byzantine church can be seen in the courtyard.

Two holy days every year were dedicated to St George: his birthday on April 23 and the day of his burial on November 15. The latter was celebrated by a large picnic attended by Christians and Moslems alike, the Moslems identifying St George with the prophet Elijah.

MAGDALA – MIGDAL

A small ancient town on the western shore of the Sea of Galilee, some 6km (4 miles) northwest of Tiberias, the town of *Mary who is called Magdalene* (Luke 8:2). The town seems to have been founded around the 1st century B.C. and was important for its fishing and as a fish products industrial centre. Its Greek name Tracheae means "place for salting the fish." Recently a fleet of several small fishing boats of that period has been discovered near Magdala, in the muddy banks of the Sea of Galilee. It was also renowned for its textile industry.

The Church of Mary Magdalene at Magdala.

During the Jewish war against the Romans Magdala was the main centre of the rebels in the area. It was fortified by Josephus Flavius, the high commander of the Jewish rebels in the Galilee, and withstood a Roman siege for a long period. When the Romans finally entered Magdala, they massacred its inhabitants and destroyed its fishing fleet. The town recovered slowly and became one of the centres of Jewish life in the Galilee in the first centuries A.D.

From the early days of Christianity Magdala was identified as the home town of Mary Magdalene and many pilgrims went there to honour her. A church was built on the traditional site of Mary's house. It was destroyed in the 7th century and rebuilt in the Crusader period, but the site has been in ruins since the 13th century. Excavations carried out since 1973 have revealed remnants of a Jewish town of the first centuries A.D. with paved streets, a villa with a swimming pool, and shops. The town had a sophisticated water-supply system fed by subterranean water ducts. Excavations also exposed the ruins of a large Byzantine monastery.

MAR ELIAS MONASTERY

Mar Elias Monastery.

A Greek Orthodox monastery on the southern outskirts of Jerusalem. It stands at an isolated spot east of the Jerusalem-Bethlehem road and offers a magnificent panorama of Jerusalem to the north, Bethlehem to the south and the Judean desert to the east. Tradition links this site to the prophet Elijah (called Mar Elias – St Elijah in Greek), who is said to have rested there when he fled from the wicked Jezebel (I Kings 19:1-3). The stone on which Elijah rested can be seen in the monastery. The site is also connected with Elias, the 14th-century bishop of Jerusalem who is buried in the monastery, and whose tomb is still a place of pilgrimage for the neighbouring Christian communities of Bethlehem and Beth Jala.

The well-fortified monastery was first built in the 6th century. Although destroyed many times, both by enemies and earthquakes, it was always rebuilt. The present structure dates from the 12th century.

In the field near the monastery is a well, known by it Arabic name Bir el- Kadismu (Well of the Repose) where Mary rested on her way to Bethlehem. Here, legend tells, Mary had a vision of two people, one rejoicing in the birth of Jesus, the other refusing to accept it.

MEGIDDO – ARMAGEDDON

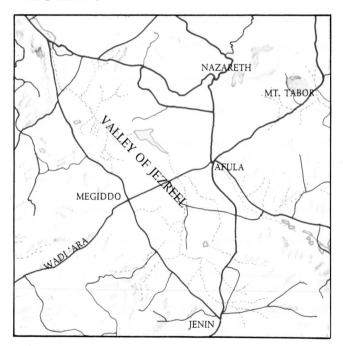

Armageddon, a mispronunciation of Har Megiddo ("Hill of Megiddo" in Hebrew), is the site where the final battle between Christ and Satan will take place (Revelations 16:16). The vicinity of Megiddo was chosen as the site of this eschatological event probably because of the memory of the many historical battles fought over and near this ancient, most strategically located city. Megiddo overlooks the opening of the narrow Wadi Ara into the Jezreel Valley. It thus held a key

Aerial view of Megiddo excavations.

position on the Via Maris, the ancient road that connected Egypt with Damascus and Mesopotamia. Its location brought Megiddo many benefits in times of peace, but recurring destruction in times of war, when armies chose the open Jezreel Plain as their battle ground. The two most famous and decisive battles fought in ancient times near Megiddo were the battle of the Egyptian king Thutmosis III against a coalition of Canaanite kings in 1482 B.C., and the battle between the Egyptian army and Josiah king of Judah in 609 B.C. (II Chronicles 25:22). In both battles the Egyptians were victorious. The first broke the Canaanite coalition and brought all of Canaan under Egypt's yoke for some 300 years; in the second Josiah was killed and the end of the Kingdom of Judah was accelerated.

Megiddo was first settled towards the end of the 4th millennium B.C. and was an important city for the following 2,700 years. Excavations carried out in 1929-1939 revealed remnants of 22 layers of occupation. During most of its long history, Megiddo was a fortified urban centre. The most important remnants of the Canaanite period (3000-1200 B.C.) are a series of temples, some of which can be seen on the site.

Victory celebration depicted on a Canaanite ivory plaque found at Megiddo.

In the Israelite period Megiddo was an administrative centre. King Solomon built a monumental gate and two palaces there (I Kings 9:15), while King Ahab refortified Megiddo and filled it with stables for his war chariots. Ahab's days saw the construction of the very impressive water supply system which leads from the city to the spring while offering protection to the inhabitants. After the fall of the Kingdom of Israel in 712 B.C. Megiddo became an Assyrian provincial capital, after which the site was deserted forever.

Megiddo is a well-kept archaeological site. Entrance is via a small museum where finds from various periods in the history of the city are exhibited. A path leading up to the mound brings the visitor to Solomon's Gate and then to the great section on the eastern side of the tell, at the bottom of which are Canaanite temples of the 3rd millennium B.C. A lookout above the section offers an excellent view of the Jezreel Valley where it is believed the battle of Armageddon will be fought. A visit to the site should end with a descent into the water shaft which leads from the summit of the mound to the foot of the slope.

MODI'IN

Today an Arab village named Midieh, this was the birth place of the Maccabees, founders of the Hasmonean dynasty. It is situated in the foothills of the Judean mountains, some 6km (4 miles) west of LYDDA. Here, in 166 B.C., Mattathias and his five sons, the best known among whom was Judah, raised the banner of revolt against Antiochus Epiphanes, king of the Seleucid empire, who tried to suppress the practice of Judaism. The tombs of the Maccabees at Modi'in are described by Josephus Flavius in his *Antiquities of the Jews* (XIII:211): "Simon built a very great monument of polished white stone, and raised it to a great and conspicuous height, and erected monolithic pillars, a wonderful thing to see. In addition to these he built for his parents and his brothers seven pyramids, one for each." Nothing remains of these

View of Midieh (Modi'in).

monuments, but some tombs cut in the rock on the hill above the village are believed to mark the place of the tombs of the ancient heroes.

A new village named Mevo Modi'in was established nearby in 1964.

MONASTERY OF ST GEORGE

A most impressive Greek Orthodox monastery, built on the steep slope above the northern bank of Wadi Kelt, some 5km (3 miles) west of Jericho. It can be reached by a dirt road branching northwards from the Jerusalem-Jericho highway. The monastery was built in the 5th century in the centre of an area already inhabited by hermits who lived in caves. The founding father of the monastery, which was first dedicated to the Holy Virgin, was John of Thebes in Egypt who became a hermit and came to Wadi Kelt in 480. In 516 John was appointed bishop of Ceasarea, but in his old age he returned to his monastery where he died in about 525. After his death the monastery was renamed after him. The most famous monk to live in the monastery was Georgias of Cosiba (St George), who spent most of his long life here, and in whose honour the monastery was again renamed.

The Monastery of St George on the mountainside above Wadi Kelt.

In the Middle Ages a local legend developed connecting the monastery and caves around it with Joachim and Anne, Mary's parents. It is said that Joachim hid here to bewail the sterility of his wife, and saw an angel who told him that he would have a daughter.

The monastery of St George was active from the time of its founding to the 9th century and then again in the Crusader period when it was rebuilt. Soon after the Crusaders left the country the monastery fell into disuse, and its ruins were described by several pilgrims. In 1878 a Greek monk named Kalinikos settled in Wadi Kelt and began the restoration of the ruined monastery. Work continued until 1901, and in 1952 the belfry was donated by the Patriarch of Jerusalem.

In the main part of the monastery are the chapels of St John, St George of Cosiba and the Holy Virgin. In these chapels can be seen remnants of ancient mosaic floors and frescoes of the 5th-6th and 13th centuries as well as numerous icons. Under the main floor are vaulted store rooms as well as the tombs of five of the early hermits of the monastery. On a higher level are a cave in the rock face and a chapel in honour of the Prophet Elijah who, according to tradition, was fed here by ravens (I Kings 17:3-6). This is based on the Medieval period identification of Wadi Kelt with the brook of Cherith where this episode in the life of Elijah took place.

MOUNTAIN OF THE BEATITUDES

The Mountain of the Beatitudes is on the north-western shore of the Sea of Galilee, above Capernaum, and is approached by a special road branching from the Tiberias-Rosh Pina road. It is one of the holiest Christian sites in the Holy Land being the place where, according to tradition, Jesus taught his disciples the Sermon on the Mount as related by Matthew.; *And seeing the multitudes he went up into a mountain... And*

The Church of the Beatitudes.

he opened his mouth and taught them saying, "Blessed are the poor in spirit: for theirs is the kingdom of heaven..." (Matthew 5:1-3), Verses 5:3-11 of the sermon begin with the words *Blessed are*, hence the name Beatitude which means "Blessing" in Latin. The Mountain of the Beatitudes is also said to be the place where Jesus chose his 12 disciples (Luke 6:12-16): *And it came to pass in those days,that he went out into a mountain to pray... And when it was day, he called unto him his disciples: and of them he chose telve, whom also he named apostles.*

In 1936 the Associazione Italiane built on the mountain the beautiful Shrine of the Beatitudes and a hospice next to it. Both institutions are run by the Franciscan Sisters of the Immaculate Heart of Mary. The church, designed by the architect Barlozzi, is octagonal, each of its eight walls commemorating one of the Beatitudes. The mosaic floor is decorated with symbols of the seven virtues of man referred to in the sermon. There is a magnificent view of the Sea of Galilee from the church and from the hospice; between the church and the monastery is a lovely garden.

MOUNTAIN OF THE PIECES

A holy site, believed by Jews and Moslems alike to be the site where the highly ritualistic Covenant of the Pieces (*Brit Bein ha-Betarim*) took place, during which God passed between the pieces of the animals Abraham had sacrificed. During the ceremony God promised Abraham *this land from the river of Egypt unto the great river, the river Euphrates* (Genesis 15:9-18).

The Mountain of the Pieces, about 1,270m (4,000 ft) above sea level, is on the slopes of Mount Hermon and is approached by the western Hermon road. On the road leading up the summit is a triple-domed shrine built by the Moslems, in tribute to Abraham whom they too venerate as their Patriarch. The central dome is green, the colour holy to the Moslems; the other two are white. The building stands on an elevated platform which seems to be much older than the building itself, and is surrounded by a grove of giant, old oak trees.

In the vicinity of the shrine are ruins of Hellenist, Byzantine, and contemporary settlements, with houses, agricultural terraces, water cisterns and tombs. Five of the latter are especially interesting. They are tower-like structures about 1.80m (5 ft 9 inches) high, surmounted by domes. Two are built of stone and are old; the other three, made of concrete, are recent. In all five the deceased was placed on the floor of the structure wrapped in his garments, rather than interred in the ground. This mode of burial, not common in Islam, seems to preserve very ancient burial customs practised in the first centuries A.D. There is no doubt that the tradition that this is the place of the Covenant of the Pieces is of Jewish origin, but the first reference to it in Jewish sources is found only in a document of 1537. Jews used to come up here on pilgrimage in November, during the week after chapter 15 of the Book

The snowy slopes of Mount Hermon.

of Genesis (recounting the Covenant of the Pieces) is read in the synagogue.

It should be noted that other places in the Holy Land, especially the PLAIN OF MAMRE, are also pointed out as the site where this covenant was made.

MOUNT CARMEL

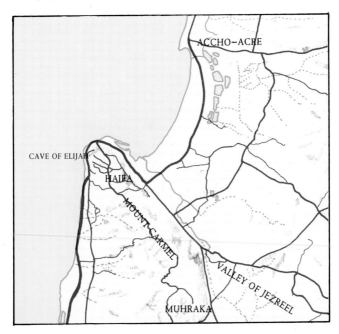

A mountain range, the north-western continuation of the hills of Samaria, rising to 500m (1,650 ft) above sea level. The Carmel forms the southwestern border of the Valley of Esdraelon. Falling steeply to the Mediterranean, it leaves only a narrow coastal plain and its canyon-like cliffs are dotted with numerous caves, some of which served as dwellings in

Caves in the mountains of Carmel.

prehistoric times. Most of the Carmel is covered with a thick deposit of good soil and abundant vegetation. It was noted as a symbol of beauty (Isaiah 33:9; Song of Solomon 7:5) and compared with Lebanon and the Bashan.

Some scholars believe that Mount Carmel is referred to by Veni, a general of Phiops I, king of Egypt, (23rd century B.C.) who describes it as the "gazelle's nose" on reaching the coast of Palestine. In the list of conquests of Thutmosis III (15th century B.C.) it is called "Holy head," or "Holy". An altar to Baal was set at the top of the mountain. Elijah lived there for some time and it was there that he confounded the prophets of Baal (I Kings 18:17-46).

The sanctity of Mount Carmel was still preserved in the Hellenistic period when a temple of Zeus stood on the

Landscape in the Carmel mountain range.

mountain. There was also an altar and an oracle there and a fragmentary inscription found on the mountain mentions a cult of Zeus Heiopolitanus. Christian tradition places the site of the altar of Baal on the south-eastern end of the mountain. A Jewish village called Husifa existed in the Byzantine period on one of the peaks of Mount Carmel, where remains of a synagogue have been discovered.

THE CARMELITE MONASTERY

The largest monastery of the Carmelite order and its headquarters, built on the promontory of the Carmel – the summit of the northernmost edge of the Carmel in the city of Haifa. Being such a prominent natural feature, sanctity has been attached to Mount Carmel since ancient times. It was holy to a pagan god named Carmel who had an oracle there. Later it became holy to the Greek god, Zeus. A foot of a marble statue with an inscription to "Zeus, god of the Carmel" was found in the garden of the Carmelite Monastery. The statue was dedicated to the god by a Roman resident of Ceasarea whose feet had been healed. This attribution of therapeutic qualities was later transferred to the CAVE OF ELIJAH in the lower garden of the monastery. The prophet Elijah is connected with various locations on Mount Carmel, one being the promontory of Carmel. Indeed, the small cave under the monastery is held by a Christian tradition to be the place where the prophet lived. The Jews connect the cave with the prophet Elisha, Elijah's pupil who is believed to have been buried there.

The present monastery, with its very ornate church, was completed in 1836. The statue in the church of Mary "Our Lady of Mount Carmel" is particularly noteworthy. The monastery is built on the site of earlier churches and monasteries of the Byzantine and Crusader periods. In the 17th century, when the monastery was in ruins, several monks were granted permission by the Ottoman authorities to live in caves on the slope of the mountain. These caves can still be visited. In the 18th century a half-completed monastery stood at the site. When Napoleon Bonaparte besieged Acre in 1799, he converted the lower floor of the unfinished building into a hospital for his sick and wounded soldiers. A monument erected in 1876 opposite the entrance to the present-day monastery commemorates the French soldiers who died there.

In the garden is a path known as Via Dolorosa with 14 plaques commemorating the stations of the Way of the Cross in Jerusalem.

Next to the monastery, at the very edge of Mount Carmel, is a lighthouse called Stella Maris-the Star of the Sea. Near the lighthouse is the former summer palace of the Ottoman governor of Acre. Today the palace serves as the hostel of the Carmelite monastery.

CAVE OF ELIJAH

One large cave and another small one behind it, on the northern slope of Mount Carmel, within the city limits of

Interior of the Cave of Elijah.

Haifa. It can be easily reached by climbing the steps from the highway entering Haifa from the south, or by going down a footpath through the garden of the CARMELITE MONASTERY on the summit of the mountain. The caves are traditionally connected with the prophet Elijah. The Jews believe that Elijah often came here with his disciples to give advice to the people who flocked to him. A Christian tradition from the Byzantine period claims that here Elijah hid from the wrath of Jezebel. The Moslems simply call the caves el-Khadr (the Green i.e., the Immortal), a name associated with the prophet Elijah in Moslem tradition. Different curative properties have been ascribed to the cave over the years and in particular its ability to cure mental ailments. Mentally ill people from all over the Middle East were brought to the cave and left alone there for three days. It is reported that many were cured. Barren women and pregnant women who wish to have a boy pray there even today.

Incised on the walls of the cave are inscriptions of Greek, Latin and Hebrew names, no doubt those of pilgrims who visited the cave from the 4th century onwards and, on one of the walls, is a seven-branched candelabrum.

The day of pilgrimage to the cave for the Jews is on the anniversary of the day Elijah is believed to have gone up to heaven – the Sunday following the 10th day of the month of Ab, usually occurring in July. Numerous people spend the day in the cave and its garden, praying and picnicking.

MUHRAKA – HORN OF CARMEL

A small Carmelite monastery on the highest summit of the Carmel Range, on the spot where the prophet Elijah is said to have challenged the priests of Baal (I Kings 18:19-40). A road branching eastward from the main Carmel Range road, south of the large and colourful Druze village Daliat-el-Carmal, brings the visitor very close to the summit. A splendid panorama of the Carmel, the mountains of Samaria,

The Carmelite Monastery at Muhraka.

Gilboa, Gilead, Galilee and Hermon, and the Jezreel Valley can be seen from the roof of the monastery. The local Arabic name of the place – Muhraka – means "scorching," in memory of the fire that came down from heaven and consumed Elijah's sacrifice (I Kings 18:38).

The monastery is not only dedicated to the prophet Elijah but also to Mary, as the Carmelites believe that the verse, *Behold, there ariseth a little cloud out of the sea, like a man's hand...* (I Kings 18:44), refers to a symbol of the Mother of God seen by a servant of Elijah after the dramatic events of Mount Carmel.

The monastery is surrounded by a nature reserve with specimens of the local flora. A leisurely afternoon can be spent in the monastery, the surrounding woods, and the Druze villages nearby which offer a variety of exotic shops and restaurants.

MOUNT GERIZIM

Gerizim, also known as the Mountain of Blessing, is on the southern side of the valley where the town of SCHECHEM (Nablus) is located. Ebal, the Mountain of the Curse (Deuteronomy 11:29), is on the northern side of the valley. The summit of Gerizim is reached by a good road climbing up from the western outskirts of Nablus.

Gerizim is the site holiest to the Samaritans, an ancient sect made up of descendants of a remnant of the original Jewish population of Samaria and people brought to the region by the Assyrians after the fall of the Kingdom of Israel in 721 B.C. The Samaritans believe that some of the events connected with the TEMPLE MOUNT in Jerusalem, such as the Binding of Isaac, occurred on Mount Gerizim. In the 4th century B.C., after they seceded from the main body of Judaism, the Samaritans built their central temple here, according to the

(left) Remains of the Byzantine church on Mount Gerizim. (right) The spot where Abraham prepared to sacrifice Isaac, according to Samaritan tradition. (above) Mount Gerizim seen from Mount Ebal.

plan of the Temple in Jerusalem. This temple was destroyed by the Hasmonean king, John Hyrcanus, in 128 B.C., but was afterwards rebuilt. It was renovated by the Roman emperor, Hadrian, and functioned for some 200 years. Having been destroyed in the 4th century A.D., the site of the Samaritan temple was given to the Christians who built an octagonal church there, which was destroyed in the 8th century by the Moslems. Today the tomb of a holy man – Sheikh Anim – is the only structure on the site, but remnants of previous structures – Samaritan, Roman and Christian – have been uncovered in excavations and can be seen.

South of the sheikh's tomb is a flat rock which the Samaritans identify as the ROCK OF FOUNDATION, from which the act of creation of the world started. The Samaritans consider the rock very holy and have fenced it. Near this stone is the place where the Samaritan community gathers every year to celebrate the Feast of Passover and sacrifice the Paschal lamb, a custom practiced by the Samaritans ever since the days when their temple crowned the mountain top. In previous generations they used to camp on the summit of the mountain for the whole week of Passover.

MOUNT OF TEMPTATION

The mountain where, according to tradition, Jesus was tempted by Satan for forty days (Matthew 4:1-11, Luke 34:1-13), hence it is also known as Mount Quarantal. The summit of this prominent mountain, overlooking the Jericho Valley, the Dead Sea, Moab and Gilead, the northern Judean Desert and the Jerusalem mountains, was first occupied by the Hasmonean-Herodian fortress, Dok – Dagon, one of a chain of seven fortresses overlooking the Jordan Valley and guarding

(left) The steps leading up to the monastery. (right) Some of the caves in the mountainside where the monks lived.

the eastern flank of the mountains of Judah and Samaria. Despite its superb location and the steep slopes and valleys which surround it and give it natural protection, the fortress was conquered by the Romans in A.D. 68.

In the 4th century a Byzantine monastery named Duka was built on the ruins of the fortress. This was the central monastery for the monks who lived in the caves on the slope of the mountain (see QUARANTAL MONASTERY). After the monastery was destroyed, perhaps in the 7th century, it was never rebuilt, although the Crusaders may have built a small castle here.

The site is reached on foot by a path that passes through the Quarantal Monastery halfway down the slope. In 1935 there was an attempt to build a church here but it never materialized.

QUARANTAL MONASTERY

A Greek Orthodox monastery halfway up the steep slope of Mount Quarantal – the MOUNT OF TEMPTATION west of Jericho. It was to this mountain that, according to tradition, Jesus was *led up of the Spirit into the wilderness to be tempted of the devil. And when he had fasted forty days and forty nights he was afterward an hungred... The devil taketh him up into an exceeding high mountain, and sheweth him all the kingdoms of the world and the glory of them...* (Matthew 4:1-11). But Jesus was not tempted and Satan went his way. The name Quarantal, given to the hill and to the monastery from the Middle Ages,

Quarantal Monastery.

is an Arabic mispronunciation of the Latin *Quarantena* – forty – commemorating the forty days of temptation. In the Byzantine period, between the 4th and the 7th centuries, the place was inhabited by hermits. They did not build a monastery but lived on the side of the hill in two rows of caves, which they turned into cells, chapels, storage rooms and water reservoirs. One such cave can be seen in the chapel of St Elias, and others are seen elsewhere in the monastery. A sophisticated system of conduits brought the rain water of a large catchment area into five caves used as reservoirs.

With the Arab conquest of the 7th century, the monks were scattered. In the 12th century the Crusaders tried to restore the place, but after a short period of occupation it was evacuated and was not in use for hundreds of years. Travellers in the 19th century reported that some of the caves were inhabited by Ethiopian monks. The present-day monastery was built between 1875 and 1905 with funds provided by the Russian Church. It is built against the almost sheer cliff and seems to be growing out of the mountain. In the monastery is a stone on which, according to tradition, Jesus sat during his temptation and many beautiful ritual objects can be seen there. Only a handful of monks inhabit the large monastery nowadays.

Quarantal Monastery is approached by the Jericho-Ramallah road. From the parking lot at the foot of the mountain one has to climb a footpath to the monastery and from there to the summit of Mount Quarantal and the ruins of the monastery of Duka in Dok. The view from the monastery of the Jericho Valley, the Dead Sea, and the mountains of Moab and Gilead is breathtaking.

MOUNT TABOR

An isolated mountain in the eastern Lower Galilee, well known for its dome-shaped form. Its location on an important intersection between the international Via Maris joining Egypt with Damascus and local roads, has made Mount Tabor important since early times. Moreover, its unique shape captured the imagination of ancient peoples who attributed divine qualities to the mountain. The verse in Deuteronomy 33:19, *They shall call the people unto the mountain; they shall offer sacrifices of righteousness...*, is interpreted as referring to this mountain. In biblical times the area around Mount Tabor was the scene of some fierce battles such as the clash between Deborah and Barak, who had grouped their army on the mountain slope, and Sisera's war chariots down in the Jezreel Valley (Judges 4:6-14). It was also the scene of an incident in the battle of Gideon against the Midianites (Judges 8:18).

The main claim of Mount Tabor to holiness stems from the Christian tradition that the Transfiguration of Jesus took place there, according to Matthew 17:1-2: *And after six days Jesus taketh Peter, James and John his brother, and bringeth them up into an high mountain apart, And was transfigured before them;*

Mount Tabor.

and his face did shine as the sun, and his raiment was white as the light. Since the 4th century Mount Tabor has been one of the holiest Christian sites in the Holy Land. Early pilgrims used to climb the difficult slopes of the mountain aided by the 4,300 steps cut into the rock. In the 6th century there were already three churches on the mountain. By the early 11th century another church and a monastery were built and were continuously inhabited by 18 monks.

The strategic qualities of Mount Tabor were recognized by the Crusader knight Tancred, Prince of the Galilee, who, in 1099, built a fortress on the summit, on the spot fortified about a thousand years earlier by Josephus Flavius in the first Jewish war against the Romans. Tancred handed the fortress over to the Order of the Benedictines who held the mountain, until the collapse of the Crusader Kingdom in 1187. In 1263 it was taken by the Mameluke Sultan Baybars. For hundreds of years thereafter Mount Tabor remained deserted and in ruins.

In 1631 the Order of the Franciscans was allowed to return to the mountain. Yet, construction activities began only in 1873 when a small monastery was built. Since then the monastery has grown in size. In 1911 a Greek Orthodox monastery and in 1925 a Franciscan church and a hostel – Casa Nova – were built on the summit.

A winding and rather difficult road leads to the summit of Mount Tabor. It is open to small vehicles only, and visitors coming by bus may reach the top by a taxi service available at the parking lot at the foot of the mountain. Once the summit is reached, a magnificent view unfolds, encompassing all the Lower Galilee. The first structure the visitor sees on the site is the gate of the Crusader fortress known as the Gate of the Winds. In 1898, the protective ditch in front of it, once crossed by a drawbridge, was filled up. South of the gate one can see remnants of the wall built by Josephus Flavius. They are easily recognizable by the alternating uncut stones and ashlars used.

The most prominent structure on the mountain is the Franciscan church built between 1921 and 1925 by the Italian architects, Antonio and Barlozzi, in the form of the Byzantine basilica that once stood here and incorporating fragments of it into the new church. This is one of the most beautiful churches in the Holy Land. The entrance to the church is flanked by two chapels; the one on the right is dedicated to Moses and the one on the left, to Elijah to commemorate the presence of Moses and Elijah during the Transfiguration (Matthew 17:3). On the walls of the central apse of the church, above the high altar, is a mosaic depicting the Transfiguration. In the crypt under the church, are the altar and fragments of walls of the Byzantine church. The rock floor of the crypt is believed to be the very spot on which Jesus stood during his transfiguration.

During excavations carried out in preparation for the construction of the Franciscan church, remnants of a Canaanite place of worship and walls of the Byzantine and Crusader churches were unearthed. All finds from this and other

Interior of the Church of the Transfiguration. (above) The facade of the church.

excavations carried out on the mountain can be seen in the small museum, the keys to which are kept by the church priest.

Northwest of the Franciscan church are the ruins of the large Benedictine monastery of the Crusader period. The foundations of the central hall of the monastery can be seen to the north and those of the refectory (dining hall) on the west. The Greek Orthodox church, in honour of the prophet Elijah who saw the Transfiguration, is another important structure on Mount Tabor. It, too, is built on the ruins of Byzantine and Crusader churches. Near it is a chapel known as The Cave of Malchizedek, commemorating the curious Greek Orthodox tradition that the meeting between Abraham and Malchizedek, king of Shalem (Genesis 14:18-23), took place here rather than in JERUSALEM.

General view of Nain.

A small Arab village in the Lower Galilee, north of Mount Moreh where, according to tradition, Jesus performed one of his well-known miracles – the reviving of the son of the widow: *Now when he came nigh to the gate of the city, behold, there was a dead man carried out, the only son of his mother, and she was a widow... And he came and touched the bier... And he said, Young man, I say unto thee, Arise. And he that was dead sat up, and began to speak. And he delivered him to his mother* (Luke 7:12-15). Despite its holiness, Nain was not frequented by pilgrims, perhaps because, as a French monk who visited the place in 1664 relates, "In the village are one hundred Arab families, wild as leopards, and therefore only few Christians come here. And there is no sign of the house of the widow." Only as late as 1880 did the Franciscans build a church in the village in honour of the miracle.

NAZARETH

A town in the Lower Galilee, the place where Mary received the Annunciation (Luke 1:26-38) and where Jesus grew up and was educated as a child and as a young man. It is one of the holiest towns in Christendom, ranking next to JERUSALEM and BETHLEHEM in its wealth of tradition, its new and ancient churches, monasteries and other religious institutions. Today Nazareth is the largest Arab town in the Galilee, and provides administrative and commercial services for the surrounding villages.

The ancient centre of Nazareth, where the market and main churches are located, is still notable for its small old houses

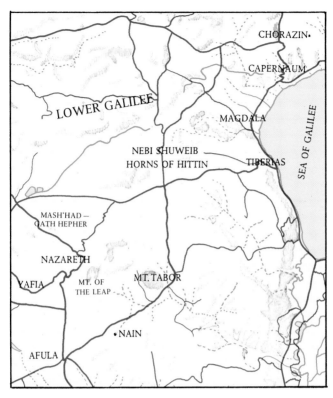

and winding alleys. From here the town expanded in all directions, and is divided into quarters according to the religion of their inhabitants – a Catholic quarter, a Greek Orthodox quarter and a Moslem quarter – each surrounding its religious buildings. There are also six mixed quarters, and above the old town is the new Jewish town of Upper Nazareth.

General view of Nazareth.

The site of Nazareth has been occupied since the Middle Canaanaite period, and remnants from those early days have been unearthed in excavations under the CHURCH OF THE ANNUNCIATION. The settlement existed in the Israelite and Roman periods, when it was only a small village, the main centre of the region being nearby YAFIA.

Nazareth is first mentioned in the New Testament as the hometown of Jesus, the place where he started his preaching and from which he went to visit towns and villages in the Galilee to teach and preach (Matthew 2:23; 4:13; Mark 1:9).

In the days of Jesus, and later in the Roman and early Byzantine periods, the Galilee was densely populated by Jews, but there was also a Judeo-Christian community in Nazareth. Traces of its presence were revealed in the form of symbols – flowers, boats and crosses – painted on the walls of a water reservoir discovered under the Church of the Annunciation. The first church was built only around 427 B.C. and its remnants, including mosaic floors, can be seen under the Church of the Annunciation. A document from the 6th century tells that this Byzantine church was originally a synagogue. Two other Christian edifices – the Church of St Joseph and the convent of the Ladies of Nazareth – were built in the 6th century.

The Persian conquest of 614 followed by the Arab conquest, destroyed the Byzantine churches and reduced Nazareth once again to the status of a small and unimportant village. The Crusaders revived the town, and in 1109 an enormous cathedral, measuring 75 × 30m (250 × 98 ft) was constructed over the ruins of the Byzantine Church of the Annunciation. The cathedral, built in the form of a basilica with three apses was very ornate and the capitals, with sculpures depicting the Apostles and people relating to them, have survived and are superb examples of Crusader sculpture. Three other churches were built in the Crusader period – the rebuilt church of St Joseph and the churches of Gabriel and St Zacharias – and Nazareth became a busy pilgrimage centre.

"Our Lady of the Fright" on the way to the Mount of the Leap.

The Crusader Church of the Annunciation was destroyed with the fall of the Latin Kingdom of Jerusalem in 1187 and again by the Mameluke Sultan Baybars in 1263. Devoted Franciscan monks attempted to hold on to the ruins of the church but were chased out time and again. In 1620 the Franciscans managed to purchase the site of the church. They built a new church over the ruins of the old one and soon afterwards added a monastery and hostel. It was not until the 19th century, however, when 12 churches and monasteries, hostels, schools and ophanages, hospitals and other religious institutions were built, that Nazareth really revived from a long period of neglect. From then on Nazareth has maintained its position as a major centre of pilgrimage, visited every year by hundreds of thousands of devotees.

CHURCH OF GABRIEL AND FOUNTAIN OF MARY

On the northern outskirts of downtown Nazareth is a fountain, still used by the inhabitants of the town. Tradition tells that by the fountain the angel Gabriel first appeared to Mary while she was drawing water. From here Mary went to her home where the Annunciation took place. A church dedicated to the angel Gabriel was first built here by the Crusaders, and over it stands the present-day Greek Orthodox church built in 1769. Remnants of the Crusader church can be seen in the crypt, especially renowned for the unique tiles that panel its walls. The tiles were manufactured in Armenia and brought to Nazareth in the Crusader period. The water of the Fountain of Mary inside the crypt is in fact conveyed into the church from a nearby spring further uphill. From here the water is piped to a fountain.

CHURCH OF ST JOSEPH

A church located opposite the CHURCH OF THE ANNUNCIATION. According to tradition the cave over which the church is built was used by Mary's husband Joseph as his carpentry workshop. Another tradition held that the cave was the dwelling-place of the Holy Family. In the crypt of the present church, completed in 1914, are remnants of Byzantine and Crusader churches. Deeper down under the crypt is the Holy Cave, and next to it – a water cistern. Both cave and cistern are cut in the rock and are remnants of the ancient village of Nazareth.

CHURCH OF THE ANNUNCIATION

The largest church in NAZARETH and one of the holiest and most highly decorated churches in the Holy Land. According to an early Christian tradition, the church is built on the site of the house of Mary and Joseph, where Mary was told that she would *bring forth a son and shalt call his name Jesus* (Luke 1:31).

The church, located in the centre of Nazareth, is a modern structure built between 1955 and 1969, over the ruins of Byzantine and Crusader churches. It is easily recognized by its high dome, which makes it the most prominent structure in

Façade of the Church of the Annunciation.

the city. The entrance to the church is from the west and on its façade are reliefs of Mary and the angel Gabriel. Reliefs of the four Evangelists – Matthew, Mark, Luke and John – overlook the entrace, and above them is a large statue of Jesus. The doors are decorated with copper panels depicting scenes from the life of Jesus. A statue of Mary stands in a niche above the southern entrance to the church.

The central hall of the church is decorated with large and colourful wall mosaics, gifts from various Catholic communities around the world. On the western wall is a mosaic made of glass rather than stone cubes, the gift of the French government. The ceiling has been fashioned in the shape of a lily, the pure white flower symbol of Mary.

Below the church is the Cave of the Annunciation, thought to have been the dwelling place of the Holy Family after it returned from Egypt. In the cave are three chapels: the Chapel of the Angel, with two altars; the Chapel of the Annunciation, with two red columns and fragments of a mosaic floor from

Inside the Cave of the Annunciation.

the Byzantine church that once stood on the site; and the Chapel of St Joseph. Another cave is known as Mary's Kitchen. Other remnants of the Byzantine as well as of the Crusader churches can be seen on this lower level.

Near the church, in the Franciscan monastery, is a museum in which are displayed five capitals of columns sent by St Louis from France as a gift to the Church of the Annunciation. These capitals are splendid examples of French sculpture of the late 13th century. When they arrived the church had already been destroyed and they were never used. In 1908 they were discovered under the church. Finds from the Roman period are also on display.

CHURCH OF THE ROCK – MENSA CHRISTI

A Franciscan church on the slope of the hill west of the CHURCH OF THE ANNUNCIATION. It was built in 1861 on a huge block of rock, on which according to tradition, Jesus and his disciples dined after the Resurrection. Hence the name of the church Mensa Christi – Table of the Lord.

THE CHURCH-SYNAGOGUE

A Greek-Catholic church, located a short distance from the CHURCH OF THE ANNUNCIATION. Here, according to a 6th-century tradition, stood the synagogue in which Jesus preached and antagonized the community (Luke 4:15-24).

MOUNT OF THE LEAP – HAR KEDUMIM

A mountain south of Nazareth associated with the events related in the Gospel of Luke when Jesus antagonized the congregation in the synagogue of Nazareth by applying the messianic words of Isaiah 61:1, *The spirit of the Lord God is*

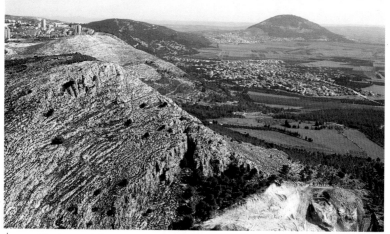

The Mount of the Leap, or Mount of Precipitation.

upon me..., to himself. The enraged citizens *rose up, and thrust him out of the city, and led him unto the brow of the hill whereon their city was built, that they might cast him down headlong* (Luke 4:16-30). Although Jesus *passing through the midst of them went his way*, a tradition developed that he leaped from the mountain. This is accepted by all Christians, although the exact mountain from which he jumped is not agreed upon. The Catholics and Protestants believe that Jesus jumped from this mountain, Jebel Kafza, or Mount of the Leap, while the Greek Orthodox hold that he jumped from a different hill, closer to Nazareth.

On the mountain, which is reached by foot from the road coming up to Nazareth from Afula, are only a few remnants of a small medieval church and several rock-cut tombs. The view from the mountain top is breathtaking – sweeping from Mount Carmel in the west to Mount Tabor in the east and the Jezreel Valley and Mount Gilboa to the south. On the southern slope of the mountain is a cave, inhabited in the prehistoric and the early historic periods. The cave became world-famous when excavations carried out there yielded about a dozen specimens of the Neanderthal Man, designated by archaeologists as the "Galilee Man." These people of the Paleolithic age had received a communal burial on the terrace in front of the cave, and are among the earliest humans ever to have had a formal burial. Because of these prehistoric remains the Hebrew name of the mountain is Har Kedumim, i.e., the Mountain of the Ancients.

NEBI MUSA

A large, multi-domed structure, located about 1.5km (1 mile) south of the Jerusalem-Jericho highway, about 8km (5 miles) southwest of Jericho, on an important intersection of regional roads. Here, according to a relatively late Moslem tradition, Moses is buried. How this tradition developed is not known, as Moses died on Mount Nebo on the eastern side of the Jordan, and *he buried him in a valley in the land of Moab, over against Beth-peor; but no nan knoweth of his sepulchre unto this*

Nebi Musa.

day (Deuteronomy 34:6). It would seem that the place was first chosen because of its strategic position, and that the tradition connecting it with Moses developed later, perhaps as a means of attracting many people who by their very presence would protect the spot. It should be noted, however, that very early stone mounds and structures of cultic nature, perhaps of the Chalcolithic period (4500-3500 B.C.), are scattered in the area, indicating that the site was holy long before the Moslems connected it with Moses. The structure as it stands today was built in 1265 by the Mameluke sultan, Baybars.

Pilgrimage to Nebi Musa used to be held every year, about a week before Easter, during the time when numerous Christian pilgrims congregated in Jerusalem. The date seems to have been chosen on purpose, to serve as a counterweight to the Christian celebrations. Thousands of Moslems used to join a festive procession from Jerusalem to Nebi Musa, where they would camp for a week during which weddings and circumcisions took place and many business transactions were finalized. This tradition has been discontinued.

Around Nebi Musa is a huge cemetery used by Bedouins of the Judean Desert for many generations, to fulfill their desire to be buried near the tomb of a holy man.

NEBI RUBIN

An Arab sheikh's tomb, said to be the burial place of Reuben, eldest of the 12 sons of the Patriarch Jacob. It is located on the southern coastal plain, about 18km (11 miles) south of Tel Aviv, on the bank of the Sorek stream. The tomb is venerated by the Moslems, who used to come here from all over the coastal plain for a yearly month of rejoicing in September. The building over the tomb has a tall and distinct tower built in the 15th century, the time when the tradition identifying it with the tomb of Reuben was crystallized. Nebi Rubin was first mentioned by Mujir ad-Din, a Moslem judge and resident of Jerusalem, who wrote in 1495 that "they say that there is the tomb of our lord Reuben [Rubin in Arabic].

Many visit the place and every year is a great feast. Many people from Ramla, Gaza and other places come here for a few days, to spend much money and read the Koran..."

The reason for attributing this tomb to Reuben son of Jacob is not known, but it may be because of its proximity to Yavneh, an important Jewish centre from A.D. 70 until about 135. Rabban Gamaliel II, one of the leading rabbis of those days, was buried in Yavneh and his tomb drew many visitors. The local people who heard the title "Rabban" may have confused it with Reuben.

NEBI SABALAN

A high mountain 814m (2,670 ft) above sea level, south of the Druze village Hurfeish in the centre of the Upper Galilee. At the peak of the richly wooded mountain is an ancient tomb, believed by both Moslems and Druze to be that of Zebulun, one of the 12 sons of the Patriarch Jacob. The tomb, from which a magnificent panorama can be seen, is reached by a road from Hurfeish. It is located in a small grotto beneath a large building which serves as a hostel for the many pilgrims who come here to honour Zebulun and pray at his tomb. The tradition associating the site with Zebulun seems to be recent, as the Jews believe that he is buried in Sidon in Lebanon along with his brother Issachar.

NEBI SAMWIL

The burial place of the prophet Samuel – Nebi Samwil – is traditionally sited on a high mountain, north-west of Jerusalem. This tradition, dating to the Byzantine period, is accepted by Jews, Christians and Moslems alike, although the Bible clearly states that Samuel was buried at Ramah, his hometown (I Samuel 25:1) which is identified with the Arab

Nebi Samwil.

village Er-Ram some 5km (3 miles) north of Jerusalem, on the Jerusalem-Ramallah road. Today a conspicuous structure that can easily be seen from the northern neighbourhoods of Jerusalem marks the site. Access to Nebi Samwil is by means of a wide road from Ramot, a northern suburb of Jerusalem.

In the central hall of the large edifice of Nebi Samwil is a tombstone, and under it, a burial cave which can be reached from the northern section of the building via a staircase. The structure itself is a Crusader church, known in the Middle Ages as St Samuel de Shiloh. The mountain top on which it was erected was called Monjoie – Mountain of Joy – by the Crusaders because from there they had their first glimpse of the Holy City in 1099. In the 15th century the church was transferred to Jewish hands and was converted into a synagogue. It changed hands again about a century later and under its Moslem owners became a mosque.

The site of Nebi Samwil is surrounded by remnants of previous settlements – orchards, water cisterns and irrigation canals. Steep steps lead to the roof, from which there is a panoramic view of Jerusalem, the Judean mountains, the mountains of southern Samaria and the coastal plain.

NEBI SHUWEIB

An old tomb, holy to the Druze community, identified as the tomb of Jethro father of Zipporah the wife of Moses (Exodus 3:1). The tomb is located on the northwestern slope of the HORNS OF HITTIN in the eastern Lower Galilee, some 10km (6 miles) northwest of Tiberias, and is reached by a road crossing the Arbel valley. The tomb is in a small room in the centre of a complex of buildings. The cenotaph is covered with a green embroidered cloth – green being the holy colour of Moslems and Druze alike. On the walls of the room of the tomb are hung woven and embroidered pieces of cloth, gifts

Nebi Shuweib.

of women in fulfillment of vows. Next to the tombstone is a small depression in the stone pavement believed to be Jethro's footprint.

Jethro, under his unexplained Arabic name Shuweib, is a central figure in Druze religion. The Druze believe that in every generation a prophet appears who is recognized as such by the people but he, in fact, receives his inspiration from a hidden prophet who communicates directly with God. The Druze believe that Jethro was the hidden prophet who inspired Moses, the recognized prophet. This tradition probably developed because Jethro gave good advice to his son-in-law (Exodus 18:19-27). The Druze venerate Jethro and celebrate the anniversary of his death with a pilgrimage to his tomb which is the occasion for a communal gathering, with great rejoicing, song and dance, and feasts.

It is not known how the tomb of Jethro came to be identified with this particular spot. The tradition arose no earlier than the Middle Ages and is first mentioned by Khosrow, a Persian who visited the Holy Land in 1047. From the 12th century on it was also mentioned by Jewish pilgrims. Jews, however, did not venerate the tomb.

NEBI YAKIN

A shrine in the mountains of Judea, where, as held by Moslem tradition, Abraham stood and watched the destruction of Sodom and Gomorrah. It is marked by a structure on a high hill some 900m (3,000 ft) above sea level, 1.5km (about 1 mile) south of the nearest Arab village Bani Naim, southeast of Hebron. Indeed, a magnificent view of all the Judean Desert can be seen from the site, but, interestingly, the Dead Sea area where Sodom and Gomorrah were located is not visible from here.

The name Nebi Yakin means the "prophet of the just law", one of the names by which Abraham is known in Moslem tradition. While he was standing on the hill watching when *the Lord rained upon Sodom and upon Gomorrah brimstone and fire* (Genesis 19:24), Abraham's footprint was embedded in the rock, and over this holy relic the monument was built. An Arabic inscription above the entrance to the structure indicates it was built in the year 963, making it one of the oldest buildings to survive intact in the region.

Remnants of settlements dating from the 4th millennium B.C. to the Middle Ages have been found near the site.

NEBI YAMIN

A domed structure housing a tomb, holy to the Moslems who identify it with the burial place of Benjamin (Yamin in Arabic), the youngest of the twelve sons of the Patriarch Jacob. It stands by the Kfar Saba-Qalqilya road in the central Sharon, and seems to have been built in the Mameluke period. The reason for attributing this tomb to Benjamin is not known. Around the tomb are ruins of a Roman-Byzantine settlement.

NEBI YUNIS

An old tomb on a hill south of the port of Ashdod, holy to the Moslems who identify it with the burial place of the prophet Jonah (Yunis in Arabic), who was sent to warn Nineveh's inhabitants of their town's imminent destruction and was swallowed by a whale on the way, as related in the Book of Jonah. The attribution of this tomb to Jonah seems to have its roots in a Christian tradition, as it is depicted on the Medeba map (a 6th-century mosaic map found in a Byzantine church in Transjordan). On this map the tomb is shown as a large building, over which is the Greek inscription "Saint Jonas." The story behind this tradition is not known.

The small hill of Nebi Yunis was occupied for hundreds of years. Ruins of what used to be an elaborate shrine, remnants of various installations and tombs and many pottery sherds are scattered on it. Today the summit is occupied by the lighthouse which is surrounded by a lovely park. The hill commands a good view of the town and harbour of Ashdod.

PLACE OF BAPTISM

A 3km (2 mile) stretch on the western shore of the Jordan River, east of Jericho, where, according to tradition, John the Baptist baptized Jesus. This act marks the ultimate role of John as the forerunner of Jesus who - once baptized - was declared Beloved Son (Matthew 3:13-17; Mark 1:0-11). The Place of Baptism is one of the holiest sites for Christianity.

The stretch is divided up into five separate sites, each revered by a different Christian denomination. In the past the

The traditional place of the baptism of Jesus.

site was frequented by numerous pilgrims of different nations who congregated there especially during the Epiphany Festival. The Place of the Baptism was particularly revered by Russian pilgrims who until the Russian Revolution of 1917, used to come from Russia, sometimes on foot, carrying their shrouds. Upon approaching the Jordan River they put on their shrouds and baptized themselves in the water in the belief that this act would ensure their resurrection. Bottled Jordan River water drawn in the Place of the Baptism was a very common souvenir taken home by the pilgrims, as it was thought to have curative powers.

DEIR EL-HABASH (Monastery of the Ethiopians)

The monastery was built in the 19th century with funds donated by the royal house of Ethiopia. Only one monk lives in it.

The chapel of Deir el-Habash.

ENCLOSURE OF THE FRANCISCANS

It contained a chapel with a small hospice built in 1935 but was destroyed in an earthquake in 1956. Today there is only a small chapel with an altar, and on the bank of the Jordan River there is another altar.

Franciscan chapel at the Place of Baptism.

MONASTERY OF JOHN THE BAPTIST

This is a Greek Orthodox establishment, called in Arabic Qasr-el-Yahud (Citadel of the Jews). The name recalls the tradition that here the Children of Israel crossed the Jordan River. The present-day monastery is a medieval structure restored in 1954. It is built over remnants of a 5th-century Byzantine church destroyed in A.D. 614 by the invading Persians and rebuilt in 1128. Two monks regularly reside in the monastery.

MONASTERY OF JOHN THE BAPTIST (SYRIAN)

It was built at the beginning of the 20th century and is now deserted.

EL-QASAIR (The Citadels)

These are earth mounds with ruins of a Byzantine church. According to tradition, it was here that the prophet Elijah's stormy ascent to heaven took place (II Kings 2:11).

(EL) QUBEIBA

An Arab village in the mountains northwest of Jerusalem about 4km (2.5 miles) west of NEBI SAMWIL. It is approached by a road leading from the main Jerusalem-Ramallah road.

House of Cleopas at El Qubeiba.

El Qubeiba became important in the Crusader period, when the village was part of the large agricultural domain belonging to the CHURCH OF THE HOLY SEPULCHRE in Jerusalem.

In 1187 the Frankish settlers had to vacate the village. However, following an agreement between the Moslems and the Crusaders, El Qubeiba returned to Crusader hands for a very short time, but was finally deserted in 1244. In the centuries following the expulsion of the Crusaders from the Holy Land, Christian pilgrims were not allowed to use the main highway from the coastal plain to Jerusalem which passed along the same route as it follows today. The Christians were thus barred from visiting ABU GHOSH, identified in the Crusader period with EMMAUS, where Jesus revealed himself to Cleopas (Luke 24:13-35). By way of compensation, the Christians declared El Qubeiba the true site of Emmaus, and this new tradition is upheld to this day by the Franciscans.

In 1872 the site of the Crusader church was purchased by the Franciscans who built a new church and a monastery there named the House of Cleopas. Excavations carried out in the courtyard of the church revealed ruins of the Crusader village.

RAMLA

The "town of sand" (*raml* meaning sand in Arabic) next to LYDDA - LOD, some 18km (12 miles) southwest of Tel Aviv. Ramla was founded in 716 by a Caliph Suleiman of the Umayyad dynasty as the capital of the newly established province of Palestine. In the first centuries following its establishment, Ramla grew in power and wealth at the expense of its neighbour Lydda-Lod. Several unique structures of the early Moslem period can be seen in Ramla, the most impressive being the Vaulted Pool, also known as St Helena's Pool, in the centre of town. Ramla became holy in the Crusader period, when the Crusaders erroneously identified it

The Mameluke sultan Baybar's heraldic device on the bridge at Lod, on the way to Ramla.

(facing page) The White Tower at Ramla. ▷

with Ramah, birthplace of the prophet Samuel and of Joseph of Arimathea (Greek for "of Ramah"). In 1150 they built a large, ornate church in honour of Joseph of Arimathea and Nicodemus who took the body of Jesus down from the cross and buried it in Joseph's family sepulchre (John 19:38-42). In 1260, after the Mameluke conquest, the church was converted into a mosque and is one of the most complete examples of Crusader architecture in the Holy Land. It can be visited only on Friday, the Moslem day of prayer.

Joseph and Nicodemus are also commemorated in the names of a Franciscan monastery and hostel established in 1390. The present-day church standing in this large Franciscan compound was built in 1902, but the old hostel has been preserved, at least in part, and in one of its rooms Napoleon Bonaparte stayed after he conquered Ramla on February 29, 1799.

Another site of interest is the White Mosque – a large Mameluke compound containing remnants of earlier structures. Especially interesting are the three huge subterranean water reservoirs in the courtyard, and the six-storey, ornate White Tower that stands next to the entrance of the compound.

SAMARIA – SEBASTE

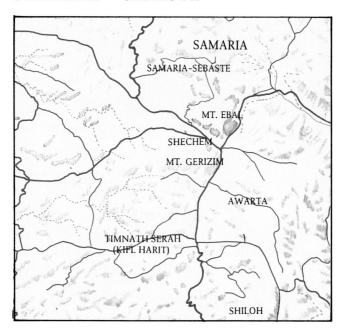

Samaria is the name of the former capital of the Kingdom of Israel as well as the name of the surrounding region.

The ruins of the ancient city are located in the northern Samaria mountains, on the road between Schechem (Nablus) and Jenin. Nearby is the Arab village of Sebastiyeh (Sebaste).

Samaria is one of the largest archaeological biblical sites in the Holy Land. It was founded in the 9th century B.C. by King Omri who bought the site from a certain Shemer (I Kings 16:24) hence, probably, the Hebrew name *Shomron* of the city.

Part of the colonnaded road at Sebaste (Samaria).

Omri started building his new capital and his work was continued by successive kings of Israel. Samaria was the capital of the Northern Kingdom until the kingdom fell to the Assyrians in 721 B.C. Archaeological excavations have revealed remains of the walls of the palace of the kings of Israel and fragments of carved ivory pieces that decorated the furniture and, because of this, this palace has been identified with the "ivory house" mentioned by King Ahab in I Kings 22:39. After the destruction of Samaria and the deportation of the majority of its inhabitants, the Assyrians populated the area with captives from other countries and made it the centre of their province. From then on Samaria was an important non-Jewish city, inhabited by descendants of these foreigners.

A second period of glory came to Samaria in the days of King Herod in the 1st century B.C. Herod rebuilt Samaria as a Roman metropolis which he named Sebaste – "the illustrious" – in honour of his benefactor, the Roman emperor,

Augustus. In those days Sebaste had a central temple (the Augusteum), various other temples dedicated to Roman gods, a theatre, a stadium, and a forum; it was protected by a wall with gates. To a later time within the Roman period belongs the magnificent colonnaded road, one of the major attractions of the city. All these public structures, which can be seen on the site, have been excavated and restored.

Sebaste was destroyed during the Jewish revolt against the Romans. It was rebuilt shortly after the Byzantine period, destroyed by the Arabs, and then again restored by the Crusaders who made it a large and important city. Its population dwindled thereafter and the town declined to the state of a small poor village. The magnificent structures unearthed in the course of archaeological excavations carried out between 1909 and 1910 and then again between 1931 and 1935, have made Samaria a major tourist attraction.

South of the acropolis of the ancient city, between it and the colonnaded road, is a small Byzantine church of the 7th century. Traditionally it is held that the head of John the Baptist, killed in the fortress of Machaerus on the eastern side of the Jordan River, was kept in this church. It is interesting to note that the Armenian church in the compound of the RUSSIAN CHURCH OF THE ASCENSION on the MOUNT OF OLIVES in Jerusalem also boasts of being the burial place of the head of John the Baptist. On the walls of the crypt under the church are traces of fresco paintings. The large Crusader church in the village of Sebaste, now used as a mosque, is also dedicated to John the Baptist.

SEA OF GALILEE – SEA OF CHINNERETH

The largest fresh-water lake in Israel, fed mainly by the Jordan River and drained by it. The Hebrew name for the lake, Sea of Chinnereth (Numbers 34:11; Joshua 13:27), is derived

The Sea of Galilee.

from the name of the most important town on its shores in the Canaanite-Israelite periods. The name Chinnereth resembles the Hebrew word *kinnor*, "harp," and this gave rise to the notion that the name derived from the shape of the lake, being wide in the north and tapering towards the south. The lake was known by other names – the Lake of Gennesaret in the Second Temple period (Luke 5:1) and the Sea of Tiberias in the Talmud.

The Sea of Galilee lies in the Jordan Valley rift, some 210m (690 ft) below sea level, and is part of the great Syro-African fault line. The hot mineral springs that issue along the shores of the lake indicate that the fault line is still active. The warm climate, abundant water, lush vegetation and plentiful fish have drawn people to the Sea of Galilee since early prehistoric times. The land around the lake has been cultivated since the very beginnings of agriculture, and many villages, town and cities have dotted the region throughout history. Beit Yerach on the south-western shore of the lake and Chinnereth on the

The Sea of Galilee at sunset.

north-western shore were major cities in the 3rd-1st millennia B.C., while from the Roman period onwards Tiberias has been the major urban centre of the region. The Sea of Galilee has a special significance for Christians, as it was in the surrounding area that Jesus was most active and performed many miracles. Places like CAPERNAUM, MOUNTAIN OF THE BEATITUDES, TABGHA and MAGDALA deeply stir the heart of every Christian.

Today the Sea of Galilee is the main water reservoir of Israel. Water is pumped from the lake and conveyed to the central and southern regions of the country. The area around the lake is one of the most popular tourist resorts in the Holy Land. The warm climate, historical and religious sites, sporting facilities, numerous hotels and camp sites and beautiful scenery draw to the shores of the lake many tourists and holiday makers.

The Roman theatre at Shechem.

Shechem, in the centre of the Samaria Mountains, is one of the oldest and most important cities in the Holy Land. Excavations carried out in 1913-14, in 1926-27 and again between 1956 and 1964 revealed that ancient Shechem was located at Tell Balata, east of present-day Nablus. The site was inhabited continuously from the beginning of the 2nd millennium B.C. to the 1st century A.D. Important remnants of fortifications and temples uncovered in the excavations, as well as written documents of the 2nd millennium B.C., testify to the fact that Shechem was the most prosperous and active Cannanite city in the mountainous region of Canaan. The Patriarchs roamed through the area around Shechem,

Stone mazzebah *at Tell Balata, the site of biblical Shechem.*

sometimes conducting peaceful business transactions with its inhabitants, such as a land purchase by Jacob (Genesis 33:19), sometimes entering into violent conflicts, such as the massacre of its population over Dinah's honour (Genesis chapter 34). Both Abraham and Jacob built altars to God in the vicinity of Shechem (Genesis 12:6-7; 33:20), thus sanctifying the town and the region. These memories of ancient holiness were perhaps the reason why Joshua chose Shechem as the place where he gathered all the tribes of Israel and where he made a covenant between them and God (Joshua 24:1-27). The plot of land purchased by Jacob became the burial place of Joseph whose bones the Children of Israel brought back with them from Egypt (Joshua 24:32). JOSEPH'S TOMB is one of the holy sites in Shechem. After the conquest of Canaan, Shechem was one of the cities assigned to the Levites. However, in the times of the Judges there was still a Canaanite temple in it known as the "House of Baal-berith" (Judges 9:4) or "House of the god Berith" (Judges 9:46). Substantial remnants of this massive temple have been unearthed on the tell, including a large *mazzebah*, a sanctified standing stone of the type common in Canaanite places of worship. For a short time Shechem was the capital city of the Kingdom of Israel (I Kings 12:25), but once the capital was transferred to Penuel, Shechem declined in importance. After the destruction of the kingdom, foreign captives from other countries were settled in Shechem by the king of Assyria (II Kings 17:24). These foreigners intermingled with the remnants of the local Israelites and constituted what was to become the Samaritan sect. The Samaritans consider Shechem, and more so MOUNT GERIZIM south of the town, holy and to this day Shechem is the centre of the Samaritan community. Samaritan Shechem was probably the Sychar mentioned in John 4:5.

After Shechem was destroyed by the Romans, a new site was selected further to the west, between Mount Gerizim and Mount Ebal, and a Roman town bearing the name Flavia

Sarcophagi in a burial cave of the Roman period at Shechem.

Neapolis was built. This site is occupied to this day. The current name Nablus is the Arabic pronunciation of the Roman name Neapolis. Impressive remnants of the Roman, and of the later Byzantine, city have recently come to light, and include a theatre, an odeon, a hippodrome and traces of the city wall.

Today Nablus is a compact Arab city with an old centre and new suburbs on the lower slopes of the surrounding hills. It is especially known for its soap which is manufactured from olive oil.

The exact location of the sites connected with Abraham and Jacob are not known. However, on the eastern side of Nablus is a very important holy site known in Christian tradition as JACOB'S WELL, and at the foot of the ancient mound is the traditional site of Joseph's Tomb.

JACOB'S WELL

Located on the eastern outskirts of Shechem-Nablus. Here Jesus asked a Samaritan woman for water, saying: *If thou knewest the gift of God, and who it is that saith to thee, give me to drink; thou wouldest have asked of him, and he would have given thee living water... whosoever drinketh of the water that*

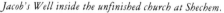

Jacob's Well inside the unfinished church at Shechem.

I shall give him shall never thirst; but the water that I shall give him shall be in him a well of water springing up into everlasting life. Jesus revealed himself as the Messiah, and said, *I that speak unto thee am he* (John 4:5-26).

The earliest church on the site was a cruciform-Byzantine style church with the well at its centre. The Crusaders built their church over it, and in 1914 construction began of the unfinished church which now stands on the site. Work on this church, a project of the Pravoslav church of Czarist Russia, was stopped with the Communist Revolution of 1917, and the building was never completed. In the centre of the unfinished church, built on the plan of the Byzantine church, is Jacob's well. It is about 35m (115 ft) deep.

TOMB OF JOSEPH

An ancient tomb in the village of Balata, east of SHECHEM – NABLUS venerated since the Byzantine period as the burial place of Joseph son of Jacob, whose bones were brought from Egypt by the Children of Israel (Joshua 24:32). The tomb is inside a domed structure at the foot of the mound of ancient Shechem. Flanking the tomb are two pillars named after Ephraim and Manasseh, the sons of Joseph.

Joseph's tomb at Shechem.

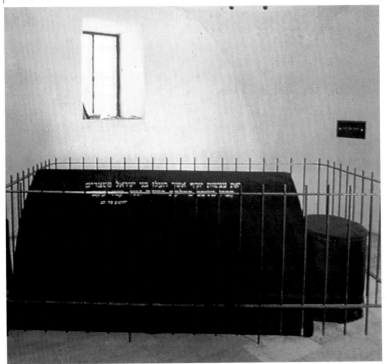

SHILOH

One of the holiest towns of ancient Israel, the home of the Ark of the Covenant for some 200 years, from the time of the conquest of Canaan under Joshua (Joshua 18:1). Shiloh was the religious and political centre of the tribes of Ephraim and Benjamin in the period of the Judges, a place of frequent

The biblical site of Shiloh.

pilgrimage (I Samuel chapter 1) and of a famous annual
festival (Judges 21:19) when the maidens danced in the
vineyards. In the middle of the 11th century B.C., after the
decisive battle of Ebenezer (I Samuel chapter 4), the Ark of
the Covenant was taken by the Philistines. It seems that Shiloh
was destroyed in the course of this battle, although the Bible
does not mention such an event. The battle marked the end
of the period of the Judges, and was followed by the growing
need for a king and eventually by the selection of Saul and
then of David and the establishment of the monarchy.

Shiloh was in ruins for about 150 years, until it was rebuilt
in the days of Jeroboam at the end of the 10th century B.C.
Occupation was then more or less continuous until the Middle
Ages but Shiloh never resumed its former glory.

The site of the mound of ancient Shiloh, locally called
Khirbet Sailun, is located east of the Jerusalem-Shechem
(Nablus) road in central Samaria, and today a new settlement
named Shiloh stands next to it. Excavations on the tell
(mound) have unearthed impressive remnants of a fortified
settlement of the 17th-16th century B.C. over which the earliest
Israelites built their settlement. Remnants of houses were
discovered in various parts of the tell, indicating that Shiloh
in the time of the Judges was fairly large and well-to-do.

South of the tell are two Byzantine churches dating to the
5th-6th centuries. Both have mosaic floors with lovely designs;
they are now protected by structures built by the Danish
expedition which excavated the site in 1926-29. One floor
depicts two does and fish flanking a pomegranate tree, echoing
the biblical verse, *As the hart panteth after the water brooks,*

Bronze weapons (left) and incense stand (right) found at the ancient site of Shiloh.

so panteth my soul after thee, O God (Psalms 42:1). An inscription on the mosaic floor mentions the brothers Porphirius and Jacob who perhaps donated the mosaic. Stones from these churches were taken in the 9th-10th centuries to repair a nearby structure known as the "Mosque of the Sixty," which originally may have been a synagogue.

TABGHA – HEPTAPEGON

The Arabic name for a small valley on the northwestern shore of the sea of Galilee, east of the Tiberias-Rosh Pina road. The name, derives from the Arabic mispronunciation of the Greek name *Heptapegon* – "seven springs" – and refers to an area especially holy to Christians – the site where Jesus is said to have performed two miracles commemorated by ancient and modern churches.

Of the seven springs which gave their name to the area, three are fairly large, the others small. The largest issues inside an enclosed pool known as Ein Nur, next to the road to CAPERNAUM. This is a hot (81°F; 27°C) mineral spring, noted for its bluish, sulphuric and undrinkable water. The pool is impressive – a deep octagonal structure built of black basalt stones on Roman foundations. The pool used to supply water to the surrounding valley.

The second largest spring is Ein Sheva, which issues into a pool inside the Franciscan compound. East of Ein Nur is a large, round pool, and next to it a small spring of fresh water known as Job's Spring. There is local tradition that Job used to come to this spring to wash himself.

On the southern side of the valley is a very pleasant hostel for visitors and pilgrims. The hostel, surrounded by gardens and trees, was initially built by the German Catholic Society for the Holy Land, which purchased the site in 1887.

CHURCH OF ST PETER

The other miraculous event believed to have occurred at Tabgha is the third appearance of Jesus after his death, as related in John 21:4-17: *When the morning was now come, Jesus stood on the shore: but the disciples knew not that it was Jesus... Simon Peter went up and drew the net to land full of great fishes... Jesus saith unto them, Come and dine... This is now the third time that Jesus showed himself to his disciples after he was risen from the dead... So when they had dined, Jesus saith to Simon Peter, Simon son of Jonas, lovest thou me more than these? He saith unto him, Yea Lord... He saith unto him, Feed my lambs...* After this event Peter's primacy was recognized. The church which commemorates these events is called both St Peter and the Chapel of the Primacy. In the Middle Ages the church that stood here was known as Tabula Domini (Table of Our Lord) or Mensa Christi (Christ's Table). The contemporary church was built in 1934 by the Franciscan Order. It stands close to the shore of the Sea of Galilee, directly on the natural rock.

The Church of St Peter at Tabgha.

CHURCH OF THE MULTIPLICATION OF LOAVES AND FISHES

The other miracle performed at Tabgha was the Multiplication of Loaves and Fishes, when Jesus fed five thousand people with

Mosaic depicting a basket of bread and two fish at the Church of the Multiplication.

five loaves of bread and two fish (Matthew 14:13-21; Mark 6:30-44; John 6:1-14). The first church on the traditional site of the miracle was built in the early Byzantine period in the 4th century. It was damaged by a landslide from the nearby hill, and over its ruins another church was built in the 6th century. This was a typical basilica with a central nave and two aisles, and in front of it was a colonnaded courtyard (atrium). The rock under the altar in the main hall of the church is said to be the rock on which Jesus put the loaves and fish. The church is especially renowned for its multicoloured mosaic floors. Near the altar the mosaic floor depicts a bread basket flanked by two fish and in the two aisles are exquisite scenes of wildlife-water vegetation and various kinds of birds. These mosaic floors have been very well preserved, and are among the loveliest in the Holy Land. When the ancient church was discovered during excavations, the owners of the area – the Order of the Benedictine monks – built a new church over it in 1935.

TIBERIAS

A town on the western shore of the SEA OF GALILEE, 212m (some 700 ft) below sea level. Tiberias was founded in A.D. 18-22 by Herod Antipas (the Herod of the time of Jesus) and named after the Roman emperor, Tiberius. Since its foundation Tiberias has been a most attractive town. The land and seascapes are beautiful and the climate is mild, especially in the winter. South of the town are hot mineral springs, the curative qualities of which have been appreciated since antiquity. Tiberias does not figure in the stories of Jesus and his disciples, although a Crusader tradition identified in it the

230

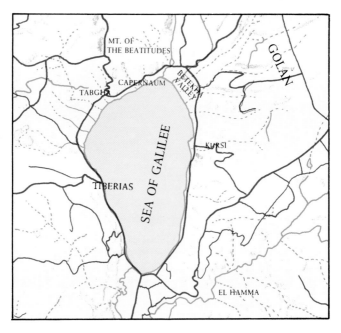

place where *Jesus shewed himself again to his disciples at the sea of Tiberias* (John 21:1), usually believed to have been at TABGHA. The Crusaders built a church in the town and today the Franciscan CHURCH OF ST PETER stands on its site. In the centuries following the destruction of Jerusalem by the Romans, Tiberias became a major centre of Jewish learning and religious life. Many important rabbis lived and were buried there and their tombs became holy places of pilgrimage for the Jews.

Tiberias fell to the Moslems in 637, to the Crusaders in 1099 and to the Mamelukes in 1247. In the 1560s the Turkish sultan, Suleiman I, granted the town, almost in ruins by then, to a prominent Jewish family of Istanbul. The activities of the family, headed by Don Joseph Nasi and

General view of Tiberias.

Donna Gracia, brought a period of revival to Tiberias. The ruined walls were repaired and a silk factory established. The walls were repaired again in the 18th century, but almost collapsed in two disastrous earthquakes in 1759 and 1837.

Today Tiberias is a thriving tourist resort with many modern hotels catering to pilgrims and holiday-makers. It is close to major holy and historical places around the Sea of Galilee and offers a variety of beaches and sport facilities.

ST PETER'S CHURCH

A Franciscan church built in 1850 in the centre of Tiberias, close to the shore of the SEA OF GALILEE, where according to tradition *Jesus shewed himself again to his disciples at the sea of Tiberias* (John 21:1). The tradition that this is the site of the

St Peter's Church at Tiberias.

third appearance of Jesus after his death, seems to be a late one, as no old ruins were found under or near the relatively modern church. More accepted is the identification of the site of this miracle with TABGHA, some 12km (7 miles) to the north.

TIMNATH SERAH – KAFR HARIT

A small Arab village in the Samaria mountains, south of the road which crosses Samaria from east to west. Here, according to Jewish, Samaritan and Moslem tradition, are the tombs of Joshua (Joshua 24:30), his father, Nun, and his friend, Caleb son of Jefuneh. The tomb of Joshua is believed to be located in the village mosque and those of Nun and Caleb, in the cemetery.

VALLEY OF AJALON

A valley in the foothills of the Judean mountains; about half way between Tel Aviv and Jerusalem. The highway today circumvents the valley but in the past went right through it. The valley won its place in history when Joshua, while fighting the five Amorite kings who had attacked the Gibeonites, witnessed a spectacular miracle there: *And the sun stood still and the moon stayed, till the people had avenged themselves upon their enemies* (Joshua 10:13). At the end of the conquest of Canaan, Ajalon was assigned to the tribe of Dan (Joshua 19:40-42). However, the Danites did not succeed in ousting the Amorites from Ajalon, but help came from the Ephraimites in the north, who subjugated the Amorites of Ajalon (Judges 1:34-35).

After Saul's first victory over the Philistines at Michmash, his son Jonathan pursued them as far as Ajalon (I Samuel 14:31). In David's administrative reorganization, Ajalon became a city of refuge (I Chronicles 6:67-69). It was later included in the territory of Benjamin (I Chronicles 8:13), and was fortified by Rehoboam against invasions from the west or the north (II Chronicles 11:5-10). During the reign of Ahaz, it ws taken by the Philistines (II Chronicles 28:18). The site of ancient Ajalon is identified with modern Yalu, east of Amwas (EMMAUS). It was known in the Roman period as Jalo.

The Valley of Ajalon.

VALLEY OF ELAH

A valley southwest of Jerusalem, extending towards the land of the Philistines, through which passed the important road from Philistia to the Judean Hills and Jerusalem. It was there that David slew Goliath. It is identified with present-day Wadi es-Samt. *Israel were gathered together, and pitched by the Valley of Elah... the Philistines stood on a mountain on the one*

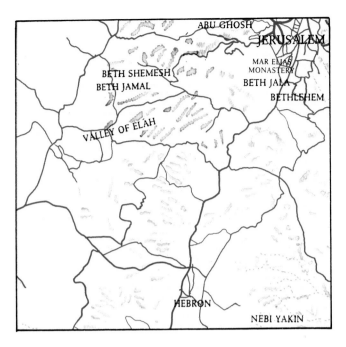

side, and Israel stood on a mountain on the other side; and there was a valley between them... So David prevailed over the Philistine with a sling and with a stone, and smote the Philistine and slew him... (I Samuel 17:2-51).

The hill of Azekah in the Valley of Elah.

YAFIA

An Arab village on the western outskirts of Nazareth, believed to be the birthplace of the Apostle James. Four churches in this village, whose population is only 30 percent Christian, commemorate this tradition.

Yafia is an ancient settlement, mentioned in the El Amarna Letters of the 14th century B.C. as Yapu. In the 1st century

A.D. it was the largest village in the Galilee and one of the main centres of the revolt against the Romans. Josephus Flavius, commander of the Galilee in the early stages of the war against the Romans, surrounded Yafia with a double wall and had his headquarters there for a time. When the Galilee fell, Titus killed all the inhabitants of Yafia and completely razed the vilage.

A synagogue brought to light during archaeological excavations shows that the village was rebuilt shortly afterwards, and that it flourished in the 3rd-4th centuries. It is especially renowned for its mosaic floor in which stones of 11 colours were used. Two fragments of the damaged mosaic are exhibited in the Israel Museum in Jerusalem. Carved stones from the synagogue are incorporated in several structures in the village, such as a lintel decorated with a seven-branched candelabrum now found in the Catholic church.

YARKA

In this village east of Acco, the largest of the Druze villages in the Western Galilee, is a holy tomb known to the local inhabitants as E-Nebi e-Zadik (the Pious Prophet). In Jewish tradition it is identified as the tomb of Hushai the Archite, loyal friend of King David (II Samuel 15:32- 37). It is not known how old this tradition is nor how it developed. Perhaps it grew out of the similarity of sound between the names Archite and Yarka.

That the tomb was venerated by Jews, Arabs and Druze alike can be learned from a description of a pilgrimage in 1742. A pupil of the Jewish scholar Hayyim Ben Attar and his followers spent a Friday at the tomb and reports that the local Arab and Druze villagers used to visit the tomb and light candles on it. They used the area around the shrine as a burial ground, a custom associated with tombs of holy men.

ITALY

ROME

POZZUOLI-PUTEOLI

POZZUOLI – PUTEOLI

The port of arrival of St Paul in Italy (Acts 28:13). There was a Christian community there and Paul stayed with the brethren for seven days. Puteoli has been identified with the ancient port of Pozzuoli, a few km from Naples.

Remains of a Roman temple at Pozzuoli.

ROME

Capital of Italy and the Christian world, a city richer than any other in the world in historic and cultural sites.

Ancient Rome occupied seven hills on the eastern side of the Tiber River, some 24km (15 miles) from its mouth. Tradition tells that Rome was established by Romulus in 753 B.C., but excavations have proved that the Palatine Hill, one of the seven hills of Rome, was already occupied by the middle of the 2nd millennium B.C. Around 800 B.C. this settlement united with others on adjacent hills to become a unified city-state by the 7th century B.C. The first large-scale project of Rome was the construction in the 6th century B.C. of the Cloaca Maxima, the "great sewer" that drained the marshy area between the Palatine and the Capitoline Hills. The dried area was thereafter occupied by the Forum – civic centre of Rome – which already in those early days included two temples, those of Venus and of Vesta. At the same time a temple to Jupiter, chief god of Rome, was established on the Capitoline Hill.

Rome revived quickly after it was sacked by the Gauls in 390 B.C. and was rebuilt on a more lavish scale. By then the

View of the Forum in Rome.

centre of all Italy, Rome soon became the largest and most populous city of the ancient world. After the 2nd century B.C. it expanded and was the centre of the largest empire of antiquity. The city benefited greatly from the influx of wealth with which many temples, public buildings and private palaces and villas were built. At the same time the neighbourhoods of the lower classes became more and more crowded and hygenic conditions were deplorable. Julius Caesar did much to improve living conditions in Rome and Augustus praised himself, saying that he found Rome a city of bricks and left it a city of marble. Rome continued to expand in the days of the Empire and many public structures were added – palaces for the emperors on the Palatine Hill; temples, the most renowned and best preserved being the Pantheon; the Colosseum for gladiatorial combats; amphitheatres; many public libraries; new forums; public baths; aqueducts and new walls to contain the expanding city. By the 4th century A.D. Rome had about one million inhabitants.

In the 1st century A.D. the event that determined the status of Rome as a holy city occurred – the visit of St Peter, a visit preserved in tradition rather than in written sources. Peter, who received the keys to the Kingdom of Heaven (Matthew 16:18-19), is believed to have been the first bishop of the Christian community of Rome, thus establishing the hegemony of the bishops of Rome who considered themselves his spiritual heirs. Peter was in Rome during the persecutions of the Christians in the days of Emperor Nero (A.D. 54-68) and it is believed that he was executed then. An early Christian legend tells that Peter out of respect for Jesus asked to be crucified head down. ST PETER'S BASILICA, the holiest site of the Catholic world, is believed to be built over Peter's tomb.

With the political decline of Rome in the 4th-6th centuries

Ancient street in Rome.

as a result of the transfer of the capital of the Roman Empire to Constantinople, and the recurring invasions of various barbarian tribes, the religious significance of the city increased. At the end of the 6th century Pope Gregorius I undertook the secular administration of Rome and by the 8th century Rome was a church state.

Throughout the Middle Ages and the Renaissance Rome was ruled by popes who were often in serious conflict with emperors and with powerful families in the city. In the 9th-15th centuries Rome was repeatedly sacked and destroyed as a result of these conflicts and only from the 15th century on did the popes initiate large-scale construction projects that made Rome the centre of Renaissance culture. Renowned artists – Michelangelo, Leonardo, Raphael and many others – were commissioned to build and decorate the city and their work has given Rome its splendour.

Rome has been the capital of Italy since 1870, while since 1929 the religious power has been concentrated in the autonomous state of the VATICAN CITY.

Rome abounds with churches, mostly commemorating New Testament events and personalities. Only those churches directly connected with biblical occurrences will be described here. Information about other churches, as well as the remnants of the Roman period, museums, palaces and parks for which Rome is so famous, can be found in other guide books.

BASILICA OF ST PAUL OUTSIDE-THE-WALLS

The original Basilica of St Paul Outside-the-Walls, built in the 4th century, was one of the first churches in Rome. It commemorates the visit of Paul to Rome where, tradition tells,

St Paul-Outside-the-Walls.

he was put to death. It is believed that the Basilica contains Paul's tomb. When built, this was one of the largest and most important churches in the Christian world. The ancient church has been damaged and repaired many times, and in the 19th century was completely destroyed by fire. It was rebuilt but still incorporates 5th-century wall mosaics miraculously preserved on the huge arch in front of the apse. The Basilica is located some 2km (1.5 miles) south of Porta S. Paolo.

THE CATACOMBS

Although not directly connected with biblical history, the catacombs – underground tombs – of Rome are among the most important remnants of early Christianity and the pilgrim to Rome should make sure to visit them. Here, in tiers of niches in the walls of long, rock-cut corridors, generations of the early Christian community of Rome were buried following the custom of the Jews of the time. The Romans were accustomed to cremate their dead. Sixteen groups of catacombs have been found in Rome and it is estimated that their total length is some 250km (150 miles).

The three most famous catacombs – St Calixius, St Sebastian and St Domitilla – are located along the ancient VIA APPIA, the main road leading from ancient Rome to the south and south-east. The catacombs were used from the 1st to the 4th century A.D. The names of the deceased were inscribed on the slabs that blocked up the niches, and the rock face between the niches was often decorated with paintings. The paintings, especially those of the earlier catacombs, where pagan motifs were adapted to Christian ideas, are of great interest. The great majority depict well-known biblical scenes such as the Story of Jonah, the Binding (Sacrifice) of Isaac, Daniel in the Lion's Den, the Good Shepherd, the Baptism and Mary and the Child and the Three Magi.

In times of persecution the catacombs served as places of refuge and later, once Christianity became the state religion and burial in the catacombs was discontinued, they became places of worship. Little chapels were built in and next to the catacombs in memory of the martyrs. With the passage of time most catacombs were forgotten. Their re-discovery in the

The catacombs of Rome. ▷

middle of the 19th century was a moving and well-publicized event and since then numerous pilgrims and visitors frequent these mysterious caves.

DOMINI QUO VADIS

A small church on the VIA APPIA, less than 1km (half a mile) from the San Sebastiano Gate where the Via starts. The church stands on the spot where, according to legend, St Paul had an apparition of Jesus. St Paul asked, *"Domine quo vadis?"* – "Lord whither goest thou?" – to which Jesus answered, "I go to be crucified anew." Hearing this Paul, who was fleeing from persecution in Rome, returned to the city and was eventually martyred.

SANTA CROCE IN GERUSALEMME

A church in the vicinity of Porta S. Giovani built by Emperor Constantine to house the relics of the True Cross discovered in the CHURCH OF THE HOLY SEPULCHRE in JERUSALEM by his mother Helena, and which, according to tradition, were brought to Rome. When built, the church was part of a large imperial palace constructed in the 2nd century in what was then the south-western extremity of Rome. The church was rebuilt in 1144 and then again in 1743-44 when it was completely remodelled and an impressive façade added.

At the end of the right aisle of the church a stairway leads down to the Chapel of St Helena, the vaulted ceiling of which is adorned by a noted 15th century mosaic.

SCALA SANCTA

A flight of steps believed to have been those that Christ descended after he was condemned to death by Pontius Pilate. The steps are said to have been transferred from Jerusalem by Helena, mother of Emperor Constantine, in the 4th century and are now in the old Lateran Palace east of the Colosseum. At the top of the steps is the Chapel of San Lorenzo which contains a depiction of Jesus believed to have been painted by a non-human hand.

TEMPIETTO

A circular building with 16 granite columns in the Doric style, surmounted by a dome. The Tempietto, a small but exquisite building built by the famous Renaissance architect Bramante (1499-1502), stands in a courtyard next to the Church of San Pietro in Montorio in Transtevere. The site on the west bank of the Tiber River in Rome was believed by some to be the place of St Peter's martyrdom. Peter's death is not mentioned explicitly in the New Testament, but is believed to have been referred to by Jesus when he said, *...when thou shalt be old thou shalt stretch forth thy hands, and another shall gird thee, and carry thee whither thou wouldst not. This spake he signifying by what death he should glorify God* (John 21:18- 19).

The Tempietto is usually closed, but entrance may be granted by applying at the nearby church. The interior is very ornate; the stuccoes on the walls of the crypt are especially noteworthy.

The Tempietto.

VIA APPIA – THE APPIAN WAY

Via Appia was the most important of the Roman roads in Italy, leading from Rome to the south and south-eastern regions of the country. It was built in 312 B.C. and in time was extended as far as Brundisium (Brindisi) on the eastern coast of Italy. Along the section of the road leading south were several stations, two of which are mentioned in connection with the arrival of St Paul in Rome – the Appii Forum and the Three Taverns. To these places, not yet clearly identified, the Christian brethren came from Rome to meet Paul (Acts 28:15).

The site identified as that of the Three Taverns.

VATICAN CITY

Situated on the western bank of the Tiber River in Rome, the Vatican is the spiritual centre of Roman Catholicism. It became an autonomous state, independent of Italy, in 1929, but its history goes back to the 4th century when the Byzantine Emperor Constantine had the first church of St Peter built over the tomb of the martyred saint. Near the church, the popes, descendants in spirit of Peter, have their residences and offices.

The most important edifices in the Vatican City are the Church of St Peter and the VATICAN PALACE which includes the library, various museums and the Sistine Chapel.

ST PETER'S BASILICA

The largest and most imposing church of the Christian world, built over the traditional tomb of St Peter who was martyred in A.D. 65 in the nearby Circus of Nero. The church as it stands today in the VATICAN is one of the great masterpieces of late Italian Renaissance, dominating the skyline of Rome with its huge dome designed by Michelangelo.

Excavations carried out between 1940 and 1950 under and next to the church revealed remnants of the Circus of Nero just south of the church. Under the church itself a cemetery of well-to-do Romans of the 1st century A.D. was found. In it was a funerary monument, and under it were found bones of a strongly-built, elderly man. On December 23rd, 1950 these were declared to be the bones of St Peter by Pope Paul VI. The location of the church has thus been verified, making it one of the most authentic holy places in the Christian world. Tradition claims that as early as 25 years after

St Peter's Basilica.

the death of St Peter a church was built on the site, but excavations have revealed that the first place of worship dates to the middle of the 2nd century. Emperor Constantine built a large basilica here with 86 marble columns dividing it into a nave and double aisles. In this basilica, adorned with numerous frescoes, mosaics and memorials of popes and emperors, Charlemagne was crowned in 800. The basilica survived until the 15th century when it showed signs of collapse and Pope Nicolas V decided to rebuild it. It took about 175 years and a long list of architects to finally complete the project. In the course of the new construction the old basilica was demolished, but some parts of it were preserved in the Vatican Grottoes (see below) and others were used in the new church. The plans and details of the new church were changed by every new architect who was commissioned to do the job, but the most influential ones were Bramante who gave the basic concept, Michelangelo who designed the majestic dome and Bernini who was responsible for the interior decoration and also designed the enormous St Peter's Piazza in front of the church.

Of the many works of art of the exterior of the church, mention should be made of the 15th-century bronze doors of the central entrance, preserved from the old basilica; Giotto's mosaic depicting Jesus walking upon the water, also made for the old basilica and transferred to the tympanum above the central entrance, and the statue of Constantine by Bernini inside the northern entrance to the church. In the interior the eye is drawn to the dome supported by four immense piers. Directly under the dome is a *baldacchino* (canopy) designed by Bernini. In the right aisle of the church, near the entrance, stands Michelangelo's *Pieta*, one of this great artist's most moving statues.

Below the church are the Vatican Grottoes, which more or less repeat the design of the church above and incorporate various architectural parts of the former basilica, placed there by the Renaissance architects. Many popes and other important church figures are buried in the Grottoes. Stairs from the left extension of the Grottoes lead to the Roman necropolis discovered in the excavations. Entrance to the necropolis may be obtained by writing to the Vatican in advance of the visit.

THE VATICAN PALACE

The Vatican Palace, adjacent to ST PETER'S BASILICA, houses one of the world's most important art collections. The immense building is open to the public with the exception of the Pope's apartments. The important part of the palace is the Vatican museums which include: the Gregorian Museum of Pagan Antiquities with Greek and Roman works of art; the Vatican Picture Gallery with outstanding works by Leonardo Da Vinci, Raphael and many other famous artists; the Stanze and Loggia of Raphael – a series of rooms the walls of which are completely covered with frescoes by Raphael; the Gallery of Modern Religious Art; the Museum of Christian Art and the Museum of Antiques. Special mention should be made of the Sistine Chapel, with the famous ceiling and wall frescoes of biblical scenes by Michelangelo. Also world famous is the Vatican Library with over 60,000 manuscripts and over 1,000,000 printed books. Some of the most precious acquisitions of the library are on display and the exhibits are changed every year.

The Last Judgement by Michelangelo in the Sistine Chapel.

JORDAN

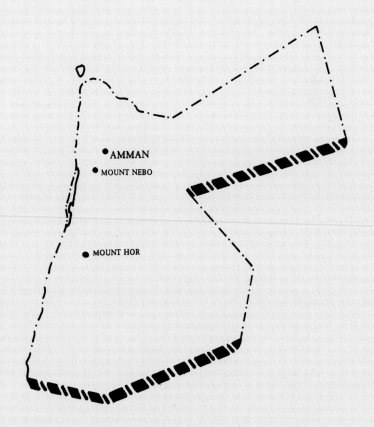

●AMMAN

● MOUNT NEBO

● MOUNT HOR

Jebel Harun, identified with Mount Hor.

A mountain in southern Transjordan, near the ancient Nabatean city Petra, identified, according to a very old tradition mentioned by Josephus Flavius, as the mountain on which Moses' brother Aaron died and was buried (Numbers 20:23-29). From the mountain, which is 1,396m (4,580 ft) high, there is a spectacular view of the surrounding Transjordanian plateau, the Arabah Valley and the Negev. The tomb said to be Aaron's is located inside a cave on the mountain, above which is a domed building constructed in 1459 – the date is part of an Arabic inscription above the entrance. The tomb is venerated by Jews and Moslems alike. Indeed, this is the site holiest to the Moslems in Transjordan. A Moslem traveller who visited the mountain in the year 925 reported that inside the cave of the tomb a dreadful noise is often heard. Jews visited the tomb for hundreds of years and some left their names inscribed on the tombstone.

MOUNT NEBO

A mountain east of the River Jordan, in the northeastern corner of the Dead Sea, some 25km (16 miles) southwest of Amman. Mount Nebo is reached from the town of Medeba. This, according to a tradition that developed in the 4th century A.D., is the mountain to which God directed Moses, saying: *Get thee up into this mountain of Abarim, unto mount Nebo, which is in the land of Moab, that is over against Jericho; and behold the land of Canaan, which I give unto the children*

Mount Nebo.

of Israel for a possession; and die in the mount whither thou goest up, and be gathered unto thy people (Deuteronomy 32:49-50). Although the mountain on which Moses died is mentioned in the Bible by name, *no man knoweth of his sepulchre unto this day* (Deuteronomy 34:6). Moses' exact burial place is thus not known and therefore no Jewish tradition in this connection ever developed. Early Christians, however, did seek the site, and by the end of the 4th century an empty tomb of Moses was shown to pilgrims on the mountain. A church dedicated to Moses was already standing on the mountain. In the following centuries this church expanded in size and a monastery, a chapel in honour of the Virgin and a baptistry were built right next to it making it one of the largest church complexes in the Holy Land.

The church on Mount Nebo was not destroyed by the Persians nor by the Arabs in the 7th century – the fate of most churches in the Holy Land – and survived with changes until the 9th century. Very few pilgrims visited Mount Nebo, and travellers have left few descriptions of the place.

Excavations carried out on the mountain in the 1930s and again in the 1970s unearthed the entire complex. The 4th-century church was found to have been adorned with particularly interesting and colourful mosaic floors which were well preserved. Especially elaborate were the floors of the baptistry and the Chapel of the Virgin. On the floor of this last chapel is depicted the Temple of Jerusalem with its two courtyards and altar for burnt sacrifices.

South-west of Mount Nebo, on an adjacent hill on which stood the town Nebo, remnants of three Byzantine churches of the 6th-7th centuries have been found. The churches of St George, St John and Lot and Procopius also have exquisite, well preserved mosaic floors. On the floors are depicted scenes from everyday life such as the grape harvest, herding, fishing and hunting, as well as scenes illustrating biblical verses, such as a lion and a cow eating together (Isaiah 11:7). One allegorical figure unique to these churches is Earth, in the form of a woman holding flowers while two boys bring her baskets of fruit. The floors are also very rich in inscriptions mentioning various donors to the churches.

It is interesting that the Moslem tradition moved the tomb of Moses to the western side of the Jordan River, to the site of NEBI MUSA.

MALTA

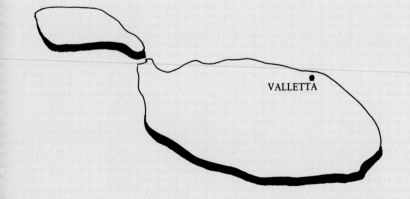

VALLETTA

MALTA

An island in the Mediterranean Sea, south of Sicily, identified with the island called Melita where Paul and his fellow passengers were shipwrecked (Acts 28:1). The island, part of a submerged ridge that once connected Europe with Africa, has been inhabited since the Neolithic period. Throughout its history Malta has been repeatedly invaded and colonized by people of various origins who left their cultural mark on the island. The spectacular temple-tombs of the late 3rd-early 2nd millennia B.C. are similar to the megalithic tombs of western Europe, on the one hand, and to the Aegean culture on the other. During the 2nd millennium B.C. Malta was invaded by people from Sicily and southern Italy, and in approximately 8th-7th centuries B.C., by invaders from Carthage. The Carthagenians, a people of Phoenician origin who spread to the western Mediterranean and colonized its shores, introduced their culture – also known as Punic Culture – into Malta. The rule of Carthage over Malta was very oppressive, and in 218 B.C. the local population appealed to Rome for help. The Romans took over control of the island and under their rule the Maltese were allowed a measure of autonomy and apparently retained their own culture which seemed "barbarous," that is non-Hellenistic, to Paul. Paul was shipwrecked in about A.D. 60 in the harbour that since then bears his name. Having survived an encounter with a venomous snake, Paul was thought to be a god by the people

A view of the port of Valletta.

(Acts 28:2-6). Tradition tells that there and then Paul converted the inhabitants of Malta to Christianity, thus making it one of the first strongholds of the new religion.

Malta fell to the Vandals in the 5th century, to the Arabs in the 9th century and to the Normans in the 11th. When the Knights of St John were driven out of Rhodes they obtained rights in Malta (1530) and in effect ruled the island until it was conquered by Napoleon in 1798. Following some 150 years of British rule, Malta became an independent nation in 1964. The capital is Valletta.

Some of the old historical buildings at Valletta.

SYRIA

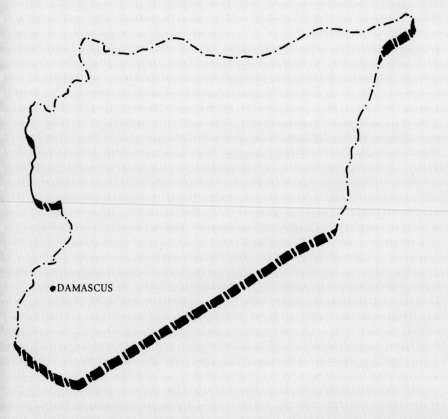

●DAMASCUS

DAMASCUS

One of the most ancient towns in the world, and today the capital city of Syria. Damascus is located in the south-western corner of Syria, quite close to both Israel and Lebanon, at the edge of the great Syrian Desert. The valley in which Damascus lies is very fertile, being watered by the River Barada (ancient Amana). Damascus, surrounded by gardens and orchards, has always seemed like a paradise to the desert Bedouins, who called it by such poetic names as the "Pearl of the East" or the "Necklace on the Throat of Beauty."

Damascus is first mentioned in the Book of Genesis (14:15; 15:2) in the days of Abraham. It is also mentioned in Egyptian records of the 15th-14th centuries B.C. Damascus was taken over by the end of the 2nd millennium B.C. by the Aramaeans, a nomadic people of the Syrian Desert who at that time underwent a process of sedentarization. Before long it became the centre of an important state. Aram-Damascus was one of

Two views of the "Street Called Straight" in Damascus.

the most powerful enemies of the Kingdom of Israel. It was subdued by David, but soon, in the time of Solomon, gained its independence. As an independent state, Damascus was in constant conflict with Israel. It fell to the Assyrians in 732 B.C., some 10 years before the fall of Israel.

In the Persian period (5th-4th centuries B.C.) Damascus recovered and regained its importance, which was not diminished in the Hellenistic period (4th-2nd centuries B.C.) when it passed from one ruler to the other. From the lst century B.C. its importance grew further, and it became the head of the Decapolis, the league of ten cities in eastern Syria and Palestine. At that time it had a large and influential Jewish community to which Saul of Tarsus (whose name was later changed to Paul) carried letters from the high priests in Jerusalem with orders to persecute the "disciples of the Lord" (Acts 9:1). When he came near Damascus, Saul had a vision of Jesus which caused him to join the Christians rather than persecute them (Acts 9:3-20).

Damascus rose to the zenith of its importance after it was captured by the Moslems in 635-6. Mu'awiya, the first caliph of the Umayyad dynasty, made Damascus the capital of his enormous empire that spread from Spain in the west to Turkestan in the east. When the Umayyad dynasty fell in 750, the capital of the empire was transferred to Baghdad, and Damascus was neglected and declined. It knew another short-lived period of glory under Saladin, who in 1187 defeated the armies of the Crusaders. In 1260 it fell to the Mongols and was badly damaged. In the 16th century the Ottomans made Damascus a provincial capital. Since 1920 it has been the capital of Syria.

The most famous site in Damascus is the Great Mosque of the Umayyad period. Its site was first occupied by a Roman temple to Jupiter, and then, in the Byzantine period, by a basilica dedicated to John the Baptist whose head was supposed to have been kept there (see also SAMARIA). In 709 the church was taken over by the caliph, el-Walid, and converted into a mosque. The mosque is renowned for the multicoloured mosaics depicting trees and landscapes that cover the walls of the central court and adjoining porticos. The mosque was destroyed by fire in 1068, rebuilt and destroyed again in 1893. Little remains of these earlier mosques in the present structure.

Another interesting building is the 'Azm Palace, the 18th-century home of the 'Azm family, governors of Syria under the Ottomans. The palace is an excellent example of Damascene domestic architecture with gracious courts with fountains, and porticos opening onto them. The ceiling of gilt and painted wood and the marble inlays on the walls are especially noteworthy.

Not far from the 'Azm Palace runs "the street which is called straight" – Darb el-Mustaqim in Arabic – where Saul stayed during his visit to Damascus (Acts 9:11). In the Christian quarter north of this street is the house of Ananias, of whom it is told, *And Ananias went his way, and entered into the house and putting his hands on him said, Brother Saul, the Lord, even Jesus, that appeared unto thee on the way as thou comest, has sent me, that thou mightest receive thy sight and be filled with the Holy Ghost* (Acts 9:17). Remnants of a Byzantine church can be seen on the site. Another place of interest is the Chapel of St Paul, situated next to the Old City wall, near the now closed Bab Kisan. Here, according to tradition, the disciples of Paul let him down the wall in a basket to save him from the Jews of Damascus (Acts 9:25).

The mountain north of Damascus, Jebel Qasyun, is holy to the Moslems who believe Abraham first recognized his Creator there. They also attribute a tomb there to Abel, son of Adam, who was killed by his brother Cain.

TURKEY

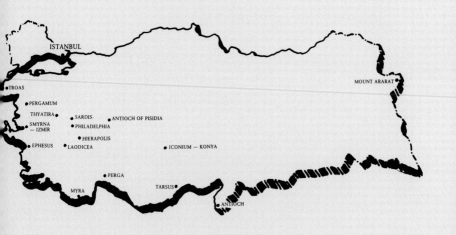

ISTANBUL

MOUNT ARARAT

TROAS

PERGAMUM

THYATIRA   SARDIS   ANTIOCH OF PISIDIA
SMYRNA   PHILADELPHIA
— IZMIR
              HIERAPOLIS
EPHESUS   LAODICEA   ICONIUM — KONYA

          PERGA
MYRA   TARSUS
                      ANTIOCH

ANTIOCH – ANTAKYA

One of the most prosperous cities of the Hellenistic and Roman periods. It is situated in the fertile plain of the lower Orontes River, close to the northern tip of the east Mediterranean coast. It is now in Turkey, very close to the Syrian border.

Antioch is one of the few cities of the ancient world whose exact date of inauguration is known – 22nd of May, 300 B.C. It was founded by Seleucus, one of the three heirs of Alexander the Great, as capital of his part of the empire. Right from the beginning Antioch was embellished by many fine temples and public buildings decorated with beautiful statues. The games and feasts held in the temple of Apollo in Antioch were known throughout the East for their pomp and splendour. In the 2nd century B.C. Antioch is thought to have had about 500,000 inhabitants of mixed origins, including a large Jewish community.

Antioch remained a very important city in Roman times, when it became known as a seat of science and learning. It played a major part in the propagation of Christianity, when Judeo-Christians who left Judea after the death of Jesus came to Antioch and spread their beliefs among the local Jews. Antioch was one of the first places visited by Paul and Barnabas, and the former lived there for several years (Acts 11:19-26, 14:22-35). Despite early persecution, several churches were built, but were destroyed in the days of the

The harbour wall of Seleucia, the port of Antioch.

Roman Emperor Diocletian (284-305). They were rebuilt in the days of Emperor Constantine, who himself consecrated a church in Antioch in 341. Antioch now became a major Christian city and the centre of the Eastern Christian Church which proclaimed its independence from Rome in 341.

A series of devastating earthquakes in 526, 528 and 529 destroyed Antioch, and soon afterwards, in 540, it fell to the Persian king, Khosrau (Chosroes). It was recaptured by Emperor Justinian and remained in Byzantine hands until 636 when it fell to the Arabs. From then on until the 13th century Antioch changed hands between the Byzantines, Arabs, Seljuks, Crusaders and Armenians. Throughout these turbulent centuries it maintained its importance, and prospered on the silk, glassware, soap and copper industries. It was destroyed in May 1268 by the Mameluke Sultan Baybars and has never since recovered. The Turks took over the small town in 1516 and renamed it Antakya.

The interesting sights in Antioch are the Archaeological Museum, renowned for the many Roman mosaic floors on display, and the Citadel on the almost inaccessible rocky summit of Mount Silpius which offers a good view of the town. The citadel was repaired many times. St Peter's Grotto at the foot of the mountain is believed to have been the meeting place of the first Christians of Antioch. Inside the cave are traces of very worn mosaics, perhaps of the Byzantine period.

ANTIOCH OF PISIDIA

Remains of a Greek temple at Antioch (Yalvac).

An ancient town on the Anatolian Plateau, some 170km (107 miles) northwest of Konya. The ruins of ancient Antioch can be seen near the small, picturesque town of Yalvac.

Antioch was founded by Seleucus Nicator in the 3rd century B.C., most probably on the site of an older, Phrygian temple. Around 25 B.C. Antioch became a Roman possession and prospered. Excavations have revealed several imposing structures from this period. On the acropolis of the city was found a propylaea (decorative gateway) dating to the time of Augustus. It opened on to a square known as the Augusta Platea, ending on the east with a semicircular esplanade. In front of the propylaea was the Tiberia Platea, built in honor of Emperor Tiberius. The square was surrounded by shops. Water was brought to the acropolis from the neighbouring hills by an aqueduct, the ruins of which can be seen about 8km (5 miles) north of the city.

Antioch was a well-to-do city when Paul and Barnabas visited it and Paul preached in its synagogue on two consecutive Sabbaths. By the 4th century Antioch was already an important Christian centre, the seat of a bishop. An inscription mentioning Bishop Optimus (375-381) was found in the ruins of a basilica that stood on the acropolis, northwest of the Augusta Platea. Another church with a cruciform layout stood a little west of the Tiberia Platea.

The decline of Antioch started after the 4th century. It was destroyed in 713 during the Arab invasion and was never rebuilt.

EPHESUS

An important and prosperous ancient city on the Aegean coast of Asia Minor (Turkey), about 75km (47 miles) south of the city of SMYRNA (Izmir). It spreads over the slopes of two hills – Mount Coressus (Bülbül Dagi) and Mount Pion (Penayir Dagi) – and the valley between them, where the ancient harbour, now silted up, once carried its bustling trade. It is now called Selçuk and is little more than a quaint and colourful large village.

St Paul visited the important Greco-Roman city of Ephesus between A.D. 55 and 58. Here he preached in the synagogues of the large Jewish community, tried to convert worshippers of the local goddess Artemis, and baptized twelve disciples (Acts 19:23-34). He encountered fierce opposition, chiefly from the priests of Artemis, and was imprisoned. Nevertheless, he laid the foundation for a Christian community which became one of the most important in the early years of Christianity. It is believed that Paul wrote part of the Epistles while imprisoned at Ephesus. According to tradition, Mary moved to Ephesus after the Crucifixion and died and was buried there. This tradition is based on John 19:26-27, which states that Jesus entrusted his mother to the care of John, who moved to Ephesus, where he spent the rest of his life and where he was buried. Thus Ephesus is connected with Mary, John and Paul, and boasts of two important edifices – one commemorating Mary and the other, John.

But the history of Ephesus starts hundreds of years prior to the events connected with early Christianity. The region was inhabited as early as the middle of the 2nd millennium B.C. by a population which worshipped the great mother goddess Cybele, later identified with Artemis-Diana. In the 10th century B.C. the site was colonized by the Ionians, and under the leadership of Androcles, Ephesus became the most important Ionic city, a centre of commerce and finance. Many fine buildings were erected in the city, most important of which was the Artemision – the temple to the goddess Artemis. During the ensuing centuries, Ephesus knew many conquerors including the Persians, Alexander the Great and the Romans. It had a period of prosperity under Lysimachos, heir of Alexander, but its days of greatest glory were under Roman rule.

From the time of Augustus to the 2nd century A.D., Ephesus was the capital and most prosperous city of the Roman province of Asia, and controlled the commerce and banking affairs of the entire region. Most of the magnificent structures to be found in the ancient city date from that period. Between the 4th and the 6th centuries, the Byzantine rulers of Ephesus constructed the basilicas of St John and the Virgin Mary, and destroyed the old pagan temples of Artemis. The marble and stones of the famous Artemision were used in the construction of the basilica of St John in Ephesus, as well as in the imperial basilica of St Sophia in Constantinople. Two ecumenical councils were convened in Ephesus, one in 431 and the other in 449, evidence of its importance in those days. In the 6th century the city moved to the hill northeast of the old site, which gradually became marshy. In its new location the city knew another period of prosperity during the Seljuk era in the 14th century. Since then the city has declined to its present state.

Archaeological excavations began in Ephesus in 1866, and since then the site has been periodically excavated, mainly by Austrian teams. Substantial remnants of the Hellenistic, Roman and Byzantine cities have been unearthed, and an ambitious project of restoration is being carried out.

Of the most important temple of pagan Ephesus-the Artemision, considered one of the seven wonders of the ancient world – there are today only parts of its foundations, situated outside the contemporary village of Selçuk. The Roman city can be entered from the north. The main street runs first southwards and then turns to the southeast, and takes the visitor along the main structures of the prosperous Roman city. These include the Vedius gymnasium, the stadium, the harbour gymnasium and baths, the theatre gymnasium, a well-preserved theatre, the agora (marketplace), with a temple to the Egyptian god Serapis next to it, the Celsus Library, now restored to its past magnificence, the Scholastica baths, the temple of Hadrian and Trajan's fountain. One walks along the

(facing page, from top to bottom) The Arkadiane Street. Remains of the ▷
theatre. Part of the agora. Remains of the temple of Artemis.

colonnaded Arkadiane Street leading to the ancient harbour, and on the pavement of the Marble Road, part of the sacred road of the city.

The holy sites of Ephesus are the two basilicas honouring the Virgin Mary and St John.

CHURCH OF THE VIRGIN MARY

Situated in the centre of the ancient city, near the harbour, this church is the most important Christian shrine in Ephesus. It was built inside a 2nd-century basilica-type building connected with the central marketplace of the city. It is an elongated structure 30m (100 ft) wide and 260m (860 ft) long, divided by two rows of columns into a nave and two aisles, with a semi-circular apse at each of the narrow ends. It is thought that this building was the corn-and-money exchange of this thriving commercial metropolis, while the apses were the meeting place of the courts of justice. In the 4th century, the city having declined, the growing Christian community erected a church in the western part of the abandoned building. A few centuries later two more churches were built inside the western half of the building, one behind the other, while the eastern half was the seat of the bishop and members of the clergy. It was here that the Ecumenical Councils were held in 431 and 449.

ST JOHN'S CHURCH

Remains of St John's Church.

This church is situated on the hilltop northwest of ancient Ephesus, above the town of Selçuk, on the traditional site of the house and tomb of St John. The church dates from the reign of the Byzantine emperor, Justinian (527-565). It is a large, cross-shaped basilica, 120m (360 ft) long and 45m (135 ft) wide, divided by massive marble-covered pillars into a wide nave and two narrower aisles, above which were galleries. The side transept protrudes on both sides of the church. In the intersection of the nave and the transept, under the central one of the six domes which formed the roof of the church, lies the crypt which contains the tomb of St John. The dust rising from the grave was believed to have curative powers and was gathered by the multitudes of pilgrims who visited this important basilica throughout the Middle Ages.

The basilica is now in ruins, but its general features, as well as marble slabs, segments of the mosaic floor and capitals can be seen.

HIERAPOLIS

An ancient town on the western side of the Anatolian Plateau in the ancient province of Phrygia, some 250km (160 miles) southeast of SMYRNA-IZMIR. Today it is a heap of ruins near the splendid spa of Pamukkale but in the past, especially in the Roman period, it was a flourishing city. There was a large Jewish community which was readily converted to Christianity (Colossians 4:13). Here the Apostle Philip was martyred in A.D. 80 and a large church of St Philip was built

(left) Remains of Roman baths near Hierapolis. (right) Cliffs formed by lime flowing from hot springs at Pamukkale.

in his honour in the Byzantine period, when Hierapolis was a bishopric. Remnants of this basilica can be seen on the site, alongside the ruins of many Roman-period public buildings – baths, an agora, theatres and a temple. Hierapolis is especially renowned for its extensive Roman-period necropolis, with tombs of various shapes, many with ornate sarcophagi. A Byzantine fortress of the 11th or 12th century dominates the site.

ICONIUM – KONYA

An important city 1,150m (3,770 ft) above sea level, on the Anatolian Plateau of Turkey, founded at the very beginning of the 1st millennium B.C. by the Phrygians, who believed that it was the first settlement to emerge from a devastating flood which had destroyed humanity. Later the town passed into the hands of the Lydians, the Persians, the Seleucids and eventually the Romans, who called it Iconium and built many fine structures there. During the early Roman period, in the years A.D. 49, 50 and 53, Paul and Barnabas visited Iconium on their apostolic missions. Paul preached in the synagogue and was rejected by the Jewish community, who chased him and Barnabas out of town (Acts 14:1-5). Between the 7th and the 9th centuries Iconium was sacked several times by the Arabs, and in 1069 it fell to the Seljuk Turks who made it the capital city of their sultanate. The Seljuk sultans beautified the city, now called Konya, and many structures of that period are still standing. In the 13th century the celebrated Moslem mystic, Jalal ad-Din ar-Rumi took up residence in Konya and made it into a centre of mysticism. His adherents were known as the Whirling Dervishes on account of their mystical dance. Ar-Rumi is buried in the Tekke of Mevlâna, a monastery, part of which is now an Islamic museum.

Today Konya prides itself on a small archaeological museum, located in a former Seljuk mosque, which houses objects from the Phrygian, Hellenistic and Roman periods. Various mosques, *medreses* (school of religious studies), and *turbes* (burial monuments) of the Seljuk period provide impressive examples of the architecture of that time. The bazaar of Konya is very colourful and lively, specializing in woven carpets made by the nomadic tribes of the area.

LAODICEA

Remains of Roman aqueduct at Laodicea.

Not far from HIERAPOLIS, Laodicea is situated on the Anatolian Plateau. It was founded in the 3rd century B.C. and changed hands several times until it was taken by the Romans in the lst century A.D. Laodicea had a large Jewish community which adopted Christianity (Colossians 4:13, 15), and was one of the seven churches of Asia (Revelation 1:11). In the 11th century Laodicea again knew a stormy period, being conquered by the Seljuks and then again by the Byzantines. From the 13th century on the town gradually deteriorated and is now uninhabited.

MILETUS

View of the ancient harbour at Miletus.

One of the most important cities of antiquity, situated on the Turkish shore of the Aegean Sea, on an easily defended peninsula close to the mouth of the river Meander. This site once gave Miletus its prominence as a port city, but as the mouth of the river gradually silted, Miletus was doomed to decline. It is not known when settlement at Miletus began, but by the 11th century B.C. the site was occupied by the Carians who were allies of Troy. In the 9th century B.C. Miletus was settled by the Ionians and became the most active of the twelve cities that made up the Ionian confederacy. Among the enterprising Miletian colonists were the famed Argonauts who sailed in search of the Golden Fleece. Miletus was an intellectual centre and among its great men were the philospher, Thales, the engineer, Anazimenes, and the geographer, Hecataeus. Miletus stook part in many struggles and was often conquered. The most traumatic conquest was that by the Persians who razed the city to the ground. Miletus was rebuilt according to a plan of its native architect Hippodemus. Under the Romans Miletus had its period of greatest prosperity. There was a large Jewish community there at that time to which Paul preached (Acts 20:16-18) before returning to Jerusalem. From the Byzantine period the city declined rapidly as a result of the filling-in of its harbours.

Remains of the Roman theatre at Miletus.

Many ruins of the Hellenist, Roman and Byzantine periods can be seen on the site, among them a magnificent theatre, the Delphinion – temple of Apollo, the agora, baths, a gymnasium, the buleuterion (senate house) and remnants of several of the city's harbours.

MOUNT ARARAT-AĞRI DAĞI

The highest mountain in eastern Turkey, towering over the junction of the Turkish-Persian-Russian borders. The mountain, 5,165m (16,916 ft) above sea level, is an active volcano which last erupted on June 20, 1840. On the northern side of Mount Ararat is the river Araxes (Turkish Aras) which

Ağri Daği identified with Mount Ararat.

flows into the Caspian Sea. Since it was identified as the
mountain on which Noah's Ark came to rest after the Flood
(Genesis 8:4), many expeditions have been undertaken to
discover remains of the Ark. Indeed, some travellers have come
down believing that they have actually seen wooden planks of
the Ark under the snow that covers the summit of the
mountain.

A track leading up the mountain starts in the village of
Iğdir and passes through the village of Başköy to the
beginning of the valley of Ahira, about 2,100m (6,880 ft)
above sea level. Here one can see five crosses hewn in the rock
and, a little further on, many caves once occupied by Christian
hermits. Higher up is Jacob's Spring which, local tradition
claims, the Patriarch Jacob caused to gush out of the mountain
when he came on a pilgrimage to Mount Ararat to see where
Noah's Ark had landed. Still further up, at about 3,000m
(9,800 ft) above sea level, is a glacier which feeds rivers and
lakes below. The water is unfit for drinking because of its
sulfurous gases and volcanic ash.

On the western side of the mountain are the small fortress
of Koran Kalęsi and an Armenian church.

MYRA

A very ancient town on the Mediterranean coast of Turkey,
some 125km (77 miles) southwest of Antalya. Today some
remains of the ancient site can be seen in the village of Demra.
In antiquity Myra was a fairly important town, renowned for
its temple of Apollo. St Paul landed here on his way to Rome
(Acts 27:5). In the Byzantine period it was an important
Christian town centered around the tomb of St Nicholas, the
original Santa Claus, who was martyred there in the 2nd
century. His tomb is shown in the crypt of the modern Church
of St Nicholas, built over the ruins of a Byzantine church.

PERGA

An ancient town in the region of Pamphylia in southern
Turkey, about 17km (11 miles) north-east of Antalya. Today
the site is in ruins, but in the past, especially in the Hellenistic
and Roman periods, it was a very important town surrounded
by a wall, in which was a temple to the goddess Artemis. Paul
and Barnabas passed here while on their evangelical missions
in Asia Minor (Acts 13:13).

PERGAMUM – PERGAMOS –
BERGAMA

A very important ancient city in western Turkey, some 109km
(68 miles) north of SMYRNA. The city, built on the upper slopes
of a high hill, rose to prominence in the 2nd century B.C. under
its king, Attalus, and his successors who made Pergamum a
most important commercial, scientific, artistic, cultural and

religious centre. The city attracted people of different nations, including many Jews and Phoenicians. Towards the end of that century the last of the Attalid kings gave Pergamum as a gift to Rome, who made it the capital of its province of Asia. The city expanded and a new quarter was added at the foot of the hill. In this flourishing metropolis was one of the "seven churches which are in Asia" (Revelation 1:11; 2:12). The decline of Pegamum was connected with the decline of the Roman Empire. It was rebuilt in the Byzantine period, but never regained its former glory.

Ancient Pergamum has been thoroughly explored and excavated and is one of the most spectacular sites of the ancient world. Noteworthy are the Asklapeion – the temple dedicated to Aesculapius, the god of healing and medicine – and the Red Basilica the original function of which is not known. Both these edifices are in the lower city. Above them rises the acropolis with its walls, temples and magnificent theatre.

PHILADELPHIA

An old town on the western Anatolian Plateau, some 150km (95 miles) west of SMYRNA – IZMIR, now called Alaşehir. It was a centre of pagan worship in the Roman period, and Christianity did not spread there as fast as in other Asian cities. Nevertheless, it was one of the seven churches of Asia (Revelation 1:11; 3:7-13). It was a rather important town in the Byzantine period, and large stretches of the walls of those days still surround the town of Alaşehir.

SARDIS

An important ancient town on the western edge of the Anatolian Plateau, once the capital of the Kingdom of Lydia. It is located about 90km (55 miles) east of SMYRNA-IZMIR. Not much is known of the early history of Sardis before it was captured by Cyrus of Persia and made the chief town of the

Mosaic floor at the synagogue at Sardis.

region. However, legend attributes to its last king, Croesus (650-546 B.C.), the magic touch that turned everything to gold as testimony of his great wealth.

Sardis was destroyed by the Athenians (499 B.C.), captured by Alexander the Great (334 B.C.) and then by the Romans (133 B.C.). As was their custom all over Asia Minor, the Romans erected many fine buildings, especially after the devastating earthquake of A.D. 17.

There was a large and wealthy Jewish community in Roman Sardis, among which Christianity spread very early. Sardis was one of the seven churches of Asia mentioned in the Book of Revelation (3:1). The Jewish community, however, remained strong and by the 4th century had built the largest synagogue known in the ancient world. Originally it was part of the civic centre of Sardis which included a gymnasium, a boxing arena and public baths. At some point however, a large and narrow hall in this complex was handed over to the Jewish community who converted it into a synagogue. The hall was divided into a front open courtyard and a main hall with a large apse in the west. The floors were covered with colourful mosaics and the upper parts of the walls with frescoes and glass mosaics, traces of which were found scattered on the floor.

Sardis retained some of its importance until the 14th century, and declined thereafter to become a tiny village.

Excavations carried out on the site have uncovered the huge civic centre and impressive remains of a temple dedicated to Artemis, the chief goddess of the city in the Lydian, Hellenistic and Roman periods. Substantial sections of the temple of the Hellenistic period (4th-3rd centuries B.C.) have come to light. The huge temple, measuring about 100 × 50m (300 × 148 ft) stood on a podium and was reached by a flight of steps. The temple had eight columns on each of its short sides and twenty columns along the long sides. Eight columns at the western end of the temple still stand there today. Under this temple traces of the temple of the time of Croesus have been found.

Colonnaded building at the gymnasium-bath complex at Sardis.

SMYRNA – IZMIR

A large and prosperous city in the central part of the coast of the Aegean Sea, inhabited from the 3rd millennium B.C. to this day. It prospered particularly in the Roman period when it was the home of one of the "seven churches which are in Asia" (Revelation 1:4; 2:8). There is no indication that St Paul ever visited Smyrna, but it had an early Christian community and as soon as Christianity was recognized as the state religion by Emperor Constantine it became an archbishopric.

Very few of the monuments of ancient periods have been preserved or excavated in Smyrna; its main attraction for the visitor is its mild climate and dried fruit delicacies.

TARSUS

One of the great cities of ancient times, it earned its place among holy sites as the birthplace of St Paul (Acts 9:11). Tarsus is situated in the Cilician Plain in southern Turkey, surrounded on three sides by the Taurus mountain range, and open on the south to the Mediterranean Sea. The whole Cilician Plain is a geologically young alluvial plain, made up of the silt of three great rivers coming down from the Taurus Mountains. Tarsus is built on the westernmost of these rivers – the Tarsus Çayi, Cydnus of antiquity. The delta is still pushing southwards into the sea, leaving Tarsus, once a great sea port of the Cilician Plain, silted up and landlocked. North of the town is the famous passage in the Taurus Mountains – the Cilician Gates. It was to this location between the sea and the mountain pass that Tarsus owed its growth and fame in antiquity. The city was one of the most important crossroads of the Near East, connecting the Anatolian Plateau with the coast of the Levant.

Because of its favourable location and clement climate, the region around Tarsus was settled as early as the Neolithic period and was one of the earliest areas in which plants and animals were domesticated and agricultural communities established. Remnants of the Neolithic and of later periods were unearthed in Gözlükule, northeast of Tarsus. From these early beginnings, the region developed so that by the 2nd millennium B.C. it formed an autonomous political unit – the Kingdom of Kizzuwadna. Growth continued into Hellenistic and Roman times, when the cities of Cilicia, with Tarsus at their head, reached their greatest development and highpoint of fame. Public baths from the Hellenistic period and a Roman theatre were found at Gözlükule. It was in the Tarsus of that period – a busy commercial centre and a meeting point of many cultures – that Saul, later named Paul, the Apostle to the Gentiles, was born.

With the constant wars between the Byzantines and the Arabs Tarsus, and Cilicia as a whole, was destroyed. The plain was virtually deserted. Armenians, fleeing from their captured homeland south of the Caucasian Mountains, settled here and established the kingdom of Lesser Armenia in the 12th century which lasted until the 14th century. Oshin, founder

Remains of the city gate at Tarsus.

of the Hethumid dynasty of Lesser Armenia, built the Castle of Lambron (now Namrun) north of Tarsus, on the first slopes of the Taurus Mountains. Some remnants of the castle still exist. After Lesser Armenia fell to the Mamelukes at the end of the 14th century, Cilicia became the winter pasture-grounds of nomadic Turkmen tribes, who grazed their herds among the ruins of ancient cities in the expanding swamps of the plain. Only towards the middle of the 19th century were attempts made to resettle the plain, first with Egyptian farmers, then with many nomadic tribes – the Cherkess, Tartars, Yuruk, Turkmen, Arabs and Kurds. The current population of the villages and town of Cilicia is a mixture of all these groups. The largest city of the plain is, however, not Tarsus but Adana.

A large but as yet barely excavated tell in the town of Tarsus contains remnants from various periods of the past and evidence of the destruction wrought by the many conquerors who came through the Cilician Gates. Among these were Sennacherib of Assyria, Alexander the Great, Seleucus I Nicanor, Tigranes the Great, Pompey, Hadrian, the Caliph el-Maymun, Bohemond the Crusader and Sultan Selim the Ottoman. As yet nothing from these waves of conquerors has come to light. The only ancient monument in the town is the Kancik Kapisi (in Turkish, "Gate of the Bitch"), an old Roman gate sometimes called St Paul's Gate for reasons of nostalgia rather than for any known connection with the Apostle.

The last word about Tarsus belongs to a conqueror of a different sort, a remarkable woman who sailed up to the town to win a heart. One autumn day in the year 41 B.C., Cleopatra, queen of Egypt, came to Tarsus where she met Mark Antony for the first time. This is how the Roman historian Plutarch describes Cleopatra's arrival:

She came sailing up the Cydnus on a galley whose stern was golden; the sails were purple, and the oars were silver. These, in their motion, kept tune to the music of flutes and pipes and harps. The queen, in a dress and character of Aphrodite, lay on a couch of gold brocade, as though in a picture, while about her were pretty boys, bedight like cupids, who fanned her, and maidens habited as Nereids and graces, and some made as though they were rowing, while others busied them about the sails. All manner of sweet perfumes were wafted ashore from the ship, and on the shore thousands were gathered to behold her.

THYATIRA – AKHISAR

A small town in western Turkey, some 100km (60 miles) northeast of SMYRNA. The present-day town is called Akhisar and is a prosperous centre of carpet-making. In antiquity it was a town of some importance, in which Christianity spread rapidly, and in it was one of the seven churches of Asia (Revelation 1:4; 2:18-29). Nothing is left of the ancient town.

TROAS

A seaport on the northwestern coast of Asia Minor, in which Paul and Barnabas stayed seven days. While Paul was preaching a long sermon, a young man named Eutychus *sank down with sleep and fell down from the third loft, and was taken up dead. And Paul went down, and fell on him, and embracing him said, Trouble not yourself; for his life is in him* (Acts 20:9-10).

Troas is situated only a short distance from ancient Troy. It was founded in the 4th century B.C. by Antigonus, one of Alexander the Great's generals and in 133 B.C. came under Roman control. Today it is a heap of ruins.

Greco-Roman remains at Troas.

Acknowledgement is here made for permission granted for
reproduction of photographs by the following:
Werner Braun; David Harris; Rolf Kneller; E. Lessing; Ministry of Tourism
Turkey; Garo Nalbandian; Zev Radovan; A.A.M. Van der Heyden;
S. Mendrea; A. Shabataev; D. Tal & M. Haramaty; Hanan Isachar;
A. Nezer; J. Sahar; Itamar Grinberg.